For Ever Valiant

The Pacific Islands

Alan Paisey

First published 2008
Copyright © Alan Paisey

ISBN 1900604302

Part of a series
Volume 1: United Kingdom
Volume 2: Mediterranean, Africa & India

Printed and bound in the United Kingdom

Published by Compaid Graphics.
T'otherside, Drumacre Lane East,
Preston. PR4 4SD. England

www.compaidgraphics.com

To Those who Flew

✳ ✳ ✳

To Those who Sustained Their Flight

CONTENTS

Part One

The experiences of veteran airmen operationally based in the Pacific Islands during the Second World War (1939-1945).

Part Two
Aircraft used by the veterans either for Training, Conversion or Combat

Geographical Note. Throughout the book, the large island of Bougainville is quoted as being in the Solomon Islands. Geographically, this is correct, but politically it was a province of New Guinea, which has since become Papua New Guinea. It has never belonged to the territory of the Solomon Islands in the political sense.

PREFACE

With the start of the twenty-first century, the powerfully formative events of the 1900s for many people suddenly seemed to recede into history - an effect not merely induced psychologically by the simple act of changing numbers from 19 to 20, but by the hope of 100 years of a different but better order from that of the last 100 years. The previous century it was felt could be safely consigned to the past.

Enough cataclysmic events in the first few years of this different - if not better - order in the new century, however, have occurred to reinforce the barrier in the mind between present and past. It is doubly difficult, therefore, to invoke and enliven an interest in those powerfully formative events. Yet, as George Santanaya, the Spanish-American philosopher, has remarked, those who forget the past are condemned to repeat it, an observation and belief echoed by Bi Yun, speaking at China's first museum on the Cultural Revolution, when he asked, "Can you forget this kind of thing? You can't. If you forget history it's a crime. It is betrayal." (*The Guardian,* Tanzania, 17 May 2006, viii). The same thought is expressed by the slogan, "What happened then matters now", as carried on the cover of current issues of the British Journal *History Today.*

Among those powerfully formative events, the First World War (1914-1918) and the Second World War (1939-1945) were foremost. In recognition of that fact, it has become commonplace to remark the gradual demise of those who took part in them, to the point of realising that the few who still survive are exceptional. If any ex-serviceman from the First World War is still alive he has to be at least 104 years old, supposing he took part only in the last year of it, in 1918, and at a disguised age of sixteen years. With regard to the Second World War, by the same tokens, a surviving participant from it has to be at least seventy-seven. The young men who volunteered for aircrew duty, however, were often above twenty years of age on application, so those who survived the war and remain alive today are typically in their mid-eighties and sometimes well beyond.

It was the chance opportunity to meet such men in a group that prompted the creation of this book as the third of three volumes. Ever since 1945, ex-aircrew members have formed associations to maintain contact with each other. A significant vehicle for doing this in New Zealand was by way of the Brevet Clubs. Their membership over the years has attracted not only native New Zealanders but those of other nationalities who have become residents and citizens of New Zealand since 1945. They have provided a means to preserve the comradeship that their members experienced and relied on during their wartime commitments. They have been able to provide a second home to provide support and encouragement to their veteran members who remain to remind us all of the effort and sacrifice it took to preserve the way of life that we preferred, when it was threatened with destruction.

By the year 2005, when the work for this volume was started, many surviving aircrew members had already overcome, or were being obliged to cope with, the infirmities that usually accompany great age. Their indomitable spirit and cheerful manner are inspirational to those of a younger age, bearing in mind that in many cases their infirmities have been caused by - or exacerbated by - wartime injury, stress, and other occupational effects. They survived a war which took a terrible and disproportionate toll of aircrew members. Today they face up to life with equal determination. They were valiant then and remain valiant now.

It has been a sad experience for me to meet several veterans with a view to including them in the book, but finding that their disabilities precluded their being able to undertake the work needed. With regard to this, I am indebted to Squadron Leader Ray Archibald DFC, AE, Mentioned in Dispatches, for meeting me and for conveying a brief overview of his distinguished experience, which is summarized as follows.

He was born in Christchurch on 7 September 1922 and flew with the Royal New Zealand Air Force from 30 November 1941 to 27 October 1945, completing five operational tours by July 1945, and subsequently serving in the Territorial Air Force and the Reserve until 8 September 1977. He was Honorary Aide-de-Camp to His Excellency The Governor General of New Zealand from 2 December 1952 to 1 December 1953.

He received the Air Efficiency Award (AE) on 13 May 1954. The citation for his being Mentioned in Dispatches (MID) early in 1945 refers to his service in 18 Squadron, flying Kittyhawks, quoted verbatim, as follows. "In two tours of duty in the Solomons this officer has completed the exceptional total of 256 hours of operational flying and has taken part in 77 missions against the enemy. He has always shown an aggressive spirit, disregard for his own safety and is a keen and most determined flight leader. Flying Officer Archibald is a thoroughly staunch and reliable officer and a valuable influence within the unit."

The citation for his award of the Distinguished Flying Cross (DFC) on 25 September 1945 refers to his service as a pilot of Corsairs in 20 Squadron, quoted verbatim, as follows. "Leader of many highly successful bombing and strafing attacks against areas heavily defended by Japanese anti-aircraft batteries, Flight Lieutenant Archibald has shown constant disregard for personal danger in a long series of important fighter bomber missions that have resulted in heavy losses to the enemy in personnel and equipment. An experienced officer who has flown 438 hours and completed 188 missions in four years of duty, Flight Lieutenant Archibald has, by his fearless leadership, contributed materially on several occasions to the safe return of bomber aircraft under his escort. He has also been particularly prominent in locating and leading attacks upon hidden targets in the jungle after undertaking individual reconnaissance flights at little more than tree top level in his keen desire to seek out the enemy. By his gallantry and devotion to duty, this officer has been invaluable to the squadrons with which he has served. "

The time will come when younger generations will wonder about those who displayed such valour and ask why, when, where, and how they did it. This book is the product of a project undertaken to contribute to the means by which the answers they seek will be met. It consisted of interviewing veterans, and using any records and written material in their possession, on their wartime experiences. Copies of this book have been presented to the National Air Force Museum Archive at Wigram, Christchurch, in the South Island of New Zealand.

The criteria for including the particular veterans in this book were that priority should be given to those whose experiences had not been previously given publicity and to those who were willing to present an account of their experiences. Each chapter is presented on an autobiographical basis. This is justified in that each veteran personally presented an oral or written account of his experience and vetted the text derived from it for this book in at least one draft before giving his final approval. Each veteran presented his account by interview(s), and variously by supplying photographs, documents, and written notes, as additional source material. Every effort has been made by reference to log books and other sources to ensure accuracy in every particular.

Thanks are due to the large number of people who were involved in the project. As well as the time and effort given by the veterans themselves, their wives offered their support and hospitality for the necessary home visits. In addition, or alternatively, sons and daughters have taken an interest and in some cases gave their active assistance, in particular Ann Riley and Wendy Wallator, with respect to their father Fred Thomas, Desmond Newfield, with respect to his father, and Karilyn Smith with respect to her father Arthur Hoskins.

Graham Goss, a veteran himself, and President of the New Zealand Federation of Brevet Clubs Inc., gave firm support to the project at its origin and circulated information to all the ten Brevet Clubs to alert eligible veterans to the project. Douglas Drake, President of the Timaru Brevet Club gave an early welcome to the project and every encouragement.

Members of Staff at the Air Force Museum, Wigram, Christchurch, gave practical help as well as their interest and support. In particular I thank Jane Praven for access arrangements to the archive and Bill Bell for assisting with communications over the photographic commitments.

In particular, I am indebted to Matthew O'Sullivan, Keeper of Photographs at the Museum, for the important contribution he has made to this book, as he did for Volumes 1 and 2, by culling and processing the aircraft photographs for Part 2 from the archives, and supplying original data bases from which I have been able to extrapolate the aircraft information provided with the photographs. His professional knowledge of aircraft, and the technical procedures needed for the storage and preparation of all the photographs in this book for publication, has been of immeasurable and indispensable value.

Walter Carter, Douglas Hawker, Maurice Stevens, and Bill Sparks - veterans themselves from other theatres of the Second World War - identified names of veterans who could be included in this book. I am grateful for their help, especially for the initial contacts and interview dates with a number of veterans arranged by Douglas Hawker.

As always, the telephone reference service of the Christchurch Central Library has been available when an obscure datum has been needed. I thank the staff for the courteous and painstaking service they maintain.

I am indebted to Squadron Leader Don Smith AFC (Retired), of the Royal New Zealand Air Force, for a professional review of Part 2 of the book. He carefully verified technical aspects of the text and the information about the aircraft, making many helpful observations and corrections. Thanks are due to Mariette Laurenson for a painstaking lay reading of the book. She drew attention to blemishes that had been overlooked. I wish to thank Sheila Smurthwaite for numerous items of help with computer processing during the entire period of the book's preparation. Any errors and imperfections still remaining are entirely my responsibility.

Throughout the work for this book I have had the sustained interest and encouragement of Air Marshal David Crooks. In addition to undertaking the research necessary to contribute the Introductory Chapter, he clarified some of the uncertain items in the Dispositions of the Royal New Zealand Air Force in the Pacific 1942-1945, identified the locations of five of the veterans presented in the book, and made arrangements for me to meet and undertake the necessary work with them.

Alan Paisey
Christchurch
New Zealand
April, 2007

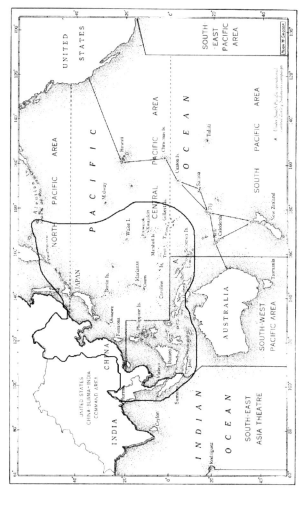

Map of the Pacific for the Second World War. The superimposed heavy line circles the limit of Japan's conquests. The lines from the United States through to Australia and New Zealand mark the air and sea supplies routes. A strategic objective of the Allies was to prevent a Japanese eastern air/sea breach of this vital link. (Map prepared by Matthew O'Sullivan, Keeper of Photographs, Air Force Museum, Wigram, Christchurch, from a copy supplied by Air Marshal David Crooks)

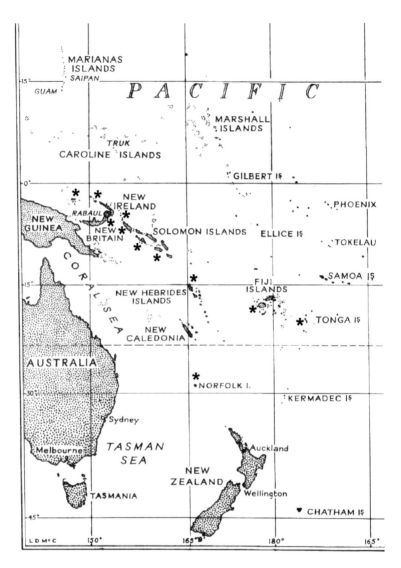

Map showing the area of the Pacific in which The Royal New Zealand Air Force fought during the Second World War. Its main bases in the islands are shown with an asterisk. They include combat and supply/staging bases. (Map prepared by Matthew O'Sullivan, Keeper of Photographs, Air Force Museum, Wigram, Christchurch, from a copy supplied by Air Marshal David Crooks)

Dispositions of the Royal New Zealand Air Force (RNZAF) in the Pacific 1942-1945

Note: All items are listed in the date order of foundation and formation

Command and Control

No 1 (Islands) Group, New Hebrides, Guadalcanal, and

New Zealand Air Task Force (ZEAIRTAF), Bougainville

No 1 (Islands) Group was formed on 10 March 1943 with headquarters on Espiritu Santo in the New Hebrides. In January 1944 it moved forward to Guadalcanal where it remained until it closed down on 1 August 1945. It was responsible for coordination with the United States command in the operational area and for providing base facilities and maintenance, supply, and administrative services for RNZAF units and activities. It also acted as watchdog for New Zealand's national interests in the employment of RNZAF units under United States operational control until October 1944.

By the middle of 1944 the Americans were shifting their effort from the South Pacific Command to support the offensive in the central Pacific and re-entry to the Philippines. Progressively, the RNZAF became the principal air provider for operations against Japanese forces in the Solomon Islands and into the Bismarck Archipelago, coming under the South West Pacific Command. Operational control of New Zealand and United States units had been exercised by the general commanding 1st Marine Air Wing, the main American formation in the area. But it was intended that the Wing should move to the Philippines and, in consequence, that a New

Zealand Air Task Force, ZEAIRTAF, be formed to take over control. It came into being on 1 September 1944 with a headquarters staff of sixteen officers and 195 airmen, located on Bougainville, and was scheduled to take control on 1 November. But American movements were becoming log-jammed so that the New Zealand take over was successively delayed until mid-1945 by which time the war was as good as over. However, ZEAIRTAF became the sub-operational control agency, relieving the Americans in practice, although they remained nominally in command. The command entities under the heading Field Headquarters were subordinate control units of ZEAIRTAF. From September 1944, No 1 (Islands) Group retained responsibility only for maintenance, supply, and administration. It remained on Guadalcanal.

Royal New Zealand Air Force Stations

Norfolk Island, east of Australia, north-west of New Zealand

Nausori, Fiji

Tonga Islands

Guadalcanal, Solomon Islands

Bougainville, Solomon Islands

Nadi, west coast of Fiji

Lauthala Bay, near Suva, capital of Fiji

New Hebrides

New Georgia

Field Headquarters

Piva, central west coast of Bougainville Island

Emirau Island in the north of the Bismarck Archipelago

Jacquinot Bay, on the south coast of New Britain

Green Island. This is in fact a small island group in its own right to the north, about halfway between Bougainville and New Ireland in the Bismarck Archipelago. It may be described as north of the Solomons.

Los Negros Island in the Admiralty Islands

General Reconnaissance (GR) and Bomber Reconnaissance (BR) Squadrons

Detached Flight, Nadi

Squadron Numbers 4,9,1,8,5,3,2

Fighter (F) Squadrons

Squadron Numbers 15, 16, 18, 20, 22, 24, 26, 14, 17, 19, 21, 23, 25

Flying Boat (FB) Units

5 Squadron, 6 Squadron, and Number 3 FB Operational Training Unit

Transport Units

Utility Flight, Guadalcanal

Communications Flight, Fiji

Detachment from 40 Squadron, Guadalcanal

40 Squadron

41 Squadron

Sunderland FB Transport Unit

Air Force Pacific Ferry Flight

Dive Bomber (DB) Unit

25 Squadron

Torpedo Bomber (TB) Units

30 Squadron

31 Squadron

Maintenance (MU) and Service (SU) Units

Number   1 MU/SU
Number   2 MU/SU
Number   4 MU/SU
Number   5 SU
Number 10 Bomber MU/SU
Number 12 MU/SU
Number 13 MU/SU
Number 14 SU
Number 25 Dive Bomber/Fighter SU
Number 30 Torpedo Bomber/ Fighter SU
Number 31 Fighter SU

Overhaul and Repair Units

Base Depot, Espiritu Santo
Field Maintenance, Bougainville
Corsair Assembly, Los Negros

Radar Units

Number 54 RDF
Number 50 RDF
Number 52 RDF
62 Squadron
Number 56 RDF
Number 58 RDF
Number 55 RDF
Number 51 RDF
Number 53 RDF
57 Squadron

Works Units

Number 2 Aerodrome Construction Squadron
Number 1 (Islands) Works Squadron
Number 2 (Islands) Works Squadron

Notes regarding the Introductory Chapter

Area designation. Where the terms "forward" and "front" are used in the text, they are applied in a general sense to the area where RNZAF units are officially recorded as having been on operations. It should be noted though that the Americans had a much more specific system of area designation. They used the terms Combat Area for an area of actual contact with the enemy, Forward Area for an area with a liability to attack by the enemy, and Rear Area in an operational theatre with a low likelihood of attack. The boundary lines, particularly near the front, were subject to continuing revision as circumstances and the scenes of action changed. Furthermore, long range aircraft might cross one or more boundaries in the course of a single mission. Since these uncertainties are confusing without explanation, even if records were available to provide it, the generalised descriptive has been used.

Geographic names. The names of territories and places are given as they were known at the time.

Titles and acronyms. Descriptive and generally shorter terms rather than official nomenclature for command areas have been used, with the single exception of ZEAIRTAF. Official titles are often cumbersome or, in the case of acronyms, meaningless without explanation. For example, the United States commander of allied air forces in the northern Solomons was referred to as COMAIRNORSOLS.

Statistics and numbers. Accurate figures are often nigh impossible to find or derive from available sources. Basic data, interpretation, derivation, and interpolation vary from one source and user to another. Data have been corroborated where possible and tested to reduce the chances of error or distortion. However, rounding off and qualifiers such as 'some', 'around', and 'about', have been used to present a picture rather than mathematical exactitudes.

Introduction

The War in the Air in the Pacific 1941-1945

Air Marshal D M Crooks CB OBE FRAeS
Former Chief of the New Zealand Defence Staff

This, the third of three volumes recording the experiences of veteran airmen in the main theatres of the Second World War, is on the western Pacific. It is an immense region, stretching over 6,000 miles from Japan in the north to New Zealand in the south, and a similar span from Hawaii in the central Pacific west to Singapore. Only on the western and southern margins does it take in significant parcels of land – the archipelagos of Japan, the Philippines, Indonesia, and some of the islands immediately north of Australia and New Zealand. Elsewhere this vast expanse of sea and air is marked only by scattered, remote, and, for the most part, tiny islands.

The Pacific was the setting for a form of warfare markedly different from the Herculean land struggle taking place on the steppes of Russia or the intense aerial contest for the skies over Western Europe and the Mediterranean. For this was a great maritime arena – the traditional stage of sea power – but maritime in this age constituted both sea and air space. Air power was to be a dominant factor, albeit that in the early and decisive stages of the war it was exercised from sea platforms, for it was in the Pacific that the aircraft carrier came of age. Land based air power became predominant as the contest moved on and the Allies secured stepping stones from which to mount the air offensive against Japanese bases and, eventually, the Japanese homeland.

The roots of the Second World War conflict in the Pacific went back to the middle of the 19th century and Japan's emergence from centuries of isolation. With moves towards an industrialised economy and the modernisation of its armed forces, Japan became increasingly involved in the contest for influence in China and adjacent territories. By 1900 it was ready to challenge Russia's position in the east and the interests of other external powers. With the total defeat of the Russian fleet at the battle of Tsushima in 1905, Japan held the key to sea power in the wider Pacific. In the upheavals of the First World War it was able to strengthen its position on the Asian mainland at the expense of China and Russia and, significantly, to gain a controlling mandate over former German held island groups in the central Pacific. Japan became increasingly imperialistic and, when criticised in the early 1930s for its aggression against China, withdrew from the League of Nations and renounced the 1922 Washington treaty on naval limitations.

The extent of Japan's ambitions was signalled in its promotion of the Greater East Asia Co-Prosperity Sphere, a none too subtle euphemism for Empire, and in its cries of "Asia for the Asians". The combination of an influential militarist element in the Japanese government and economic sanctions by the United States led to growing belligerency and diplomatic confrontation. The Japanese armed forces were well equipped, its army and air forces gaining experience from years of fighting in China. In September 1940 Japan joined Germany and Italy in the Axis pact, and moved into Indo-China. The stage was set for war and it was not long in coming.

Japan's entry into the Second World War came on 7 December 1941 with successive surprise attacks on Pearl Harbour in Hawaii, Hong Kong, Malaya-Singapore, and the Philippines. The United States fleet was severely mauled, Hong Kong succumbed in two weeks, Singapore fell on 15 February 1942, and by the end of April the Japanese were in control of the Philippines, Indonesia (the Dutch East Indies), and Burma. Meantime, they had struck south and were firmly lodged in New Guinea, the Solomon Islands, and the Gilbert Islands. These conquests brought them within air striking distance of Australia, and, within a possible further step, of posing a direct threat to New Zealand. Beyond the Solomon Islands, and within their reach, lay the New Hebrides (Vanuatu), New Caledonia, Fiji, Tonga, and Samoa - an arc of islands that provided the last defensive screen before New Zealand, and the critically important staging points in the air link from the United States to Australia and New Zealand.

In just four months, in a series of spectacularly successful actions, Japan had established control over a huge swathe of the western Pacific, had picked up the rich resources of South East Asia, and had even struck briefly at Ceylon in the Indian Ocean. The lines of expansion matched those envisaged in the Co-Prosperity Sphere. With such success so quickly achieved, what more incentive could there be for them than to reach out for further riches and at the same time extend and strengthen their defensive perimeter? This was a prospect that held little comfort for those in the southern Pacific. Australia, with its greater resources, was the strategic power with a priority for stemming further Japanese advance to the south and for providing a base from which to mount future counter offensives. New Zealand, though for the time being less directly threatened, also assumed a new strategic importance. It was realised that if the latter were occupied by the Japanese then Australia would be cut off from the United States. If, on the other hand, Australia were compromised as a base, then New Zealand would become the vital and last back-stop. Whether or not Japan had the capacity for such further moves could not be fairly judged at the time, but it was clear that the possibilities could not be ignored.

These then were the concerns and considerations facing the United States, Australia, and New Zealand when two actions took place that were to sway the future course of events. The Battle of the Coral Sea on 4-8 May 1942 frustrated a Japanese attempt to capture Port Moresby, the main allied base on the south coast of New Guinea, and thus parried a step in the growing threat to Australia and New Zealand. The Battle of Midway, northwest of Hawaii, a month later, on 3-4 June, was a resounding defeat for the Japanese. The loss of four large aircraft carriers brought them down to near parity with the United States Pacific Fleet and was to prove a turning point in the Pacific war. These actions had significance for New Zealand that, although not known at the time, went far beyond the immediate outcomes. The Japanese had planned to extend their south eastern perimeter with early attacks on Fiji, New Caledonia, and Samoa. But the reverses of the Battles of the Coral Sea and

Midway caused a reappraisal of their position, and in July the plan was set aside, at least for the time being. In fact, these and subsequent events were to expose serious shortcomings in Japan's war-making strategy.

Japan's heavy dependence on imported raw materials was the main reason for its move on South East Asia, but the supply stream by which these resources were carried to Japan was seriously affected as their sea lines became progressively exposed to attack. Their industrial capacity was not geared to the rates of attrition replacement or the expansion of production required for a prolonged conflict. Manufacturing facilities were generally concentrated and thus vulnerable to strategic air attack. Dispersal attempts were too late to be effective and production declined disastrously during the final stages of the war.

While these effects were to become more telling as time went on, other negative factors also appeared as the first flush of success began to fade. Imperial ambition had clouded any hard-nosed appreciation of long term consequences and the demands of consolidation. Military action was often driven by opportunism rather than by the pursuance of a measured strategic aim. The armed forces were in many respects better tailored for blitzkrieg-like tactical operations than for sustained warfare. This was especially so in respect of the shape and employment of air capabilities, which were subservient to and split between army and navy control. Their air support role was successful in the early stages of fast moving tactical action on land and at sea but, lacking centralised direction and a coherent air power doctrine, Japan was not able to mount sustained bombing offensives, to marshal resources for long term conflict and, in the end, to provide an effective air defence of the homeland. These economic and politico-military factors progressively degraded Japan's war-making capacity and denied it any chance of victory. However, that was not obvious during its early military rampages, nor did it diminish the capacity for stubborn resistance by their forces lodged throughout the western Pacific and across South East Asia to the gates of India. To break that grip was destined to take three years of bitter struggle.

When Japan entered the conflict, New Zealand had already been on a war footing for over two years, having immediately joined with Britain on the outbreak of hostilities on 3 September 1939. During that time the primary role of the armed forces at home was to raise and support the expeditionary ground force despatched for service in the Mediterranean theatre and to train personnel for service with the Royal Air Force (RAF) and the Royal Navy. Units were also raised for local defence, modest air and ground forces during 1940 were sent to Fiji – which was a New Zealand defence responsibility - and latterly two Royal New Zealand Air Force (RNZAF) units were despatched to Malaya-Singapore. By December 1941 New Zealand had some 90,000 men in the armed forces, with over 50,000 of them overseas - these figures from a population of just over one and a half million. The further military demands of war in the Pacific, together with a commitment to make a maximum effort in food production for Britain and for the American forces in the Pacific, were to place a strain on New Zealand's resources. By September 1942 there were 154,000 men in uniform, 30% of the male work force, and by 1943 war expenditure had reached 53% of national income. Such were the circumstances in which the country was braced to meet the threat from Japan.

The New Zealand defence force was kept at bare minimum levels in the period between the First and Second World Wars. An air arm was gazetted in 1923, but in practice it remained only in a token form until the mid-1930s when developments in Europe and eastern Asia led to rising concerns for defence. With the country still recovering from the Great Depression, little could be spared for the armed forces, and there were questions about the future shape of defence. While staunchly loyal to Britain and the concept of collective Commonwealth defence, the government had reservations about reliance on the Singapore base and a long range response by the Royal Navy as a guarantee of security in the Pacific. It was also haunted by the still recent pain of tragically high Army casualties in the First World War. While maintaining the options for response depending on the need at the time, the government was increasingly drawn to the possibilities of an air based defence capability. Such a course was nourished by an uncomfortable awareness of vulnerable maritime approaches far removed from the sources of naval reinforcement. From the mid-1930s the possibility of future war could not be ignored and New Zealand began a programme of preparatory measures. The Royal New Zealand Air Force was established as a separate service in 1937 with a strength, including reservists, of 250, and a handful of dated aircraft. It was an important first step.

The role and organisation of the fledgling air force were based on the recommendations of a Royal Air Force Officer, Wing Commander, The Honourable Ralph Cochrane, who was sent to New Zealand in response to a request by the government for advice on air defence. Taking account both of New Zealand's geographic situation and the likelihood of a call to support Britain in the European theatre, he recommended the establishment of a home based long range maritime air strike force, and a flying training capability that could meet local requirements and provide a flow of pilots to the RAF. The strike force was to have a capability for rapid deployment to the Pacific islands or Singapore. There was provision for reserves with a capacity to form additional squadrons as required and for building up supporting services and air armaments. These were visionary, practical, and persuasive proposals. With remarkable alacrity the government accepted the recommendations and within three months had passed the necessary legislation, created an Air Department, launched the RNZAF as an independent service, and persuaded Cochrane to remain in New Zealand as the first Chief of Air Staff of the new service. It also approved the purchase of thirty Wellington bombers, advanced aircraft in their day, to equip a two squadron strike-reconnaissance force. There was nothing like the threat of war to focus the political mind!

With conflict looming there followed two and a half years of intense activity as development plans were progressively revised upwards. Orders were placed for additional aircraft, armaments, and support equipment. Territorial squadrons were activated, new bases constructed, and further training provisions made for both air and ground crews. In 1938 the British government accepted a New Zealand proposal in principle that on the outbreak of war the

RNZAF would set up a scheme to train a thousand pilots a year for the RAF. Important progress was being made but there were a number of factors that placed limits on what could be achieved. The New Zealand resource base was only a small population and a modest industrial capacity, mainly geared to processing the produce from farming. Aircraft, machinery and other items of advanced equipment had to come from abroad. But Britain, New Zealand's main source of such supplies, was striving to meet the demands of its own expansion programmes. Consequently, RNZAF requirements inevitably slipped down the order of priorities. As the RAF was re-equipped with new types of aircraft, some second-line and obsolescent aircraft were released to New Zealand, although few had arrived before war broke out. However, some 230 Vildebeests, Vincents, Baffins, Gordons, and Hinds saw service in the RNZAF. These venerable biplanes were far from ideal but better than nothing. They played an important part in providing coastal patrols and operational training during the early war years.

Though much had been achieved, much remained to be done when war came in September 1939. RNZAF strength was still only 1,000 personnel and it still had no modern combat aircraft. A small contingent was in Britain preparing to fly the Wellington bombers to New Zealand but, a full week before war was declared, the government placed the personnel and aircraft at the disposal of the RAF for use in the defence of Britain. It was an act of extraordinary generosity, motivated by the priorities of the hour, but which also underlined the closeness of ties with Britain and between the RNZAF and the RAF.

For the first two years of war the energy and resources of the RNZAF were largely directed to the development and operation of a training programme that would meet the aircrew quotas set under the Empire Air Training Scheme (in July 1942 renamed the British Commonwealth Air Training Plan). But there was also a need for air and ground crews to service the training establishment, to meet air garrison and patrol commitments in the south Pacific, and to upgrade local defence in New Zealand. On the outbreak of war with Japan the personnel strength of the RNZAF was about 10,500 - of whom 5,500 were serving overseas, either with the RAF, training in Canada, or with RNZAF units in Malaya-Singapore and Fiji. First line aircraft comprised 36 Hudsons, 35 Vincents, and 3 Singapore flying boats. In Singapore, No 488 (NZ) Squadron was based at Kallang equipped with the Brewster Buffalo, an under performing and by then an obsolescent American fighter. No 1 Aerodrome Construction Squadron was based at Tebrau in southern Malaya with detachments elsewhere. Although located in South East Asia, these two units were very much part of the Pacific story. They were the first New Zealand military units to be engaged with the Japanese onslaught, the remnants of both returning to New Zealand to form or become part of units that served elsewhere in the South Pacific.

The debacle that resulted in the loss of Malaya and Singapore was the outcome of inter-war neglect and dated strategies. When it was belatedly recognised that the key to defence was air power, not battleships and guns, the response was too little too late. With Britain stretched to the limit in Europe and the Mediterranean there was simply neither the time nor the resources to put in place what was required – a modern, radar based control system, high performance fighters, and modern strike aircraft. When the blow struck there were nominally some 160 aircraft available to meet the Japanese attack, including obsolete biplanes, but no modern fighters. With low serviceability rates the on-line figure was probably closer to 100. Whatever the precise figures, they proved woefully inadequate.

No 488 (NZ) Squadron was still working up and had to combine air defence duties with an intense training programme during most of December 1941. From early January, as Singapore came under increasingly severe air attack, the Squadron was engaged in a rising tempo of combat operations and by the 24th it was down to two usable Buffaloes. It was allotted nine Hurricanes which were immediately thrown into the fray but on the 27th these were caught on the ground refuelling and all but one were damaged. All other squadrons were in a similar state as the withdrawal of air units to Sumatra was already under way. 488 Squadron flew out its remaining four aircraft on 2 February 1942, the rest of the unit withdrawing to Batavia over the following ten days. This withdrawal was just in time for by then much of Singapore was in Japanese hands. It capitulated on 15 February. The much depleted Squadron acquired some additional aircraft but most were destroyed when they got caught up in a Japanese parachute assault on Palembang airfield on 14 February. The remnants of the unit were evacuated from Java on the 23rd and were recovered to New Zealand via Australia. The survivors became the nucleus of No 14 Squadron formed in April 1942, to become one of the early fighter squadrons in the Pacific.

The lot of No 1 Aerodrome Construction Squadron was no less adventurous. The unit was formed in New Zealand in July 1941 and completed its move to Malaya in October. Its work began on the construction of a bomber airfield and then moved on to fighter strips in Malaya and Singapore. As the Japanese pushed down through Malaya, the unit suffered the indignity of having its role turned into equipment salvage and the demolition of the facilities that it had worked so hard to build. One member was moved to observe that it would have been easier to build mines into the foundations during construction. Nevertheless, the unit saved its heavy equipment, hauled it south to Singapore and loaded it on a freighter, only to have the further indignity of seeing the vessel sunk at the wharf by Japanese bombers. The unit was evacuated just before Singapore fell, its personnel eventually making their way back to New Zealand via the Dutch East Indies and Australia. Many of them were to serve later in works units in the South Pacific.

Of the many RNZAF aircrew serving with RAF squadrons in Malaya and Singapore some were lost in action, some became prisoners of war, and some made their way to Australia and New Zealand. Many of these survivors were also able to serve later in the Pacific.

From the outbreak of war in 1939 the RNZAF had built up a substantial infrastructure of airfields, and maintenance and supply facilities, but it was geared primarily to the support of a training role, as was the organisation. With the Japanese advance and New Zealand's exposure to attack, the RNZAF had now to take on an active operational role in its own right. The most urgent requirement was for modern combat aircraft, a need that had been pressed for some time. Under existing agreements these could be met only from British quotas of American aircraft but to date New Zealand had rated low on the priority ladder. However, a few aircraft were in the pipeline and the situation improved steadily with America's entry into the war and the establishment of direct supply arrangements. The arrival of Kittyhawks from March 1942, and additional Hudsons, enabled the RNZAF to form fighter units and more bomber reconnaissance squadrons. But there were other needs. Aircrew training was at once increased to meet the Pacific requirement and there were major intakes for ground crew to support the new operational commitments – over 16,000 recruits were enlisted in 1942. Organisation and command arrangements were revised to reflect the operational stance and to mesh in with the wider allied command set-up, of which New Zealand was to be a part.

After the fall of Singapore and the Dutch East Indies there was a review of strategic boundaries, the United States assuming responsibility for the whole of the Pacific, including Australia and New Zealand. This responsibility in turn was split in two - the South West Pacific, under General McArthur, stretching from the Philippines south to include Australia, and the Pacific Ocean area, under Admiral Nimitz, comprising the rest of that vast area. The latter was further subdivided into Northern, Central, and the South Pacific – the latter including New Zealand and the island area to its north. The United States Naval Commander South Pacific established his headquarters at Auckland, the whole of New Zealand, except for home defence, coming under his operational control. The relationship also opened up a line of support that included aircraft and this was to be reflected in the number of navy type aircraft flown by the RNZAF later in the war.

In the early stages of holding and counter-offensive operations, RNZAF squadrons were slotted into American establishments and control arrangements. This worked well but as the range of functions and the variety of units increased, it became necessary to form an RNZAF forward headquarters to effect better coordination with the American command and to attend to a rising level of national interests and responsibilities. Early in 1943, No 1 (Islands) Group was set up in the New Hebrides and by the middle of the year it had under its command eight fighter and bomber reconnaissance squadrons, several radar units, and a variety of maintenance and supply facilities, scattered across nearly 2,000 miles of island groups. Later, in 1944, when New Zealand became the predominant air provider in the Solomons, an RNZAF air task force (ZEAIRTAF) was also formed to exercise operational control of the area.

The conduct of air operations in the Pacific proved hugely challenging. Distances were immense and almost always over trackless expanses of water. Weather in the tropics was always an unpredictable factor. Within the hour fair skies could become a maelstrom of violent thunderstorm activity that was dangerous to fly through, that blotted out small island bases, and presented a special hazard for aircraft returning low on fuel. The torrential rain that poured from these storms made life a misery for those who had to maintain aircraft and provide services in primitive conditions. Aircraft dispersals, tent lines, and vehicle tracks, could become a sea of mud within minutes. There was humid heat and prickly heat, there were flies and dysentery, there were mosquitoes and malaria. And yes, there was also the enemy, in the air with his high performing Zero fighter, and on the ground - often within shooting distance of the airstrip.

All of this was compounded by a general paucity of established facilities everywhere, but in the combat zone through the Solomons and to the north, a total lack. Following assault landings, and usually within restricted beach-heads, shore handling facilities, roads, airfields, and support bases, had to be built from scratch and in the face of enemy action. The challenge was met with some remarkable achievements of which the following is but one example. Nissan Island, north of the Solomons, was chosen as the site for an airfield to facilitate the air assault on Rabaul, the main Japanese base in the South Pacific. The island was covered with dense jungle and totally devoid of facilities, but garrisoned by the Japanese as a staging point for vessels supplying their forces in the northern Solomons. In February 1944, a New Zealand force, after some en-route attention from enemy bombers, made an amphibious landing and within days had secured the selected airfield site. Engineers moved in and nineteen days after the first troops went over the beach, RNZAF and American fighters were using the strip.

Long supply lines were a universal feature of the Pacific theatre. The need for a military air route to link New Zealand with the United States in the event of war had been highlighted by Squadron Leader L.M. Isitt of the New Zealand Permanent Air Force from the early 1930s. But air leg distances were formidable, there being no landing places over much of the route. Trans-Pacific flight was then limited to a few pioneering attempts. However, New Zealand surveys and Pan American Airways proving flights from 1937 had at least mapped out the most practical route when the Second World War started, but it required much work in the construction of airfields and staging facilities to make it suitable as a wartime air supply and ferry route. When war broke out New Zealand had completed two airfields in Fiji and by the end of 1941 American work was well advanced on the further stepping stones north to Hawaii. The distance was daunting, involving some 7,300 miles from the American west coast to New Zealand, but the link was vital. For the 2,400 mile leg from California most items for on-move by air were first shipped to Hawaii. Similarly all but very long range aircraft were moved by sea and re-assembled for air ferry to the South Pacific. In June 1943 an RNZAF ferry detachment was based in Hawaii to re-assemble and test aircraft before they were despatched south.

The greatest challenge to this vital supply route was that posed by the enemy who, by April 1942, was poised to strike at New Caledonia and through Fiji to the east, thereby taking out the southern staging points. For even if the central posts were held a further eastward routing would have so lengthened the final leg to New Zealand as to make it impractical as a supply line. The prospect of such a development made even more urgent the need for allied action to stem the Japanese advance and secure the air link as a prelude to preparations for the counter offensive.

First priorities for South Pacific Command were to establish a toe-hold in the southern Solomons, to secure the New Hebrides as a forward base, and to protect New Caledonia and Fiji as staging points. These considerations determined the immediate roles and locations of RNZAF units – bomber reconnaissance and maritime patrol in Fiji and New Caledonia, fighters and radar support in Tonga. As the air campaign progressed and more combat aircraft became available from the United States, additional squadrons were formed and existing units were re-equipped. Corsairs replaced Kittyhawks, Venturas supplemented or replaced Hudsons, Avengers and Dauntlesses were used for dive bombing, Catalina flying boats were introduced for maritime patrol and sea rescue, and C47 Dakotas and Lodestars for air transport. Altogether some 750 of these aircraft types were brought into service with the RNZAF.

As the counter offensive gained momentum, New Zealand units were progressively committed to the front line. By November 1943 there were ten squadrons in theatre and a year later that number had risen to eighteen. The employment of New Zealand squadrons spanned the classical functions of a tactical air force – fighter defence and escort, medium and light bomber attack, anti-shipping strike, close air support of ground forces, maritime patrol, and general reconnaissance. There was no lack of variety. Altogether twenty-five squadrons served in the forward area, many of them for several tours, and two New Zealand based transport squadrons provided up to twenty-two flights per week to the front in round trips of some 4,500 miles. They moved priority freight, mail, and 37,000 passengers – the latter figure a reflection of the RNZAF's active personnel rotation policy. An unsung but vital service was provided by ten radar units operating in often remote sites from the Solomons to Tonga.

While working closely with the Americans at all levels, the RNZAF still had to provide its own infrastructure of maintenance, supply and administrative facilities. The overheads were high where practically everything had to be carved out of the jungle - the RNZAF even had to operate its own sawmills. In every respect it was taxing of effort. The geographical spread of air operations and their support was immense for a small air force, stretching over

3,500 miles. In northern hemisphere terms, that is equivalent to the distance from London to beyond the Persian Gulf.

The conduct of war in the Pacific theatre was very different from that in Europe or elsewhere, save perhaps Burma. The Pacific was a primitive frontier environment where the challenges of nature rivalled those of the enemy. New Zealanders responded well and wrought wonders of improvisation in maintaining rates of operational effort under trying conditions. The potential for adverse effects on health and morale were countered by an effective policy of rotating people and units. Peak RNZAF strength in the south Pacific was 7,800 but due to the turnover programme the number who actually saw service in the theatre was probably around 15,000.

By early 1945 the Americans had regained control of the central Pacific, and isolated the Japanese forces remaining to the south. They continued to resist but as they were no longer a threat, the scale of air operations was progressively reduced. When hostilities ceased in August, thirteen RNZAF squadrons were in the forward area operating from a scatter of bases through the Solomons to islands north of New Guinea. New Zealand land and naval forces were also engaged in the southern Pacific but, in accordance with American priorities, the major contribution was air force. It was not glamorous work but it was very important, both as a contribution to the allied military effort and as a statement of New Zealand's place in the Pacific. Significantly, New Zealand's signatory to the Japanese surrender document was the RNZAF Chief of Air Staff, Air Vice-Marshal L M Isitt.

The valiant service of 11,000 RNZAF aircrew members who flew with the RAF in Europe and elsewhere, illustrated in Volumes I and II of this series, was a matchless experience in the exercise of air power on the grand scale. It yielded a wealth of expertise that served the RNZAF for decades. But the coming of age for the RNZAF in a full sense, that which comes only with the need and opportunity to exercise all the functions of an air force, and which was to shape its future development, was the war in the Pacific. This was the legacy of those who served there with equal valour.

It cannot be said with certainty how many New Zealand aircrew saw service in the Pacific, available records being incomplete and often confusing, but it would appear to be in the order of 2,400. Like their compatriots elsewhere they did their duty truly and well. They braved enemy fire, the elements, uncertain landfall, and the vagaries of airborne machinery, to do the daily job. Here though, there was no prospect of compensating comfort on returning to earth – no halls of residence, no pubs, no alternative company. For most men it was a case of camping out – in a bad climate. But they adapted with good cheer and, as one might expect of the sons of pioneers, with practical good sense and often ingenious improvisation in the air and on the ground. They got on well with their American allies and earned their respect. As the United States Army Air Force history notes, American bomber crews had a preference for RNZAF close fighter escort. They served their country with honour and distinction. They were part of that extraordinary generation of New Zealanders.

These notes provide but an outline of the setting for their achievements. For those who seek a more comprehensive account there is the *Royal New Zealand Air Force* by J M Ross, part of the New Zealand official history series covering the Second World War. As with the two earlier volumes of *For Ever Valiant*, the personal experiences recounted here are a valuable and welcome complement to the official histories. Here we are again reminded that there are lessons to be taken from the hard won past, that the world can be a dangerous place, that there is no substitute for preparedness. To ignore those realities is to do less than justice to those who served us so well.

David Crooks
Wellington
New Zealand
January 2007

PART ONE

The experiences of veteran airmen operationally
based in the Pacific Islands during the
Second World War (1939 -1945)

Chapter 1.

Exchange to Exchange

Graham Goss

From Exchange to Exchange

Like those of many other New Zealanders, my family origins were of a mixed and chequered nature. I was born in Christchurch on 21 June 1924, one of two children, my mother having been born in 1898 in Kirwee, Canterbury, of Scottish parents. My paternal grandfather emigrated from England in the 1860s to Australia. My father served in the Australian Army in the First World War but, being unable to find work in his trade as a carpenter in Launceston, Tasmania, where he was then living, he decided to emigrate to New Zealand in 1919. He met my mother to be, Irene Sylvia Fairbairn, in New Zealand, while he was working on a farm near Kirwee.

Many years later I discovered that, accompanied by her sister, my mother was required to travel all the way by sea to Hobart and then by horse and carriage to Launceston to be vetted as the prospective wife of Roy George Goss. She evidently passed the test, since they were promptly married thereafter in 1920, my elder brother Harold William being born in 1921, the year in which my father was able to secure a job with New Zealand Railways. This employment was an asset for the family, his small but steady income carrying us through the depression years of the 1920s and early 1930s, which infused privation into so many families.

We were living in Middleton, about eight miles south of Christchurch on the main trunk line. It was a small village that included four railway houses, one of which we occupied. We had neither gas nor electricity in the house. As we were located in the area between the Paparoa and Waimarie Councils, neither authority could make up its mind about which of them had the responsibility to supply power to the village houses until 1938, so I had to do all my schoolwork in the light of a kerosene lamp. We depended on a coal-fired range in the kitchen for cooking and heating, at the back of which was a pipe that supplied hot water. When a fresh supply of coal was needed, on a word from my father my brother and I would go on an expedition to collect it. It was surprising how much coal used to fall off the trains.

A neighbour of ours, Mr Piggy Stewart, was the manager of Green's Bacon Factory, beside the Metropolitan Racing Course. He often passed us on our way to school in his coupé car with a couple of pigs on board, but if he had no pigs as passengers he used to stop and offer us a ride in the back of it. A Chinese market gardener lived at the no exit end of Lunn's Lane. He used to dam the small stream which ran through his property to wash his vegetables before taking them to market in Christchurch, stacked in large cane baskets on a four-wheeled cart drawn by two horses, along the shingle-surfaced Blenheim Road. When our journey to school coincided with his trip to market, we used to hang on the back of his cart with our feet lodged on the rear axle. He always used his horse whip on our fingers to compel us to drop off. In spite of his antipathy to our habit, our family maintained cordial relations with him. My mother often sent me to his hut with a batch of scones or other goodies. Each Christmas in return he used to bring us seven pounds of peas, a jar of stone ginger, and some firecrackers for the New Year celebrations. He never complained to my parents about my free rides.

Another character of my boyhood was a contractor named Fred Falloon who lived along Blenheim Road. With a draught horse and dray he carried shingle to building sites from a pit near the railway line near our home. As young boys we always found it fascinating to watch him remove the horse from the shafts and throw the nose bag over the animal's head to fortify the animal enough to pull the heavy load of shingle, which he busily shovelled onto the dray while the horse was eating.

Half a mile away was the boundary of Sockburn Airfield as it was then known. It was the location of Henry Wigram's historic initiative to interest the government in military flying in the middle of the First World War. He assembled a small number of young men for initial flying training there before sending them to England to join the Royal Flying Corps on the Western Front in France. From that modest beginning, the airfield grew as a military flying training facility, eventually becoming the largest training base in the whole country for the Royal New Zealand Air Force during the Second World War. The base and the locality were aptly named after Sir Henry Wigram, who in due course was widely recognized for the fundamental service he had rendered to military aviation.

My first recollection of Wigram was of walking down Lunn's Lane to the airfield where Charles Kingsford Smith, a Squadron Leader in the Australian Air Force, arrived on 11 September 1928, having piloted the first aircraft ever to cross the Tasman Sea. He flew from Australia in an aircraft aptly called the Southern Cross. I was carried on my father's shoulders to see his arrival and was overawed by the crowd, estimated to be over 30,000 – a remarkable percentage of population turnout for Christchurch at that time. The whole area was packed, the people standing shoulder to shoulder, both men and women all wearing hats in the custom of the time. The excitement, mounting as it did to the point of being palpable as the sound of aircraft drew nearer, left an indelible impression on me.

The Southern Cross came in sight escorted by a number of aicraft drawn from the small fleet of newly acquired Avros, Bristol Fighters, and Gloster Grebes belonging to what was then known as the New Zealand Permanent Air Force – prior to its becoming the Royal New Zealand Air Force in 1937. On landing, the other crew members, consisting of T H Williams, C T P Ulm, and H A Litchfield, descended from their aircraft with the aircraft's Captain, Charles Kingsford Smith, to be mobbed by the crowd. Each was presented with a silver fern brooch trailing black, white, and green silk ribbons. Charles Kingsford Smith managed to drop his brooch in the melée, and was unable to recover it, but it was found by a young girl who held on to it for sixty years until 1988, when, in her mature years, she presented it to the Air Force Museum at Wigram airfield where it had first been presented, lost, and found. The crossing of the Tasman Sea was a harbinger of the era that would shrink the vast ocean surfaces of the southern hemisphere in both war and peace – and mostly in that order. New Zealand honoured the achievement by awarding Charles

Kingsford Smith the rank of major in the New Zealand Permanent Air Force.

I went to school in Wharenui Primary School, located in Matipo Street in Riccarton, Christchurch, spending my time there until 1936 when I was twelve. I was runner up to be Dux of the school but Laurie Turner, who later served in the Second World War and completed a full career as an Officer in the Royal New Zealand Air Force, pipped me to the post. He has dined out on his victory for years.

After primary school I went to Christchurch Technical College to complete a four years' full time Engineering Course. For the first year of it I travelled by train into Christchurch, its arrival time always compelling me to miss the first lecture. To compensate, I had to stay on later in the day to catch up on the missed work before catching the local train, called the Springfield Train, back home. The course imposed lots of homework. The Engineering Course was biased towards mechanical engineering but included work in other branches of the discipline. We had a workshop for lathes, a blacksmith's department, which I enjoyed very much, and an electrical engineering side. In my fourth year at college we visited various industrial enterprises as part of the course, such as the Addington railway workshops, Mercer Stainless Steel, the Tramway Workshops, Scott's Foundry in Manchester Street, Ballin's Brewery, and the Irwin Electrical Company. When we were at the last named, our teacher, Harold Kirby, was upset over the prolific swearing of Harry Irwin, who hosted our visit. Teachers and teaching being generally a world of propriety at that time, the manner of Harry's speech represented an affront to the conduct that schooling tried to inculcate. School culture was formal. The teaching staff all wore academic black gowns and imposed a tough discipline.

In February 1941, at the end of the four years' course, I joined the engineering branch of the New Zealand Post Office as a junior technician in the automatic telephone exchange in Hereford Street in Christchurch, at the age of sixteen and a half. How different the conditions and circumstances governing a young man's first employment have become. My brother also went to college. After three years of study he became an apprentice to a flour miller at Fleming's Mill. When it burnt down, the firm re-located at Hornby. Our parents were conscious of the depression that made employment difficult to find in the 1930s. They were like so many people at that time in believing that security was the main objective in seeking a job, and that government employment was security writ large.

I was still at college when war broke out on 3 September 1939. We were all very aware of what was happening in the wider world. The College produced a quarterly magazine which, by 1941, was already reporting the names of past students who had become aircrew members in the United Kingdom and the Mediterranean but were listed as missing or killed in action. For me it was very impressionable, as I knew many of them by name. I didn't expect to be called up but I had been a member of the Air Cadet Squad which the college had first formed in 1936, as an initiative with foresight, being the first college in the country to do it. Limited to twenty-four students, a member needed to be a second year engineer to be eligible for membership. Monday afternoons were devoted to its activities. I wore a khaki jacket, shorts, and the traditional pointed Kiwi hat – dubbed the lemon squeezer - with gold and green college colours as a hat band. I became used to wearing a uniform. These Monday afternoons were spent at Wigram, which by 1941 had assumed such growth as New Zealand's largest aircrew training centre, that it could best be described as an air base, in the terminology of the later war years. We cadets were able to undertake many small chores for the staff, while all around us the place was alive with personnel, whilst aircraft were constantly taking off and landing. In my third year as a student I was promoted to work in a hanger refuelling the Baffin and Vildebeest aircraft. I spent an entire week at the base once each year, in addition to the regular Monday visits. The base was conveniently close to home for me, only a short bike ride away.

For the week-long visits, the aircraft section of the Air Cadets underwent special training at Wigram Aerodrome. It was divided into three groups, each individual being placed in the charge of an Aircraftman. Every moment was interesting and educational as we carried out work using various types of machines. Each of the three groups specialized in one of the different branches of the work, respectively engine-fitting, airframe rigging, and photography. A fitter Cadet spent time in the aerodrome workshop where parts of the engines and machines were overhauled and cleaned. A number of rigger Cadets were occupied throughout the entire week assisting in the dismantling of a two seat aircraft which was due to be rebuilt. The Cadets handled every part of the work and thereby were able to gain a thorough knowledge of the aircraft's construction and controls.

At various times during the day the pilots brought their aircraft in to be refueled. As the machines did not turn easily on the ground, Aircraftmen and Cadets held the wing tips to manoeuvre them into position. The boys assisted when aircraft engines were being started and maintained a readiness for these duties and others whenever a formation was taking off or landing. At other times there were special tasks for the Cadets, such as filling the bombs that the pilots used for practice bombing at Lake Ellesmere.

On one occasion the Officers of 3 Squadron who were undergoing a refresher course at the base, spent most of the time undertaking formation flying and aerobatics. The machine guns which were used during these mock battles did not fire real bullets but took photographs of the opposing aircraft to determine the potential effectiveness of the gunnery. Only the pilots of the New Zealand Permanent Air Force flew the big Vickers Vildebeest torpedo bombers. There were six other types of aircraft at Wigram, mostly obsolescent, only one of them being still used in England at the time. At the end of our week's stay at Wigram, some members of the section were given an aerobatic flight in training aircraft. Some lucky ones were in the air at other times, but I was not one of them.

With my interest in the base quickened by the duties incurred in the Air Cadet Squad, I began to spend every spare moment that I could find there. With a neighbour I used to hang about the Canterbury Aero Club, which was also located at Wigram, polishing aircraft and doing any odd jobs that came our way, hoping to get the free flight that never in fact materialized. Instead, I had to take my first flight by paying ten shillings of my own hard-earned money for fifteen minutes over Christchurch in a Monospar aircraft.

During the College vacations for four years I was never short of things to do. The Blenheim Road sawmill sometimes had an odd job or two for me when I wasn't picking raspberries at Middleton Road orchard. I still had time to cut cocksfoot, which had to be stooked, flailed by hand, and bagged, the seed fetching nine pence per pound. Evidently I made a small private living in one way or another as I could afford to visit the Centennial Exhibition in Wellington in 1940, while I was still at college, staying with a cousin in Petone. In the beautiful January weather of 1940, I indulged the delights of the Exhibition daily, especially the rollercoaster, together with visits around Wellington, including the Massey Memorial, and a factory or two. Just catching the train into Wellington Railway Station with its throng of people from all the suburbs was a fascinating experience.

In the 1930s, although my father was in a permanent job, his wages being modest, my mother supplemented his income by taking a job over at the Bush Inn, where P Burke & Company were caterers for the race meetings. She stayed in it for twenty-seven years. The additional income she earned guaranteed that my brother and I were well cared for, and well clothed. Father cut our hair. I think he invented the tennis ball haircut. I never had shoes until I was thirteen, having always worn boots. Father was very green fingered, a truly wonderful gardener, producing more than we could eat ourselves. We just gave the surplus away to other needy families. My mother was a superb cook on the kitchen coal range. Girdle scones, sponges, and roasts came out of that oven in constant profusion. I used to think how lucky I was to have such a mother and father.

With one influence and another on me I began to look forward to going into the Services. When I went to the Telephone Exchange I made an application to join the Air Force at sixteen and a half. Eventually I embarked on the required pre-entry courses. My parents signed for me to enlist under the age of twenty-one but I am quite sure they believed the war would be finished before I was old enough to get into it. Dr Scannell did my pre-entry medical examination in the Dominion Building in The Square in the middle of Christchurch. He told me that I was a bit short in the leg but added that he thought my legs might grow a little more. I attended night school for the pre-entry studies, joining more mature men who had had very little, if any, secondary education. I became friendly with a chap of thirty whose limited education left him struggling with the course, but I was able to coax him along. On completing the course I was still too young to enlist so I moved on to the advanced pre-entry course, the teacher for which was Ted Lunn, one of my former teachers at the Technical College, who later became a long serving Education Officer in the Air Force. When he saw me he asked me to come forward and sit in the front. One day in front of the class he asked me to state Boyle's Law. I promptly did so, after which he never troubled me again. I later met him in the Air Force when I was based in Ohakea in 1946, and was able to exchanges experiences with him.

Along the way, my fellow students had all received their notices to report for duty. I reached my eighteenth birthday while working at the Telephone Exchange but I had still not been called up, so with a flash of inspiration I asked my foreman if I could put through a toll call to T A Barrow, the Air Secretary. When he came on the line, I told him who I was and what I had done. He said to me, "Mr Goss, you will have a telegram within twenty-four hours." The telegram duly arrived, ordering me to report to the Initial Training Wing at Rotorua on 23 July 1942.

The Air Force had taken over a number of properties in Rotorua to cope with the surge in the town's population. The rapid concentration and increase in personnel in Air Force bases were more than building contractors could meet in the short term by way of the customary Nissen huts and other temporary housing characteristic of military camps everywhere. I was accommodated in Brent's Hotel.

The Initial Training Wing issued our uniforms and other kit, gave us medical checks, vaccinations, and inoculations. Lectures were held in makeshift places all over town, such as the cinema and the Town Hall – to which we always marched, as we did to everywhere else, as a squad. Having arrived on a Friday, I had to turn out on Sunday morning for my first Church parade in the street, outside Brent's Hotel. It was in July with twelve degrees of frost. Once we were lined up, the shout went out for all Roman Catholics and Jews to fall out. Having been brought up in the Anglican Church, I knew the order did not apply to me but I suddenly became confused, in not understanding what was taking place. A lad standing next to me did his best to enlighten me by muttering, "That's because we bloody protestants can't be trusted to go to church on our own."

While I was in Rotorua I developed the mumps. On reporting sick I was sent to Princess Gate Hospital. The power of group identity had already taken hold of me as I became concerned that my sojourn in hospital would mean being relegated to the next intake of recruits. I actually sat the Armaments examination in hospital, but before I started writing someone checked the room, and turned over the mattress to make sure that I had not squirreled away any cheat sheets.

In the event I stayed with the course and passed to qualify for a posting to the Number 3 Elementary Flying Training School at Harewood on 4 September 1942, flying the Tiger Moth. Assigned to Pilot Officer Arthur Claydon as my instructor, I soon inferred that we were not going to get along very amicably. After a few hours of dual flying there were no signs that I would be flying solo. Progress was partly hampered by my being in hospital again for a few days. Flying started at 0500 hours on days when the seasonal strong north-westerly winds were blowing.

I made better progress after changing to Pilot Officer Mitchell as my instructor, going solo soon thereafter. But on 19 October 1942 in Tiger Moth DHNZ797, having amassed 9 hours and 45 minutes of solo flying and 23 hours and 40 minutes of dual instruction, I seemed to lose a sense of control on returning to base. After first one, and then a second, abortive approach to a landing, the attention of a number of people around the airfield focused on my predicament. The fire engine and ambulance were warmed up, just in case they were needed, and my instructor

13

came out in the jeep, waiting for me. By the time of my fourth attempt, half the station was watching. My fifth attempt had the making of a reasonably good landing but it was fifty feet too high, resulting in my overshooting. I held off too long and stalled, one wing dropping down, causing severe damage to the undercarriage, wing and fuselage, but I escaped uninjured.

Having been checked on the spot for injury, embarrassingly I then had to carry my parachute around the perimeter of the airfield to the office of the Flight Commander. I was given three days' leave. My logbook was duly endorsed but I was allowed to complete the course, finally amassing 42 hours of dual and 40.5 hours of solo flying. However, at the end of the course, three of us were called in by Squadron Leader Morry Archibald, the Chief Ground Instructor, who announced, "LAC Goss, LAC Glengarry, and LAC Harris, your flying training has been terminated. Do you wish to remuster as a navigator, wireless operator, or bomb aimer?" Without drawing breath I chose navigator. The three of us were sent to Rongotai, Wellington. We were there until March 1943, until we were sent back to the Initial Training Wing at Rotorua to repeat the initial training course for new recruits – a total waste of time as far as I was concerned.

After some interim initial training in navigation at Rongotai from 27 November 1942, I was sent on leave on 1 April 1943 before leaving from Auckland for Canada on the *Matsonia*. It was in part a hospital ship - although it was not marked as such - since it carried wounded United States marines from the fighting in the islands. It had its own armament, consisting of anti-aircraft guns on both sides of the bridge and on the stern. The thirty-two Air Force personnel were detailed to man these guns. We received no systematic instruction and practice, just cursory directions as to what to do. We spent four hours on duty and four off. Fortunately we were never called upon to fire the guns. I dread to think what our level of gunnery performance would have been if the ship had been subject to a determined attack by Japanese aircraft.

The voyage was uneventful as it happened, but life on board was not as salubrious as might have been expected of an American ship that was considered to be a luxury liner. But after all, the ship was at war. We had only two meals per day. In the American way we lined up for breakfast, consisting of strange food. The voyage left us hungry and hollow legged but we bought canteen biscuits at the first opportunity to save the day, on disembarking at San Francisco, from where we travelled by train to Vancouver to take the Canadian Pacific Railway through the Rockies, destined for the Brandon Manning Depot. Arriving to a Canadian summer, having left a New Zealand summer, we were dispatched for navigator training to the Number 7 Air Observer Flying School of the Royal Canadian Air Force at Portage La Prairie, Manitoba.

After twenty-one weeks of classroom instruction in nine subjects, and six air assignments in Anson aircraft, which involved 70 hours and 30 minutes of flying by day, and 40 hours and 20 minutes by night, I received my navigator's wing and was commissioned with the rank of Pilot Officer. After some leave in New York early in November 1943, I had to report to Halifax, Nova Scotia, to await a posting. I was one of twenty newly qualified navigators from our course who embarked for the Pacific on 16 December 1943 aboard the USS *General John Pope* from San Francisco. We disembarked at Noumea, New Caledonia, on Christmas Eve 1943, to be airlifted in a United States Air Force Dakota to New Zealand on Boxing Day.

I was posted to 31 Squadron that was being formed in New Zealand to fly Avenger aircraft in dive bombing operations. I took my first flight on 19 January 1944 and was eventually crewed with Flying Officer Tom Worsp as pilot, and Sergeant Neville Williams as wireless operator/ air gunner. Our first serious mission, apart from all the flying training that was necessary to achieve Squadron efficiency, was to ferry a replacement aircraft to Number 30 Squadron, the first and only other Squadron formed to fly Avengers. It was already operating in the battle zone, based on Bougainville Island. We returned to the Gisborne base in a Dakota on 14 April.

After ten days of pretty tough jungle survival training before leaving New Zealand, the Squadron moved to Piva North airstrip on Bougainville, where we were under the control of Marine Air Group 24, in the company of an American Dauntless dive bomber

After twenty-one weeks of classroom instruction in nine subjects, and six air assignments in Anson aircraft, which involved 70 hours and 30 minutes of flying by day, and 40 hours and 20 minutes by night, I received my navigator's wing and was commissioned with the rank of Pilot Officer. After some leave in New York early in November 1943, I had to report to Halifax, Nova Scotia, to await a posting. I was one of twenty newly qualified navigators from our course who embarked for the Pacific on 16 December 1943 aboard the USS *General John Pope* from San Francisco. We disembarked at Noumea, New Caledonia, on Christmas Eve 1943, to be airlifted in a United States Air Force Dakota to New Zealand on Boxing Day.

I was posted to 31 Squadron that was being formed in New Zealand to fly Avenger aircraft in dive bombing operations. I took my first flight on 19 January 1944 and was eventually crewed with Flying Officer Tom Worsp as pilot, and Sergeant Neville Williams as wireless operator/ air gunner. Our first serious mission, apart from all the flying training that was necessary to achieve Squadron efficiency, was to ferry a replacement aircraft to Number 30 Squadron, the first and only other Squadron formed to fly Avengers. It was already operating in the battle zone, based on Bougainville Island. We returned to the Gisborne base in a Dakota on 14 April.

After ten days of pretty tough jungle survival training before leaving New Zealand, the Squadron moved to Piva North airstrip on Bougainville, where we were under the control of Marine Air Group 24, in the company of an American Dauntless dive bomber squadron, a New Zealand Corsair squadron and a New Zealand Ventura squadron. The Japanese were over 80,000 strong on the island and given to making occasional artillery attacks against the base, but the United States Navy maintained enough firepower generally to deter them. Nevertheless we always carried a revolver and a jungle knife on the base and kept them under our pillows when sleeping.

We lived three to a tent which was mounted on a wooden surround three feet in height. Ablutions were a problem, the water being invariably brackish. Food was plentiful but with little variation, notably featuring the wartime meat invention called Spam, cooked in many different ways. The hot and humid climate required a daily dosage of salt tablets, together with an anti-malaria tablet. Insects could be lethal. So could the Japanese. Occasionally we had to jump into foxholes when Japanese aircraft came over, usually at night, but we were reluctant to do so to avoid the centipedes, whose bite could induce an immediate coma, or serious nausea or paralysis.

Our first mission was on 27 May for a strike with twelve100 pound bombs to Hospital Ridge at Rabaul in New Britain, taking off at 0745 hours. To prepare for the dive we had to climb to 14,000 feet, where we were oxygen starved and very cold. I well remember the bursts of anti-aircraft fire around us and the acrid smell of cordite. I had to operate the stinger gun during the actual attack, while navigation duties were in suspense. On pulling out of the dive I leapt up, thinking I had been hit, but the cause of my discomfort was the collection of hot bullet cases from my own gun which had accumulated around my partly bare legs while I had been sitting in the gun position. On subsequent raids we lost an aircraft on 31 May, 5 June, 14 June, and 1 July before the tour ended on 28 July, when we flew our aircraft in stages back to New Zealand, the total flight time taking 16 hours and 40 minutes. Targets for the tour variously included air fields, supply dumps, troop concentrations, barges, enemy crops, and targets of opportunity.

The crews from these lost aircraft were mostly killed on their stricken aircraft's impact with the ground. It was difficult to bale out from an Avenger in a 60° dive attitude. Pilots used to open their canopies during the dive to facilitate their own escape if needed, but the navigator, positioned in the rear of the aircraft and encumbered with radar equipment and the stinger gun, often flew with his parachute hung on the side of the fuselage, imperiling his escape should he need to take it. Our pockets were full of rations, maps, and other items that could support survival if it were possible to bale out successfully.

It was probably easier for the crew of an Avenger to evacuate their aircraft if it could be put down on the water. One evening when I was on duty as Orderly Officer at Gisborne in New Zealand before the tour, I received a call from station PABX, the Women's Auxiliary Air Force operator on duty telling me that she had received a call from a local farmer who claimed he had seen an aircraft disappear into the sea. Since night flying was in progress, I contacted the control tower to find that indeed contact with one of our aircraft had been lost whilst it had been on the downwind leg of the landing circuit. Tom Worsp took off in a Harvard with its landing light on to search the area of the sea over which aircraft flew in making their approach to the runway. He sighted a dinghy with the three crewmen in it. Two of them were in good shape, but the navigator, Sergeant Sam Newton, who had graduated with me in Canada, was bleeding profusely from an injury to his chin. On jettisoning the rear door of the aircraft while it was sinking, he had collided with the flare tube which had folded under the pressure of water.

Following the tour with 31 Squadron, I was sent on a three weeks' refresher course in navigation to Bell Block, New Plymouth. A simulator tactical floor with new technology provided a revolving screen of landscapes and seascapes - as viewed from a navigator's cabin - containing natural features and enemy shipping. It made a very realistic means to exercise the trainee's skills and test his knowledge. I then received a posting to the aircrew pool at Hobsonville, where I was subjected again to the rigours of a formal base, including formalities and parade ground marching, but also the chance to fly in a Walrus flying boat, that as a type had become largely obsolete.

The days of the Avenger as a dive bomber had been short and were by November 1944 on the wane. I was posted to Fiji, to Lauthala Bay to join the Number 3 Operational Training Unit for a conversion course to the Catalina flying boat, taking my first flight on 14 December 1944. The contrasts between the navigator's work station, facilities, and the performance characteristics of the Catalina, compared with those of the Avenger, could scarcely have been greater.

Although my first operational missions were unsuccessful searches for overdue aircraft, I was soon involved in conveying important personages around the area. After flying with several different crews for my earliest flights - which included the transport of Mr Alexander Grantham, Governor of Fiji, for a tour of the Lau Islands - I settled down with the same crew from 20 February 1945 until the cessation of hostilities in August. My colleagues were Squadron Leader Ken Smith, the Captain – later, as Wing Commander, the Commanding Officer of Number 6 Flying Boat Squadron; Flying Officer Neil Carr-Smith, co-pilot; Flight Sergeant Andy Beattie, flight engineer; Sergeant Joe Laird, fitter 2E; Sergeant Swannie Horton, fitter 2A; Sergeant Bill Jarman, 1st wireless operator; Sergeant Dave Knight, 2nd wireless operator and air gunner; and Sergeant Warren Shaw, air gunner.

The work of 6 Squadron was to patrol an area of the Solomon Islands between Guadalcanal, Malaita, Santa Isabel, Choiseul, New Georgia, and Vella La Vella. It was a vast area to cover for anti-submarine searches, shipping movements, the rescue of downed aircrew members, and sometimes the transport of supplies to islands with no airstrips. We never spotted an enemy submarine but we did carry out the last rescue of a downed aircrew member of the war. With the cessation of hostilities, aircraft and people had to be evacuated from the islands and repatriated. The Catalina flying boats of Numbers 5 and 6 Squadrons were stripped down to help in the huge task of ferrying New Zealand's military personnel back from the war zone to their own country, carrying on average fifteen passengers per trip.

On 8 August 1945, our aircraft was sent to drop leaflets over Nauru and Ocean Islands to advise Japanese garrisons that an Australian destroyer was on its way to accept their surrender. They were obviously aware of their situation, following the dropping of the first atomic bomb on Hiroshima on 6 August. They signalled our arrival with white crosses clearly visible on the ground. It was a long trip, taking just under eleven hours. We stayed overnight at Tarawa Island before taking an eight hours' flight back to base.

Prior to our final departure from Halavo Bay, we received a Mayday call on 19 September to rescue a Corsair pilot who had been forced to ditch in the ocean south of Guadalcanal. Local natives picked him up in an outrigger canoe. They took him ashore but then brought him out to our aircraft which landed close to the beach. This was the last 'Dumbo' mission of the Pacific war zone.

Our aircraft, PBY5 4017, was the last to leave the station, flying out from Halavo Bay on 24 September to Hobsonville. Married men were then sent on leave but I was posted to the Air Sea Rescue Utility Flight there, but with a diminished demand for this unit's services, we were used to take part in the repatriation of New Zealand military personnel from Australia. On Boxing Day 1945 we took off for a flight of 10 hours and 25 minutes to Rose Bay in Sydney, returning with twenty-two mostly Army male and female passengers two days later. It happened to be a tough return journey through two parallel cold fronts and a severe electrical storm for half of the flight of 9 hours and 45 minutes. Most of the passengers were very ill. That was my last flight as navigator in a Catalina.

After some leave, I returned to Hobsonville to find myself posted to Number 2 Bomber Reconnaissance Squadron based at Ohakea, flying Ventura aircraft. Following familiarization exercises with the aircraft, I took part in the daily meteorological flights taken out over the Tasman Sea at 15,000 feet to gather the weather data, such as air temperatures, and cloud formations. As a diversion, our aircraft was sent to search for a yacht, missing on Lake Taupo, the great lake in North Island, but without success. One of our aircraft was lost on 28 February 1946, a search over many days failing to find it. Decades later its remains were discovered in the Tararua Ranges.

I never settled down comfortably with the Ventura aircraft or the work required of it. Having flown for a total of 31 hours and 5 minutes on these peacetime assignments, I decided to apply simultaneously for a permanent commission in the Royal New Zealand Air Force and a four year extended commission in the Royal Air Force, hoping that one would come to pass. Meanwhile, after some deliberation, I decided to leave the Air Force, with effect from 16 April 1946, returning to Christchurch to work as a technician in the automatic telephone exchange. It was while I was on a professional training course in Wellington in January 1947, that I received news that I had been accepted by the Royal Air Force. Ironically, only two weeks later I received a similar four year engagement offer from the Royal New Zealand Air Force. I accepted the former – a decision heralding a substantial change in my life.

By this time I had amassed an overall total of 743 flying hours by day and 80 hours and 40 minutes by night in the Royal New Zealand Air Force. Of these, 200 hours and 15 minutes were flown by day and 1 hour and 55 minutes were flown by night in the Avengers of 31 Squadron, most of them spent in attacking twenty-four specified targets and a further eighteen flown to attack targets of opportunity, always escorted by Corsairs, Dauntlesses, and other Avengers, with the exception of a few solo flights against targets of opportunity. The 272 hours and 20 minutes spent flying in the Catalina were all in daytime. They included 130 hours and 20 minutes for eighteen operational missions and the one rescue of an airman from the ocean.

In July 1947, with four other ex-Royal New Zealand Air Force wartime airmen, I embarked on the passenger freighter *Australia Star*, a 12,000 ton cargo ship with accommodation and facilities for twenty-four passengers, for a four weeks, five star voyage via the Panama Canal to the United Kingdom. I had to report to RAF Uxbridge, a few miles to the west of London, to await a posting. I was sent first to the Transport Command Conversion Unit at Bircham Newton, then to the Number 1382 Transport Conversion Unit for Dakota aircraft at Wymeswold. At this time, conditions in Britain were generally poor. Rationing in foodstuffs and clothing prevailed. With the cessation of the American aid that had flowed during the war years, British people found themselves worse off in many ways than they had been during the war itself, while Marshall Aid poured into the Continental countries in abundance. At the latter base, the accommodation was basic with inadequate heating, such was the shortage of fuel. Fortunately, the decision was taken by the authorities to close Wymeswold and transfer us to North Luffenham. On the scheduled day of departure at 0810 hours, the fog descended and stayed for three days.

Between July 1947 and January 1948 I was posted to seven different stations as part of my conversion training to transport operations in RAF Transport Command, including paratrooping at Netheravon, near Salisbury, and glider towing, amassing 67 hours 5 minutes flying by day and 31 hours 45 minutes by night. I was then posted to the Far East Command at RAF Changi in Singapore on 13 March 1948 to serve with 48 Squadron flying Dakota aircraft, with detachments to Kuala Lumpur and Kaitak, Hong Kong. It was the time of communist insurgency in Malaya. Tin mines were being blown up, and rubber plantations burnt. I flew many routes, including Carnicobar Island, Kuala Lumpor, Kuching, Labuan, Saigon, and Kaitak. Other destinations on routes flown included Saigon, Surabaya, Darwin, Alice Springs, Adelaide, Ceylon, and Japan. The Transport Command Examining Unit visited Changi Base every six months to test all pilots, navigators, and wireless operators, regarding their qualifications to carry important public and service passengers. By three stages between 4 January 1949 and 24 November 1950, I reached the very highest grading, the VVIP category, that qualified me to fly the Royal Family.

In January 1949 I was assigned to Kaitak in Hong Kong at the time of the growing ascendance of the communist forces over the nationalists in China. The former were poised to overrun Nanking and Shanghai. We were engaged in flying Embassy staff out from those two cities. Flight times involved were: Kaitak to Shanghai 5 hours 30 minutes; Kaitak to Nanking 5 hours 10 minutes. Our Dakota in its tropical configuration was ill-equipped to carry VIPs. We had no heating system for passengers to relieve the winter temperatures in flight across China. The conditions in Nanking during the revolutionary war made landing there something of a challenge.

Our last assignment was on Friday 26 February 1949 carrying a British Army diplomatic courier and his eleven bags of diplomatic mail, plus six embassy staff, destined for Canton and then Kaitak, Hong Kong. We were ordered on a Grade 1 diversion. Initially I ignored it, being confident our ETA at Canton would still leave twenty-two minutes of daylight. A second firm order, however, came to divert to an airfield at Swatow, about 120 miles north of Kaitak.

On landing there we were surrounded by soldiers with fixed bayonets. A lady embassy member of staff spoke at length to their leader in Cantonese. Eventually a British Customs Officer arrived, convincing the soldiers that we were friendly and expected normal diplomatic courtesies, in being committed to give assistance to the Major who had top priority with his diplomatic service mailbags. We had to be accommodated with the Customs people overnight.

The Major embarked the next morning for Hong Kong on a Norwegian ship with his mailbags. With his bags he was due to fly to Britain on the next BOAC flight out of Hong Kong. The airfield authorities refused to refuel our aircraft unless they were paid in United States dollars. After a delay, dollars were sent out by the government from Hong Kong, enabling us to leave on the Monday. Arriving at Kaitak, the civil aviation authorities impounded my log sheets and investigated why I had not responded to the first diversion notice. However, I was able to justify the action taken, my calculations on examination showing that we could have reached Canton in safety in daylight. The discussion finally put an end to our week-end's internment - a sojourn that was not entirely unwelcome, since we were invited to parties and were able to play tennis. Fortunately the Governor turned out to be Sir Alexander Grantham, who I had ferried in the Catalina from Fiji in February 1945, so our ultimate fate rested in good hands.

I returned to Changi in June 1949 when the Squadron moved to Kuala Lumpur for six months, dropping supplies to the British Army forces engaged against the communist insurgents. I flew from Changi with supply drops to the Gurkhas, the Suffolk Regiment, the Malay Regiment, the Seaforth Highlanders, and the Coldstream Guards, with an average flight time per drop of 1 hour 30 minutes. One particularly interesting trip on 3 August 1949 was to transport Brigadier Erskine from Kuala Lumpur to Quatah, a trip of 1 hour 40 minutes, owing to the fact that two months later, on 28 October 1949, we had to search for a missing

Auster aircraft with Brigadier Erskine aboard. On one occasion we flew to Borneo to collect twenty-three Dyak trackers who had been contracted by the British Forces for three months to serve with the Gurkhas in Malaya.

The Squadron returned to Changi in January 1950, and I resumed flying all routes until January 1951, when we again went to Kuala Lumpur for supply dropping. During this time two Valetta aircraft – VR 485 and VR 495 were sent to 48 Squadron for tropical trials, crew familiarization, route flying, and supply dropping trials. I did nineteen flights in them from 26 June 1950, with a total flying time of 35 hours and 5 minutes. My last flight for 48 Squadron took place on 11 February 1951 before I embarked with my wife and baby daughter on the *Empire Windrush* for the United Kingdom. Considerations over further duties in the Royal Air Force were governed by the fact that my contracted service time was drawing to a close. After a delay, the Air Ministry offered me a permanent appointment in the Royal Air Force but my wife Valmai and I decided to return to civilian life in New Zealand.

In my flying career I amassed 798 hours 25 minutes by day and 80 hours 40 minutes by night in the Royal New Zealand Air Force, and 882 hours 50 minutes by day and 57 hours and 15 minutes by night in the Royal Air Force.

My brother-in-law, who had been a prisoner of war in Japan for three years, and I formed a family retail appliances business which lasted for twenty-seven years until, with his premature death in 1977, I sold it. For a brief period I became an inspector for the Inland Revenue Department, a job that opened up for me a different dimension of life from that of all my previous experience in that it brought me up against a wider range of people, their problems, their behaviour, and financial intricacies, than I had previously encountered. It was a challenging learning curve for me.

Early in 1982, I was appointed to the position of Secretary Manager of the Wellington Stock Exchange Trading Floor. The most important part of the job was to make sure the trading floor was ready on time for business five days each week. I had to ensure that everything ran as smoothly as possible, that all the staff members were doing their jobs, dealing with complaints, and most importantly that all rules and regulations were being strictly observed. It was a challenging work environment in which we had to cope with the crash of 1987 and the phasing out of the outcry system in favour of full electronic automation, which was achieved on 21 June 1991. When I first started in the job it was considered to be a good morning's work if NZ$1 million of business took place in a morning. By the end of my time there the market was averaging about NZ$20 million in one day. I later took a position with a brokering firm for ten years until finally retiring in 2003.

My wife Valmai died in 1997. We had three daughters and two sons, all of whom have remained in New Zealand. I have seven grandchildren and two great grandchildren.

Two voluntary occupations have given me particular satisfaction over the years since leaving Air Force service. I was for many years the Verger at St Paul's Cathedral in Wellington, a position that involved me heavily in so many important public and national occasions in the Cathedral. I served through the terms of office of three Deans and enjoyed the wonderful choral music over many years. On leaving the Royal Air Force late in 1951, I completed four years on the Air Force active reserve which required annual refreshment training in navigation, general administration, and flying in the Bristol Freighter and Hastings aircraft. Throughout the years I have kept in close touch with ex-aircrew members by joining the Brevet Club, being a lifelong member of the Wellington Branch, and President of the National Organisation of Brevet Clubs.

~~~

Graham Goss flew as pilot in the first, and as navigator in the rest, of the following aircraft, listed in experiential order.

Tiger Moth
Anson
Avenger
Catalina
Ventura

Charles Kingsford Smith arriving in Christchurch in the first aircraft to cross the Tasman Sea, 1928, an event witnessed by Graham Goss as a boy of four on his father's shoulders. From the original painting of the event by the official Air Force artist M. Conly, held in the collection of the Royal New Zealand Air Force Museum

Graham Goss aged thirteen as a student at Christchurch Technical College in 1937

Vildebeest aircraft at Wigram in 1939, Photograph taken by Graham Goss as a cadet

Graham Goss at Rotorua on entry to the Air Force, July 1942

Graham Goss as trainee pilot flying the Tiger Moth at Harewood, Christchurch, September 1942

An Avenger aircrew at the Operational Training Unit at Gisborne in 1944. L-R: Graham Goss, navigator; Tom Worsp, pilot; Neville Williams, wireless operator/gunner

31 Squadron personnel at The Officers' Mess at Gisborne in February 1944

The 'Grey Wolves' Squad of trainee navigators at Rongotai awaiting a posting to Canada for advanced training in 1943. LAC G H Goss 428757 is at the left hand end of the middle row

Navigators' Course in front of an Anson in Canada 1943. Graham Goss is second from the right hand end of the back row

Graham Goss in an Avenger over Gisborne in 1944

Avengers on their way to a target in New Britain in 1944

31 Squadron Avenger navigators in Bougainville in 1944. The back row includes Sergeant Scott, Pilot Officer Cameron, Pilot Officer Metcalfe, and an unidentified navigator, with Pilot Officer Norman and Pilot Officer Goss in front

Lieutenant Craig Morrison DSO and Lieutenant Jack Loftus of the Fleet Air Arm, experienced navigators for torpedo bombing, who were seconded to 31 Squadron. Craig Morrison was shot down and killed over Rabaul

Picture theatre built by New Zealanders at Halavo Bay, Tulagi
Island in 1944. Note the crude canvas canopies for protection
from the rain. Smoking was allowed.

Avengers at Piva North airstrip in Empress Augusta Bay,
western central Bougainville, in 1944. Note the smoking
volcano of Mount Bagana in the background.

Avenger at Piva being loaded with bombs for a mission in 1944

Avengers preparing for take off at Piva in 1944

Avengers attacking
Rabaul in 1944. From
the original painting of
the event by the official
Air Force artist M.
Conly, held in the
collection of the Royal
New Zealand Air Force
Museum

Graham Goss in the
Royal Air Force on the
right with Roy Owen of
the Royal South African
Air Force in Trafalgar
Square, London, on 12
March 1947. Note that
Roy is wearing a new
style uniform with no
large side pockets

Catalina crew at Lauthala Bay in Fiji in 1944. L-R back row: Wing Commander Ken J Smith, Captain; Flying Officer Neil Carr-Smith, second pilot; Flying Officer Graham Goss, navigator; Sergeant Billy Jarman, 1st wireless operator/air gunner; Sergeant Dave Knight, 2nd wireless operator/air gunner; L-R front row: Sergeant Andy Beattie, engineer; Sergeant Joe Laird, fitter 2 electrical; Sergeant Swannie Horton, fitter 2 airframe; Sergeant Warren Shaw, air gunner

Chapter 2.

In Unlikely Places

George Gudsell

In Unlikely Places

Looks sometimes belie age. I have been fortunate in that although I have had my share of those physical disabilities that come with advancing age, and although I sometimes feel every one of my eighty-eight years, I am frequently taken for a younger man. Having been born in Ashburton in the South Island of New Zealand on 15 June 1918, I was the youngest of three boys. My parents themselves were both born in New Zealand. A fourth boy died at an early age. All three of us were born during the First World War which brought such losses to the young male population of New Zealand - and suffering to their families - in disproportionate magnitude to the total population of the country.

All three of us, ironically, being war children, were destined to serve in the Second World War, all in the Royal New Zealand Air Force. One was a navigator, while the other – having lost two fingers during his employment as an electrician by grabbing a live power line – wanted to train as a member of aircrew but found that his disability made him ineligible. Nevertheless, he served as an electrician in Air Force ground staff postings in the Pacific war zone. All three of us volunteered.

My own primary and secondary schooling were completed in Ashburton. On leaving school finally at the age of seventeen from Form 6, I went to the then New Zealand University at Canterbury in the following year,1937, where I completed the required two years of professional training to be a teacher. At a later date I graduated with a BSc degree in chemistry from Victoria University in Wellington.

My first appointment was to the primary school at Kaikoura on the coast to the north of Christchurch. In my leisure time there, I became accustomed to the pleasure of fishing, which, in those days, when the claims on the products of the sea and rivers were so muted as compared with those of the present age, I found to be outstanding.

It was a matter of professional satisfaction to discover that I could establish a good rapport with the children. They seemed to respond well to me and my teaching style. Although I was only in that school for one year, it was a thoroughly enjoyable experience and in some senses I was sorry to leave, but the call of a career lured me into applying for and getting a post at the Christchurch Boys' High School, that had already acquired a good standing and has since become a prestigious institution.

The headmaster gave me a call asking if I would take a job there with the opportunity to live in the boarding establishment. By that time we were aware of the gathering threats to world peace, and all the implications that war could have for each of us of enlistment age. I was interested in returning to Christchurch, where I had completed my teacher training, as my girlfriend lived there. I later married her. While I was still at Kaikoura, I used to travel to Christchurch for the weekends. One night early in September 1939, she and I went to a film in the State Theatre. On leaving the cinema, we were confronted by youngsters selling newspapers on the footpath, with a big placard on which was the single word WAR. I remember the scene so clearly. I remember also the realization that quickly descended on me that it was likely my life would of necessity be changed by it. It was a storybook situation, the occurrence of an event over which one had absolutely no control, yet which was able to disturb one's life to its very fundamentals. Although a teacher, I was not on the reserve occupation list, so I wrote immediately to the authorities to volunteer for service in the Air Force which had become my first choice, as I had developed a fascination for the still relatively new activity of flying. During my school days I was a builder of model airplanes, and started a model aircraft club with other boys. I used to borrow my mother's kitchen whisk, put a hook on the end of it, and use it to wind up the elastic for the model aircraft.

I have good reason to believe that my application for aircrew training was the first of the avalanche of thousands which subsequently poured into the government department concerned.

I wrote a letter direct to The Secretary of the Air Force, saying only "I want to be a Pilot", and signing it, "George Gudsell." My two brothers had not applied at that time, but they both joined up soon afterwards.

On their being informed about it, the school authorities offered no objections to my action. Although my application was in the van, several thousand other such applications followed quite speedily from young men all over New Zealand who were anxious to enlist as aircrew members. In spite of there having been considerable notice that war was looming and would undoubtedly involve New Zealand, the authorities had not been able to put in place either the practical organization to cope with the emergent number of applicants or the administration to oversee the smooth running of it.

Fortuitously, the first six months of the Second World War gave some respite for the authorities to take the substantial measures needed for the effective recruitment and deployment of aircrew trainees. Nevertheless, a log jamb developed, preventing me from actually entering the Air Force – in terms of donning its blue uniform - until early in 1941. By that time of course the whole of Continental Europe had been overrun by the Axis powers. The war had assumed serious and already monumental proportions. Although during 1940 I was physically still a civilian, I was required to attend elementary theory classes on many aspects of flying, as part of an extended pre-entry course by correspondence.

It must be borne in mind that at that time the majority of young people left school after completing primary schooling or at most after perhaps only two years of schooling at a post-primary level. Since I had already completed high school and attended university, the mathematics and other subjects involved in this study course presented me with no difficulty. Meanwhile I remained in teaching through 1940 and into 1941 until I received an instruction to go to Levin in North Island. I turned up there in civilian clothes at 10.00 am on Sunday morning, 23 March 1941, and by 2 pm I was in uniform. The course there substantially constituted an induction into the Air Force for intending members of aircrew. It included six weeks of parade ground drill and physical training, together with classroom studies in such diverse subjects as mathematics, the theory of flight, elementary navigation, and how to fire a machine gun.

From Levin I was posted to Taieri in the south of South Island near Dunedin to take the initial flying training programme in the Tiger Moth. I had only one instructor at Taieri, Flying Officer Duncan. My first flight was on 12 May 1941, taking off into the wind. I encountered no problems during my flying there but was always aware that risk and danger were at stake. One of my friends, who had been at school with me in Ashburton, was on the same course but crashed his Tiger Moth and was killed. We lost two trainee pilots on the course out of thirty, both killed in accidents. Such accidents were far from rare but all attributable, as far as explanations and justification were concerned, to the exigencies of war.

This particular course was the very first to send initially trained pilots to Canada for the further stages of pilot training under the newly formed Empire Flying Training Scheme, which had been established but was still in its early stages of development at this time in mid-1941. About nine trainees from our course, and a similar number from two other Initial Flying Training Schools – those at Bell Block, New Plymouth, and Whenuapai – formed the first contingent to sail from New Zealand to Canada.. The rest of us were sent for further training to various stations in New Zealand flying Oxfords and Vildebeests. No Harvards were available at that time. They arrived in 1941 for use as advanced trainers at just about the time I finished my initial training.

Before going solo I flew for 8 hours and 35 minutes in the Tiger Moth with an instructor. I think that was a pretty normal performance. Altogether at Taieri I amassed 46 hours of flying, 25 altogether with an instructor and 21 hours solo. I was rated a good average at everything - as pilot and navigator, and for instrument flying.

I was posted from Taieri to the Service Flying Training School at Wigram where I trained on the Airspeed Oxford, which was still new to New Zealand as a training aircraft, my course being either the first or second course to use it. Prior courses had been using all single engined aircraft, including the obsolescent Vildebeest and Gordon. The twin-engine Airspeed Oxford was to become the standard trainer for trainee pilots who were preparing to fly bombers, the Harvard being the aircraft on which those destined to fly fighters were trained. While I was at Wigram, the first Harvard arrived, but I didn't fly one at that stage. At Wigram I flew only Oxfords, aggregating a total flying time of 86 hours dual and solo in them.

After Wigram I received a posting. The Chief Ground Instructor told eight of us to go to the clothing store to get Officer's uniforms before going on leave for two weeks. This was welcome news as I had married on Christmas Day 1940, less than three months before entering the Air Force. We had decided to marry in spite of the risks. My wife in particular was aware of them, as her own father had been a soldier at Gallipoli and suffered disfigurement as a result of having been shot in the nose.

The slightly ominous news was that after leave I had to report to Rongotai, Wellington. I duly turned up there at the appointed time, dressed in the new blue serge of a Pilot Officer's uniform, complete with my newly awarded wings carefully sewn onto the tunic by my wife. I had not been informed of the purpose of the journey to Wellington but soon discovered that the small group of twenty-two pilots and twenty-nine ground crew members assembled there was being sent to Singapore by ship, all the passengers on which were bound for the same place.

Our intended destination occasioned no qualms. Winston Churchill had referred to Singapore as "our impregnable fortress in the East." In our minds we may even have recognized that we could have been dispatched elsewhere, to far less safe and salubrious places. It was already clear that in Europe members of aircrew were taking heavy casualties, New Zealanders among them.

Whatever else Singapore had to offer in terms of our military future, its one unmistakable offering was its characteristic climate. Coming from New Zealand, the tropical contrast in the weather was a shock. I was wearing a complete uniform designed to be worn in a cold climate but I was forced to shed my jacket in unmilitary fashion, arriving only in my trousers and shirt, but still drenched in sweat. Many of the others seemed to have anticipated the need very well, having already donned tropical uniform. Within a few hours of arrival I followed their example with relief. No one thought of advising us before we embarked about the differences of climate.

It was late in September 1941 before we were settled into some kind of regular duty days. A duty day had little to commend it. There were no aircraft for us to fly. It was virtually a matter of filling in time. I worked at the combined Headquarters for all three services, answering the telephone. Perhaps in one sense it was a significant if humble job, in that I first received all incoming messages for the most senior commanders and then had to relay them. At the time hostilities had been taking place in far off Europe, but since June they had been greatly extended by the German invasion of the Soviet Union of Russia. In Singapore, British Army, Air Force, and Navy personnel continued to enjoy a relatively peaceful life at a quiescent station.

On 10 December 1941, only three days after Japan's attack on Pearl Harbour, further news came through that substantial numbers of Japanese transports, escorted by strong naval forces, were heading south towards Malaya. This information evoked the need for an immediate response in Singapore. In the event it soon became apparent that the available forces in Singapore were less than sufficient in kind and number to deal with the new style of warfare that Japan had unleashed in the Pacific. I became aware in the headquarters that the different service chiefs were arguing about the best way to counter the threat posed by the task force in question that was patently ultimately aimed at Singapore itself.

In terms of the assets available to them, the chiefs had no air power of consequence with regard to the distances involved, the numbers needed, and the types of aircraft actually to hand. The actual total aircraft in Malaya, at the point of its being attacked, consisted of seventeen Hudsons, thirty-four Blenheim light bombers, twenty-seven obsolescent Vildebeest torpedo bombers, ten Blenheim night fighters, three Catalinas, four Swordfish, five Sharks, and forty-one Brewster Buffaloes. The only aircraft that could have served as air cover for a sea-borne pre-emptive strike against the enemy task force were the obsolescent Brewster Buffaloes of 243 and 488 Squadrons, but they didn't have the range to cover ships out in the China Sea. In surface ships, the Navy lacked destroyers, cruisers, and other escort vessels, but had the use of the two capital ships, *Repulse,* an older, inter-war battleship, and the *Prince of Wales,* of recent vintage.

I well remember the chiefs arguing as to whether it was feasible to send these two battleships to intercept the Japanese fleet without either sea or air escorts. Ironically, only two months later, even as Singapore fell, the Kriegsmarine managed to achieve the passage of the battlecruisers *Scharnhorst* and *Gneisanau,* and the heavy cruiser *Prinz Eigen,* from Brest back to Germany through the English Channel, in the teeth of every effort made by the British on sea and in the air to destroy them. The enemy chose to make the attempt during atrocious weather. Although they had been previously damaged by repeated aerial attacks whilst docked or moored in Brest, the success of their dash through the Channel was mainly due to the huge air umbrella which the Luftwaffe mounted from their short range bases to cover them.

I listened to the discussion of the options open to them and heard them come to the reluctant decision to send the two battleships without escorts or air cover. The fate of the two ships is now history. They were both sent to the bottom by determined attacks from the air. The days of the invincible surface capital ship were over. I took a call from a voice that informed me that the two ships had been lost. I simply said, "Thank you," and put the receiver down. How could I forget the silence which met me when I announced to the assembled chiefs, "Gentlemen, the ships have been sunk." Air Vice Marshal Sir Robert Brooke-Popham, Commander-in-Chief of the British forces at that stage, was present.

The disbelief that Japan could be capable of such lightning and effective moves was almost palpable. Hong Kong fell on Christmas Day 1941, yet complacent attitudes prevailed long enough to ensure the inadequate defence of Singapore itself, particularly that of skepticism, if not contempt, for the seemingly disorganized percolation of Japanese infantry units on bicycles moving southwards through Malaya. The British Army was compelled to retreat to Singapore on 1 February 1942. A fortnight later, on 15 February 1942, Singapore surrendered.

I left Singapore for good on 12 January 1942. Of the twenty-two pilots brought by ship from New Zealand, only five of us were left in Singapore by this date. The rest had all been sent away to various places. The five of us had almost nothing to do. Suddenly, however, we were posted to 100 Squadron of the Royal Australian Air Force, which had been flying Vildebeest aircraft at Changi. On arriving at the airfield, we went into a hangar to find to our complete surprise a row of five beautifully painted white aircraft. They were Bristol Beaufort torpedo bombers, a new type of aircraft recently introduced into the Royal Air Force in Europe.

The pilots flying the old Vildebeests were envious of our assignment to fly the new Bristol Beauforts. But their envy was misplaced. These particular aircraft had been among the first to be produced in Australia. They incorporated all the faults that could be imagined. It is not an exaggeration to say that every flight taken caused something to fall off or malfunction. As a result, the decision was made to take them back to Australia by ship for a thorough overhaul. The five of us also went to Australia, flying in a civilian Short Empire Class four-engine flying boat of Imperial Airways. It was filled with women and children who were escaping from Singapore. We had to leave all our personal belongings behind. Mine included all the gifts given to me by my wife and family when I left New Zealand. They were locked in a locker in Changi but I never saw them again. We went to Australia with the expectation that we would learn to fly the Bristol Beaufort and return to Singapore to join in its defence, but events dictated otherwise, not least that of the devastating fall of Singapore itself.

We were posted to Richmond near Sydney for four months, training to fly the Beaufort, but by the time we had finished the course, Singapore had been conquered by Japan. Instead, I was sent formally on detachment to D Flight of 100 Squadron of the Royal Australian Air Force based at Nhil, where I flew operationally on anti-submarine patrols up and down the east coast of Australia, reporting shipping movements, particularly those from the United States. Ships that were reluctant to identify themselves had to be coerced into doing so. I used to bank away while opening the bomb doors to show the depth charges we were carrying. This was sufficient to persuade them that we were in earnest. Japanese submarines were apparently active in the area. I saw the wreckage of one ship off the mouth of the Brisbane River.

On 1 May 1942 the five of us were sent back to New Zealand on the *Boschfontein* out of Sydney Harbour. After being back for only a short while we heard of the attack on the Harbour by three Japanese midget submarines, and realized how close the imminence of the real products of war in the shape of sudden death was becoming.

My return to New Zealand led to a joyful reunion with my wife and my first sight of the baby daughter who had been born while I was in Singapore. After taking some leave, I was posted to Number 3 Squadron based at Whenuapai, where I found out that I was the only pilot on the Squadron who had flown operationally up to that date on active service, the others having been confined to New Zealand. The Squadron was still equipped with Vildebeests but within days the first Lockheed Hudson arrived. While I was there I took the opportunity to fly a Vildebeest, albeit unofficially.

I went to the islands for my first tour on Hudsons, arriving at Espiritu Santo on 19 October. Between October and December, 3 Squadron was operating from Pallikulo airstrip on Espiritu Santo, flying sea searches and anti-submarine patrols around the allied fleet anchorage in Segond Channel. I moved to Guadalcanal on 23 November 1942, as part of a detachment of six aircraft and eight crews, forming a Search and Patrol Group of the Air Search and Attack Command as part of United States Task Force 63. Our location was a muddy and depressing place. All accommodation consisted of tents pitched on mud. Frequent air raids by the enemy by day and night drove everyone into foxholes in the mud. Given disrupted sleep, long flying hours, and the stress of tropical heat and ailments, our existence was unpleasant and tiring. Guadalcanal was still occupied by the Japanese, with the exception of our airstrip and its immediate surround. Our tents were pitched in the gullies, subject to sniper fire from the ridge tops.

The year 1942 was a year of desperate fighting in all quarters as the Americans, supported by its Allies in the Pacific tried to stem the advance of Japanese forces. In the first five months of the year on land the Japanese Army achieved spectacular conquests throughout the islands and to the very gates of India. On 5 May, however, the United States triumphed over a Japanese fleet at the Battle of Coral Sea and again at the Battle of Midway on 3 June, blunting the enemy's control of the sea, and damaging its control of the air. American troops invaded Guadalcanal on 7 August. The gravity of the struggle against the Japanese was brought home to me graphically on Guadalcanal. I was once on duty in the control tower flashing aircraft to take off and land, horrified at the loads of wounded United States marines who were being ferried in and out. One aircraft was dripping blood when it landed.

My own experience of the force of enemy pressures during this year of Japanese victories occurred during November 1942. The Squadron was daily engaged in reconnaissance patrols to sight and plot the movements of enemy shipping and land units. On 24 November we spotted a tanker and two transports, escorted by a destroyer. I flew in low to make as clear an identification of the ships as possible but ran into three enemy Nakajima E8N1 seaplanes of the Japanese Navy which were circling the convoy on escort duty. They engaged us, three against one, but after twenty minutes of hesitant action they broke off their attack.

Their reticence, however, was not repeated on the second occasion of my direct confrontation with the enemy whilst engaged in finding their convoys at sea. On sighting a Japanese fleet only three days later, I was able to close in at 1,000 feet to determine the details of the convoy but whilst doing so our

Hudson was dived on by three enemy land based fighters. In their first attack they put the top turret out of action. Immediately I knew that we had to take stern and determined action if we were to survive. Normally one Hudson, albeit with adequate defensive armaments, would be no match for three enemy fighter aircraft.

I ordered Flying Officer R M McKechnie to fly the aircraft while I went up into the astro-hatch to direct the fight in a do-or-die situation. We had nothing to lose by making the best of it. It was in the event fortunate that we carried a second pilot. In common with the practice of the Royal Air Force in its European operations in the early years of the war, bomber aircraft in 1942 still included two pilots in the crew. The loss rate in Europe however led to a discontinuation of the practice by the Royal Air Force – a policy change that was also adopted by the Royal New Zealand Air Force later in the war.

The action lasted seventeen minutes. We survived a large number of passes but managed to spoil the effectiveness of the attacks. Perhaps the Japanese pilots' gunnery was not as good as it could have been. Perhaps our own gunnery was better than could have been expected. It was certainly measured and accurate for our purposes of survival. They eventually broke off the engagement and retired. In flying out from the land perhaps by that time their fuel had become low. They only scored three hits without injuring any of the crew.

The engagement, linked to finding an enemy convoy, earned the appreciation of the United States Command. I was awarded the United States Air Medal with the following citation, quoted verbatim.

"For meritorious achievement while participating in aerial flight in command of a reconnaissance bomber, serving with a Marine Aircraft Group during action against three enemy Japanese fighters southwest of Vella La Vella, Solomon Islands, on November 27, 1942. After relaying to his home base a complete report on the hostile task force which he had sighted, Flying Officer Gudsell, amid a hail of bursting antiaircraft shells, precariously hovered over the surface vessels to obtain further important information by closer observation. When suddenly set upon by three fighters who blasted the top gun turret out of action and then concentrated their attacks on the stern of his bomber, he employed such skilful evasive tactics and fire control that the Japanese aircraft were forced to break off the engagement and retire. With superb airmanship and courageous leadership, he brought his plane through perilous action under fire against heavy odds to return to safety without injury to the crew and with only a minimum of material damage."

While temporarily in the New Hebrides for resting and test flights just before Christmas 1942, the Squadron's Commanding Officer called me in to ask a favour. He explained that a consignment of beer for us was in the bottom of the hold of a ship out in the harbour but could not be unloaded before Christmas Day. He wanted me to fly to New Caledonia in an available Hudson aircraft. We stripped the aircraft of every movable object that wasn't vital for the flight, even our parachutes. I took only the navigator and wireless operator in the empty aircraft, without a map. None of us had been to New Caledonia before. When we reached the island we flew along the coast until we saw an airstrip where we landed. An American in a jeep turned up to ask what he could do for us. He told us that the New Zealand forces were fifty miles away at a place called de Gaiac. He offered us petrol, which I refused while asking him to forget that we had landed in the wrong place.

Our Commanding Officer had radioed ahead to de Gaiac to explain our mission. A truck awaited our arrival to take us to the Army stores where we spent the rolls of notes, that had been collected in the Squadron, on ninety dozen bottles of beer and three cases of whiskey. I estimated the weight of our purchase at one and a quarter tons – heavier than any bomb load we had ever carried. We put an overnight guard on the aircraft and spent Christmas Eve in great fashion.

Early on Christmas morning we set off on the return flight, a journey of about 250 miles, to our own base. The whole Squadron was gathered at the side of the runway as I took the Hudson in to touch down as gently as I could. My future would surely have been in jeopardy if I had broken a single bottle. The altitude during the flight had kept the beer cool, so we delivered a Christmas present in the best possible condition.

I was transferred to 6 Squadron with Catalina flying boats during 1943. The primary work of the Squadron was to maintain ocean and coastal patrols, particularly on or near the flight paths of allied bombers and fighter bombers going to and from their targets among the numerous islands. Occasionally we had to perform other duties. I once flew two mercy missions from our base at Lauthala Bay in Fiji to take native patients with maternity complications from Ono-I-Lau to hospital in Suva, the capital of Fiji. The first took place on 9 May 1943. The second was on 11 June in the same aircraft but with a different crew, including Flight Lieutenant Gallagher, Flying Officer Steel, and Flight Sergeant (later Sir Edmund) Hillary - who, in 1953, with Sherpa Tensing, was the first man to conquer Mount Everest - as the Catalina's navigator. In July 1945 I was called to a tribal conference in Lau where I was presented with a 'tambaua', a mounted whale's tooth, a traditional tribal honour bestowed on me specifically for those successful missions.

In February 1944 I was grounded and repatriated for hospital treatment by Tony Marsh, the Medical Officer at Lauthala Bay. He left the reason for his decision on record. "As a result of a prolonged period on operations without appropriate rest he was suffering from chronic fatigue." I eventually returned to flying the Catalina as an instructor at the Number 3 Operational Training Unit in 1945. During my time there I had the opportunity to fly the obsolescent Walrus single-engine flying boat.

I ended my war service with the rank of Flight Lieutenant at the earliest opportunity when peace was declared, being actually the first man to sign out at a tent set up for the purpose in Anderson Park, Wellington, on the eve of VJ Day. However, I heard the Prime Minister declare on the national radio that the government would be sending a representative contingent of servicemen and women from New Zealand to participate in the Victory Parade in London, planned for 1946. Those interested were asked to send a telegram to say so. My wife was enthusiastic but I felt that only those with a longer row of medals than I would be chosen. She finally persuaded me. There happened to be a Post Office across the road, so it was the easiest thing to walk into it and send the telegram. To my surprise a note came note back immediately from the government department concerned telling me to report to Ohakea. My wife Melva had to stitch a patch on the seat of my uniform trousers, which in the interim I had been using for gardening and had worn rather thin. I duly reported and was sent off to London.

My first job on arrival was to buy a new uniform at Reeves. It was needed. Before the Parade itself I was invited by the British Government to Hampton Court Palace on 11 June 1946 for an Evening Reception to meet the King and Queen. Although I had welcomed the end of the war and the chance to return to civilian life, the fortuitous experience of my visit to London gave me a different appreciation of the opportunities and responsibilities of service life.

Consequently, on my return to New Zealand after the exhilarating events of the Victory Parade, I returned to teaching for a short while but then decided to go back into the Air Force when I was offered a job, as an Education Officer with promotion to the rank of Squadron Leader. I served in this branch of the Royal New Zealand Air Force until the normal retirement age, becoming Deputy Director of Educational Services at Air Force Headquarters from 1952 to 1959. In 1962 I was appointed Officer Commanding the ground training wing at Wigram, with the rank of Wing Commander. I later served as Director of Educational Services for the Royal New Zealand Air Force, and finally as Director of Defence Education in the Ministry of Defence until my final retirement from the Air Force on 15 June1968. Although a formally non-flying Officer in my post-war career in the Air Force, I was able to supplement my wartime flying a little with some unofficial flying during the 1950s and 1960s in a Harvard. By the end of my service years I had amassed 1,718 hours of flying.

~~~

George Gudsell flew as pilot in the following aircraft, listed in experiential order.

> Tiger Moth
> Oxford
> Beaufort
> Hudson
> Vildebeest
> Walrus
> Catalina
> Harvard

Photographs and the specifications of these aircraft may be found in Part 2, listed in alphabetical order.

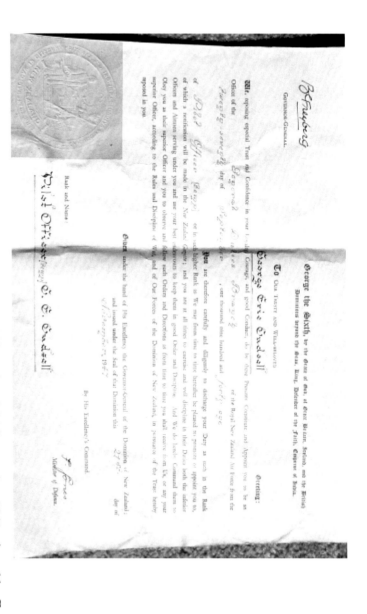

Document of George Gudsell's commission as a Pilot Officer dated 27 September 1941, signed by F Jones, Minister of Defence, and headed by the signature of the Governor General of New Zealand, B C Freyberg

George Gudsell, wife and baby daughter in early 1942

George Gudsell in
1942

Captain Lloyd R Gray, United States Naval Attaché to New
Zealand, reading the citation at the presentation of the United
States Air Medal to Flying Officer George Gudsell. L-R:
Captain Gray; Air Commodore G T Jarman, Deputy Chief of the
Air Staff; Flying Officer George Gudsell; and an unknown Air
Force Officer

A tourist at the entrance to a Japanese underground bunker of
the Second World War on Guadalcanal, August 1992

Wing Commander George Gudsell's three
unusual medals. L-R: Australian Campaign
Medal, Singapore and South West Pacific;
United States Air Medal; Solomon Islands
Commemoration Medal

Chapter 3.

Youthful in War and Peace

Keith Hall

Youthful in War and Peace

Born in Oxford, a small town thirty miles north-west of Christchurch, in December 1924, I was still not quite of school age when my parents decided to move into Christchurch city itself. Father had established a trucking business of a general nature, his loads including regular contracts for the delivery of mail, the carriage of wool bales from farms to the market, and the delivery of enormously long wooden piles for the construction of the bridge in the nearby Lees Valley to provide an alternative to fording the river. I was the youngest of five children. The others have pre-deceased me except for one sister.

In 1930, my father, being no longer a young man, sold the business and retired. Consequently I completed all my schooling in Christchurch – at the Elmwood Primary School and then Christchurch Boys' High School, leaving the latter at the age of sixteen to take a job as an office boy at Pyne Gould Guinness Limited, Stock and Station Agents, an important and well-known firm, where I remained until after the start of the Second World War.

By 1943 all young men became eligible to be called up for the armed services on reaching the age of eighteen. Those who joined the Army could not go overseas until they were twenty-one, but those who joined the Navy and the Air Force could do so once they had qualified at the conclusion of their training. My own turn came in April 1943 when I received my call up as recruit number 435961. I was one of a batch of 600 who had opted to join the Royal New Zealand Air Force. We were directed to report to the Omaka airfield at Blenheim, a town at the north end of the South Island. At that time the railway network was incomplete in the South Island, so we were transported in a large convoy of trucks for part of our journey between Oaro and Kaikoura to enable us to rejoin the railway to Blenheim. The journey from my home in Christchurch to Blenheim – a distance of some 250 miles - took twelve hours.

One of the first tasks we were set on arrival was literally to make our beds. We were shown a stack of oat straw and a pile of sacks. By stuffing the straw into two sacks and then sewing the two together we could make our own mattresses. It was important to overestimate the amount of filling needed to allow for it to settle and become compacted under one's weight. If it were underestimated the result could be a pretty hard night's sleep - and it was plenty of sleep that we needed to sustain us for the unaccustomed physical nature of our new life. For the first two weeks we spent a great deal of time on the parade ground, learning to march, to take up a variety of formations in our squads, to respond to orders, and to be alert and responsive as a group.

At the end of these two weeks each man was issued with a service rifle, together with instructions for using it, and keeping it clean and ready for use. The parade ground drills continued under the imperious commands of the drill Sergeants and the watchful eyes of Officers. It was the basic testing time for all aspiring aircrew members. We could not afford to be sluggish and unresponsive. The best efforts of every man were expected at all times. Anything short of the best from any man led to his removal from the stream of intending aircrew members. Physical fitness and good health were checked regularly, supplemented with a few injections and vaccinations, suitable for our forthcoming service obligations.

After two months of such initial training and induction experiences, I was transferred to Palmerston North in the North Island, to learn the basics of navigation, meteorology, mathematics, aerodynamics, armaments, and other subjects needed to be a competent pilot. It was a matter of going back to school again but with what a difference. The concentrated motivation was there. As my passion to be a pilot grew, in competition with all the other members of the course, so my determination to cope with my studies and to pass the examinations at the end of it became a fixation. After six weeks we duly sat the examinations, all of which had to be passed by a recruit if he wanted to proceed further in the long process of pilot training.

My reward for passing the examinations was a posting to Rotorua for two more months of classroom studies. Of the 600 who had arrived at Blenheim as volunteers for aircrew training, around 350 were sent to Rotorua. Of the latter, 130 were selected for pilot training, some seventy others being sent to Canada to train as navigators or airgunners. The entire process amounted to a giant sifting machine in which those who failed to meet the exacting standards of performance set were remustered to other appointments and trades in the Air Force.

It was not until 18 September 1943 and my posting to the Number 2 Elementary Flying Training School at Ashburton, that I achieved the direct acquaintance with an aircraft which meant more than the casual sights and sounds I had experienced as a layman. The Tiger Moth, as the ubiquitous primary pilot training aircraft in so many parts of the world during the Second World War, was to be the fulfilment of my efforts to qualify through the various stages of pre-flying training. It usually took eight to ten hours of flying with an instructor before a trainee could fly alone. I first went solo after taking the full ten hours, the landing for which was described by my instructor as heavy. The Tiger Moth bounced about in any strong wind and was particularly vulnerable in a strong north-westerly wind. It could land at the slow speed of thirty-five knots, coming to rest necessarily of its own accord, as it had no brakes.

The two months of training on the Tiger Moth included every aspect of flying, including cross-country navigation, aerobatics, and stalling. It was an intensive course. By 1943 the training system had been well developed, demanding exceptional efforts from its trainees. Of the six trainee pilots in my hut, I was the only one to complete the course. One was killed in training, two were judged as lacking the aptitude for flying, and two chose to opt out. Towards the end of the course, therefore, I had the hut all to myself.

After completing sixty hours of solo flying in the Tiger Moth, I was rated as a potential pilot for multi-engined aircraft and posted to Wigram for the advanced flying training course on Airspeed Oxford aircraft. The course of trainee pilots there was split into two sub-groups. For one week one group flew in the morning and attended classes in the afternoon, the other group taking the same programme in reverse. The following week the two groups changed their time slots. By this method, trainees could have as wide an experience of weather conditions as possible and also became accustomed to the demands of flying at all hours. Night flying was later introduced, much of which could be accomplished in the darkness of the evening, but when it was necessary to fly late towards the midnight hour, we were still required to rise with reveille at 0600 hours. Shortage of sleep plus the taxing nature of the training, especially the gunnery and bombing practice, for which it was essential to turn in a good performance to stay in the course, all conspired to make us very tired at times. Of the original 600 applicants with whom I reported initially at Blenheim, only ninety finally secured their wings – forty five at Wigram, including me, and a similar number at Woodbourne, flying Harvards, to be fighter pilots.

Life at Wigram was relatively luxurious. Accommodation was in comfortable buildings. The base boasted facilities and amenities for use in our leisure time, and we were actually waited on at table. These were conditions that I never found bettered in any other posting during the whole of my service. After four months, those of us who completed the course were awarded our wings at a Station ceremony, to which parents were invited, on the tarmac on 24 January 1944. Air Commodore Sir Robert Clark-Hall was 'The Officiating Officer' for the occasion. Newly and proudly qualified, we were sent on leave for two weeks. Four of those graduating were retained to be trained as flying instructors, six were earmarked for service in the Pacific, including me, and the rest were sent to England for operational training. Ten of the forty-five graduating pilots were commissioned as Pilot Officers, including me, the rest being made Sergeant Pilots. My commission was gazetted on 18 March 1944, last on the list.

Following my leave I reported to New Plymouth in the North Island for further training for service in the Pacific theatre of the war, where the vast amount of flying that had to be incurred for every flight over the ocean required special navigational competence. Consequently I flew as navigator in Anson aircraft with an excellent instructor to gain a wider knowledge of navigational methods.

With the navigational course successfully concluded, I was posted to Number 4 Squadron in Fiji, flying Hudson medium bombers. At that time it was still the practice to have two pilots in multi-engined combat aircraft. I became second pilot to Flight Lieutenant Tom Shand, who in the post-war years became the Minister of Labour in the Holyoake government. He was a great Captain and a fearless pilot.

Our operational flying consisted mainly of convoy escort work and anti-submarine patrols. We typically took off at 0200 hours or 0300 hours to rendezvous with convoys that had left western seaboard ports of the United States for Guadalcanal, New Guinea, or Australia. They used to sail across the Pacific between Fiji and New Zealand. We usually carried depth charges for attacking enemy submarines on our flights which lasted six or seven hours. For detecting an enemy submarine we had the use of an early type of radar that was effective enough even in murky weather. At a height of 5,000 feet, it could pin point a vessel at a distance of forty miles, allowing us to home in on it. After screening an area ahead of a convoy we used to signal an all clear to it on an Aldis Lamp with a flashing green light.

Our base was at Nausori, about fifteen miles from Suva, the capital of Fiji. It was built on marshy ground made usable for aircraft by the use of Marston matting, a network of interlinked steel plates. This posting was a suitable assignment for me to gain some operational experience and to consolidate the knowledge and skills acquired in training. After two months the Squadron flew back to Whenuapai in North Island, New Zealand. Tragically, but not without precedent, two aircraft were lost on the way with a total loss of twelve members of the Squadron, all of them well known to me after having lived and worked with them for two months. As so often happened in the Pacific, far more losses of aircraft and their crews occurred as a result of accidents or bad weather than as victims of enemy ack-ack or fighter aircraft.

On arrival, those of us who had been second pilots were posted to Ohakea for six weeks for conversion to the Ventura bomber, and command training as Captains of this higher performance aircraft. As successor to the Hudson, the Ventura was capable of around 300 mph at sea level if well trimmed and with a little nose down. It carried a heavier bomb load than the Hudson but in requiring 100 knots (about 125 mph) to take off it needed a longer runway. Its landing speed of 110 knots was unusually high. It had a complicated fuel system which was the cause of a few accidents. However, the Ventura was an updated warplane and the most sophisticated bomber used by the Royal New Zealand Air Force during the Second World War in the Pacific.

I gathered a full crew consisting of a navigator, a wireless operator, and two airgunners. We were posted to Number 3 Squadron being formed at Whenuapai, but after only two weeks there we were unexpectedly and precipitately sent as a replacement crew to Number 9 Squadron at Nausori on Fiji, a return to where I had started my operational service. This move was probably prompted by the loss of an aircraft and its crew, but I never enquired about the reason for our transfer. I reported to the Squadron's Commanding Officer, Wing Commander A C Allen, AFC, on 2 February 1945. He was an ardent smoker who blew smoke and ash over those who sat in the front row at briefings. The rear seats in the briefing room tended to be very popular.

New crews like ours were usually assigned positions to the rear of any formation – where they were more vulnerable to attack from enemy fighters and from ground fire, enemy gunners having been alerted by the arrival of the first few aircraft leading the attacking formation. They were also tasked for the less interesting jobs, one of which fell to us.

The particular version of the Ventura in use at Nausori was the United States Army type B34 which was inferior to the United States Navy type PV1. It had an unsatisfactory layout for the aircrew's work stations and leaked badly in heavy rain. The Air Force decided to withdraw them from front line service in favour of using them at home for training and other purposes. We were one of the crews allocated to fly them back to New Zealand via Norfolk Island.

We took off on 14 March 1945 at 0700 hours only to discover after about an hour's flying that we had lost contact with base. This necessitated a return for radio repairs that were completed in time to take off again at 1000 hours. We hoped to be able to check our course by the Manuva Reef - which was about three hours of flying and about half way to Norfolk Island. Unfortunately, during the three hours' delay of our flight the tide had covered it, denying us a marker for our direction.

Shortly after having passed the point of no return, we ran into a tropical storm. As it was my practice to fly at only about 100 feet above the ocean in bad weather, I started the descent from 8,000 feet. I reversed our course to do a figure of eight, whilst losing height and setting the altimeter at 100 feet and facing the front at right angles. As we entered the rain and wind, however, the window alongside me blew out, with the effect of sucking out all the navigator's maps and other moveable objects for navigation and other purposes.

It took fifteen minutes to pass through the worst of the weather, after which we climbed to 1,500 feet, taking an estimated course, which we checked by whatever means we could use. The navigator asked the wireless operator to call up Norfolk Island for a radar position, but what we were given turned out to be inaccurate. In drawing nearer to Norfolk Island we picked up the tower on our own radio which thankfully was still in working order. The controller told us we were forty miles out to the south-east of Norfolk Island and heading for Australia. I immediately turned on the radio compass which swung round 130°, showing that we were well past Norfolk Island. The correction being made in time, the Island appeared out of the haze and we landed safely, but perhaps with a touch of good fortune. As the tail wheel touched the runway the port motor cut out from a lack of fuel. It took the ground staff two days to repair the damaged window. After an uneventful flight for the rest of the way to deliver the aircraft to Whenuapai, we were put on a Dakota transport and sent back to Fiji without delay.

The Squadron then moved to Emirau Island, situated almost 100 miles west of New Ireland and a similar distance south of the Equator. We landed at an airstrip carved out of the jungle and made of crushed coral. My first combat mission was to the Japanese stronghold at Rabaul in New Britain. For a number of crews it was their first offensive operation, so there was tension in the air as we were briefed and prepared for the take off. I had an extra concern in that one of my engines did not develop a full rich mixture during the preparations for take off – a failure with the potential for a cut out when I opened the throttles for the full power needed to leave the ground with a heavy bomb load. In the event my worry was unnecessary. The airstrip itself, being located on a cliff some ninety feet above the sea level, provided an increment of assistance - when we were taking off and trying to retract our undercarriage - rather comparable to taking off from an aircraft carrier.

The Squadron's aircraft took off at twenty second intervals, our watches having been synchronized at the briefing. The strict timing necessary for Squadron activities made me time conscious for life. It was actually a court martial offence for a pilot whose aircraft was not in the right position to take off immediately on receiving the green light from the control tower at the commencement of an operational mission. Once airborne, each aircraft flew a circuit of the airstrip and then took its place in the formation which had been assembling overhead.

The flight path was in a southerly direction. I was assigned to the ninth position in the formation of Venturas which, as a whole, then made a rendezvous with sixty United States Army B25 aircraft – Mitchell medium bombers. It was a magnificent sight, giving one a great sense of power and security on a beautiful day with a clear sky and the vast blue expanse of ocean below. As a background, it created such a paradox in the mind for viewing the imminent torrent of death and destruction that would be visited on the unfortunate enemy on the ground.

In such a large formation it was imperative to remember the vital disciplines. There must never be a radical, impromptu movement. The aircraft's speed, direction, and station must be maintained rigidly at all times, requirements that needed concentration, but proved to be tedious work for the six or seven hours' of flying that the round trip involved.

The mission went smoothly enough. We bombed from 12.000 feet - a height at which we should have been using oxygen, as I learned later. But we didn't have it and suffered no ill effects. One of the gunners went down into the bomb bay to watch our bombs explode but his effort was fruitless as we were pattern bombing, a procedure whereby, as soon as the Formation Leader released his bombs, all the rest of the aircraft followed suit. On identifying the target, the Leader dropped his bombs a little short of it as a marker, the bombs of the following aircraft being expected to hit it.

As soon as we had dropped our bomb load we turned away from the target and the anti-aircraft gunfire, which was rising at about 1,000 feet per second, a rate which gave us twelve seconds to avoid it. We had to continue to follow the Leader but if he turned too tightly it was difficult to keep station without losing height. I used to find that both my hands were stiff on arriving back at our base from a mission like this - so long I had been hanging on to the control column with one hand and to the throttle quadrant with the other, in trying to stay in formation. We landed at thirty second intervals, those of us at the rear end of the formation having to remember that we had used up more fuel than those in the front of it. The judgement of distance on the final approach to landing had to be accurate, since it was essential for each aircraft, on completing its landing run, to turn quickly off the runway so that a following aircraft did not run into the tail of it. The aircraft in the rear of the formation, being light on fuel, often did not have the option of making another circuit and a second attempt. Consequently, the need to be precise and prompt increased progressively once the first aircraft had touched down.

Emirau was quite a pleasant place. Although it was near the Equator, in being an Island in the middle of the ocean the sea breezes made living conditions tolerable. The mosquitoes, however, could be a nuisance. Our tents were surrounded by protective nets and we slept with nets around our beds. The food was adequate but not very appetizing, consisting of a range of dehydrated items. When prepared for a meal they appeared as a thick soup-like mixture that could only be eaten with a spoon. The only meat in our diet was canned. Without refrigeration, of course, nothing lasted more than a few hours. Our supplies came by sea, the vessels carrying them needing to anchor two miles off shore, there being no harbour. The ships were unloaded onto barges that maintained a continual supply of food, fuel, bombs, ammunition, spare parts, and all the other things that were needed to maintain a whole Squadron – its aircraft, its aircrews, its staff members, and its large number of ground crew members – in its precarious occupation of such an unsuitable spot, as well as the Australian anti-aircraft gun crews who were in place to protect the base from aerial attacks by Japanese aircraft.

As we regularly flew in conjunction with the United States Marine Air Corps, and were in disproportionate numbers to them, we were briefed for our operational sorties by an American Colonel. The Americans were always helpful and generous, proving throughout to be an indispensable ally for the fight to prevent a Japanese hegemony in the Pacific.

In contrast to flying in such aerial armadas, we flew many times alone on solo patrol missions over the jungle at only thirty feet above the canopy. This practice was quite exhilarating and called for constant vigilance. There was always the possibility of a sudden surprise burst of gunfire from a hidden Japanese strongpoint, so we could not afford to be negligent. But in addition, an occasional coconut tree that reached for the sky perhaps as much as twenty feet above the general canopy level had to be smartly circumnavigated. Even so, it was not uncommon for us to return to base with some foliage caught under our aircraft. One pilot on such a patrol who thought he had been hit by an anti-aircraft shell discovered that a parrot had crashed through the windscreen and covered the navigator with blood, bones, and feathers.

One of our favourite patrol haunts was the road on New Ireland which ran from Kavieng to Cape St George – a distance of about 480 miles – which we could fly in four hours. The road was of course the main means for the Japanese forces to deploy their units and to supply them throughout the Island. Although they did use it during daylight, they were canny enough to realize that our aircraft did not operate at night, so that was when they undoubtedly made the best use of it.

On one of these flights we were seeking an enemy radar station that was jamming a Green Island radio post manned by Australians and New Zealanders. In patrolling low hills at a height of 3,000 feet behind a village called Po Village, we failed to realize that our map reading was astray. We had overlooked a big beach area at Namatanai which was home to a Japanese airfield. After patrolling for an hour over land, trying to find the radar station, we decided to turn out over the sea where we could relax for a while and drink some water. However, as we came out of a valley to cross the coast line I suddenly noticed the airfield and the flat land around which bonfires seemed to be burning.

Simultaneously I saw a cloud of what appeared to be snowballs coming towards us and realized too late that I was looking at cannon tracer. What I had taken to be bonfires were the perimeter ground defences going into action. As we had descended to only thirty feet from the ground we were unable to depress our own guns to retaliate. The tail gunner called me up urgently to put on some speed as the tracers were catching up with us. We must have avoided the worst of the onslaught but one shell ripped through the aircraft, damaging our IFF system – the apparatus for identifying ourselves to ground stations when asking for permission to land. It started to catch fire so I ordered the wireless operator to throw it overboard via the flare chute, an order which he promptly executed with great satisfaction.

In ridding ourselves of the threat to our aircraft, however, we were left with no means of identifying ourselves to friendly forces. The ground defence armaments around our base were in the hands of the Australian Army. Australian gunners had by that time gained a not entirely undeserved reputation for firing freely at aircraft they couldn't identify. Since it was the case that incoming aircraft could be unfamiliar types or that weather conditions made it difficult to identify familiar aircraft types, it had been known for

71

them to fire at allied aircraft. They were not alone in this. In the United Kingdom throughout the Second World War ground gunners were responsible for bringing down aircraft of the Royal Air Force as a result of misinformation or misidentification.

I approached our airstrip with a zig-zag movement in trying to convey that we had a problem but I was unable to delay the landing whatever happened, being low on fuel. I should have called up control with the code for this very circumstance - 'My cockerel is not crowing' - but in the anxiety of the moment I completely forgot about it. On landing we found that the control tower had spotted us first and had informed the gunners of our identity.

Very soon I was pleased to be told by the Station Commander, Wing Commander Allen, that the next day I would fly as his number two on a bombing mission to Rabaul. Apart from the fact that it was an easier position to keep than those I had previously been used to flying on massed aircraft sorties, I felt honoured to be assigned to it – a reaction which made the highlight of the tour for me. As a young pilot of only twenty years, I was always conscious of needing to live up to the expectations of the Squadron and to make a contribution to the Squadron that would match that of older and more experienced pilots. Altogether on this tour I flew thirty operational missions, grateful for the long months of training which enabled me to pull my weight and to stay alive.

By this time in the war, although the Americans and New Zealanders were more or less in control of the war in the air, the Japanese Army with some 100,000 men on New Ireland and New Britain presented a powerful foe for allied land forces. In the event our aircraft were able to give allied land forces strong support of both a strategic and tactical nature. In doing so, our aircrews were aware of the summary nature of the treatment they were most likely to receive on the ground in the event of being shot down and surviving.

After my tour of two months, I returned with the Squadron to New Zealand where it was scheduled to be converted to flying Dakota aircraft. The first Dakota aircraft had arrived in New Zealand from the United States to be formed as 40 Squadron early in 1943. Those remaining after the end of their war service were transferred to the newly formed National Airways Corporation.

Since the Dakota flew as an unarmed aircraft, my two gunners were posted to other squadrons. It soon became known that the Squadron would be training and preparing to take part in an airborne landing on Borneo to recapture the oil wells that had been taken by the Japanese. No one at that time had foreseen the precipitate end of the war with Japan that the use of the two atomic bombs – respectively dropped on Hiroshima and Nagasaki – would produce. It must be said with a degree of emphasis that, whatever subsequently has been made of that cataclysmic event, the relief that descended on those of us who were putting our lives at risk and were facing the prospects of an extended war and its inevitable heavy casualties were profoundly grateful for it and have remained so. As a result of it at the time, all such on-going plans and preparations for the further prosecution of the war were suddenly terminated with the Japanese surrender on 14 August 1945. The purpose for our Squadron's existence ceased.

At Ohakea I undertook a conversion course for flying the Dakota before returning one month later to Whenuapai, having been posted to Number 40 Squadron that was equipped with Dakota transport aircraft used to carry personnel - mostly being repatriated - and for maintaining supplies to the many New Zealand Air Force units scattered throughout the Pacific Islands. Our flights, apart from the many passengers, included cargos of meat, aircraft spares, and on one occasion, a consignment of 7,000 pounds sterling in Australian currency to pay the Australian Army on Norfolk Island.

Flying the Dakota provided a considerable contrast – both with regard to the experience of piloting the aircraft itself, and the style of life which went with it - to flying the Ventura. The flying gear we had to don for the latter included a parachute of course, which we didn't carry in the Dakota. Our flying suits in the Dakota could be simple and shed of all the bits and pieces which I had to carry for operational purposes in the Ventura. The Dakota itself was a benign and predictable aircraft to fly, cruising along at 125 knots and without the difficulties and vices that were part of the price to be paid for having in the Ventura a high performance type of machine.

In transferring from the Ventura to the Dakota I no longer had to think about bombing and strafing or about being attacked from the ground or the air. My job suddenly became the straightforward flying of an eminently flyable aircraft, a type that had already been widely used for over ten years and was destined to remain in use in some parts of the world into the twenty-first century. During the Second World War it had proved to be a work horse for many purposes in transport, troop carrying, airborne assaults, glider towing, and re-supply duties.

In the Pacific, where its use was confined to passive transport work, the Dakota was always subject to the vagaries of tropical weather in common with all other military aircraft, and which occasioned so many losses of every type of aircraft. Only three Air Force Dakota aircraft were lost altogether during and after the war but it is believed that a tropical storm accounted for the loss of one of them from the Squadron as it was engaged in the repatriation of Royal New Zealand Air Force personnel from the islands. On the morning of 24 September 1945 at 0530 hours, Dakota NZ3526 took off from Pallikulo, at Espiritu Santo in the New Hebrides Islands, for New Zealand. It was piloted by Flying Officer Jack Hoffeins, who had been a fighter pilot in the Mediterranean during the war. Contact was lost with the aircraft and it failed to arrive at its destination, vanishing without trace. The death of its four crew members and sixteen passengers was the largest total loss of Royal New Zealand Air Force personnel in one day for the whole war.

We had to deal with cold fronts ourselves on a number of occasions. I used to fly manually through them. It was usually a bumpy experience. No vents could be opened, otherwise the heavy rain would force its way into the aircraft. To ensure a safe passage through them I used the radio altimeter which gave a red light if we were under 100 feet above the sea, a green if we were over 100 feet, and an orange if we were right on the target level of 100 feet. Such fronts were more often than not of a short duration.

Fronts were usually about fifty miles wide, requiring ten minutes to cross.

The post-war military flying was a new way of life for me. Since hostilities had ceased, there was time to see the world of the Pacific in different light. The Squadron's aircraft flew independent missions, one going to Norfolk Island, one to Fiji, and one to Espiritu Santo. Occasionally I spent three weeks on detachment on Guadalcanal, from which to fly to Manus, St Mathias, Jacquinot Bay, Bougainville, Espiritu Santo, Green Island, and a few other islands where there had previously been hard fighting between the Japanese Army and the American Marines and troops of the New Zealand Third Division. Such a three week detachment called for a heavy work load of 120 hours of flying, the longest day's flying of which took ten hours and ten minutes, covering some 1,200 nautical miles. This inter-island work was mainly to ferry some 1,500 Air Force and Army personnel, due for repatriation, from their scattered locations to Bougainville, from where the pre-war passenger Wellington to Lyttelton ferry ship *Wahine* took them home.

My crew consisted of a co-pilot, who was newly appointed, and two members of the former Ventura crew who stayed with me - the navigator, and the wireless operator. We became a close knit team, living together in the same huts in the various outlandish places that we visited. It was a good life. The four of us crew members were all single men so we could indulge an adventurous but carefree existence. Living conditions were rough and ready in places but there were compensations in the form of good pay, plenty of cheap cigarettes, a variety of places to visit, and responsibilities to be undertaken.

Often, when flying cargo back to New Zealand from Espiritu Santo, we tracked via New Caledonia to spend the night at Tontouta, after three and a half hours in the air, before undertaking the seven hours flight the next day to Auckland. Tontouta, being a large United States base, had plenty of diversions for young men, the highlight of which was the Saturday night dance attended by the American nurses from the base hospital.

In our youthfulness, we were perhaps sometimes guilty of being a little cavalier. On one occasion we were eating canned peanuts while flying between Espiritu Santo and Bougainville. It suddenly appeared to me that we had strayed off course and I remarked as much to the navigator, but he assured me that we were on the correct compass bearing. A moment later, having eaten all my peanuts, he picked up my empty can to dispose of it but as he did so the compass moved seven degrees. He promptly cursed the peanut can but had no difficulty in rectifying our course as it was a fine day, making it easy to establish our bearings from Guadalcanal and other points.

Being young, however, guaranteed the stamina to endure taxing undertakings. Shortly after the war ended, the New Zealand government, being immediately exposed to the post-war realities of trade and competition, could not afford to maintain its purchases of aviation fuel from the Americans. Consequently, we had to fly non-stop from Espiritu Santo to Auckland, an arduous flight time of ten hours. It was always a welcome sight to see Cape Maria Van Dieman and North Cape loom out of the mist after such a long and tedious flight.

Being young enabled us to overcome the discomforts and mishaps with a certain amount of panache although we could not afford to be too nonchalant. On one occasion, when flying between 12,000 and 14,000 feet, the Dakota's heating system failed, the superchargers jammed, and we had to fly without oxygen. At first we were unconcerned, but after an hour or two our lips and fingernails turned blue, other signs of oxygen starvation also beginning to show.

From mid-October to mid-November 1945 we were based back in New Zealand, flying full loads of passengers from Auckland to Christchurch, and in reverse, in one day. This diet of flying did not appeal to any of us. My crew members urged me to apply to the Squadron Commander, Wing Commander A R Kirkup, to post us back to the island runs – an application that was successful. We resumed the old familiar flights and took on new ones as far north as the Admiralty Group of Islands above New Guinea.

On 20 November 1945 I flew Dakota 3544 carrying sixteen passengers from Whenuapai in New Zealand to Tontouta and then on to Espiritu Santo, returning the following day over the same route with a similar number of passengers. The last leg of it – the flight from Espiritu Santo to Whenuapai – lasted for nine hours. It was my last flight as pilot in command of an aircraft of the Royal New Zealand Air Force.

I had amassed forty-three flying hours for eight operational missions in Hudson aircraft, 277 flying hours for thirty operational missions – which constituted a full tour – in Ventura aircraft, and 303 hours for eighty-one trips in the Dakota.

My demobilization being due, I considered three options regarding my future employment - taking a permanent commission in the Air Force, applying to join the civilian airline that was to become the National Airways Corporation, and leaving flying altogether. On weighing up all the pros and cons I opted to return to Pyne Gould Guinness Limited, the firm I had left as an eighteen year old. I was demobilized on my twenty-first birthday, 19 December 1945, with a gratuity of 500 pounds and three months' leave on full pay.

I resumed employment in the grain and seeds department of the firm, my position being only a cut above that of office boy, the job I had left behind three years earlier. In those three intervening years, however, I had accumulated significant responsibilities and authority, and had developed a wide outlook on life. I had learned the importance of time and timing, punctuality, and working to time with other people. To be punctual in arriving over the target and discharging one's bombing attack before inviting the attention of the ground defences had taught me a great deal about co-operation with others and the use of time. All in all, therefore, my return to the constraints and low stimulation levels of this job in a civilian context was initially something of a drastic contrast for me.

The maturing experience to which I had been subjected at such an early age proved to be an asset in my civilian employment. The firm I rejoined conducted a highly diversified business providing a comprehensive range of agricultural and household goods, and services - such as banking and insurance - for farmers. In contemporary vernacular terms it was a one-stop-shop for the farming community. To cope with their endemic cash flow difficulties, farmers could obtain all their needs from the firm in advance of their future disclosed sources of income - such as sales of wool, crops, or land – which were used as collateral.

After four years in a modest position in the firm, I was appointed as its agent at Rakaia, a post which I held for four years until being appointed as agent and then branch manager at Waimate, South Canterbury. In 1958 I held the post of manager at the large Ashburton branch for thirteen years before moving to my final appointment as manager of the important Timaru branch. In 1974 I was invited to join the Board of Directors for the whole company, representing South Canterbury, an appointment necessitating frequent trips to headquarters in Christchurch.

Having retired from flying at an early age in 1945, I opted for a second retirement in 1980 at the age of fifty-six - but only in turn to take on the life of a sheep farmer. I bought land for the purpose near Timaru and farmed it until 2002, the year in which my wife died, ending fifty-two years of marriage. Our offspring of three girls and one boy have scattered themselves around the world – two in Australia, one in Canada, and one in France. Their world has been so different from mine.

~~~

Keith Hall flew as pilot in the following aircraft, listed in experiential order.

> Tiger Moth
> Oxford
> Hudson
> Ventura
> Dakota

Photographs and the specifications of these aircraft may be found in Part 2, listed in alphabetical order.

Keith Hall as a trainee pilot in front of an Oxford training aircraft at Wigram, 1943

Keith Hall, second from the left, on being commissioned in 1943, with friends in front of an Oxford. L-R: Douglas Hamilton, Derek Hamilton, and Stuart McCallum

Ventura aircrew L-R: Sergeant Andy Andrews, gunner;
Flight Sergeant Trevor Thorp, navigator; Pilot Officer Keith
Hall, pilot; Sergeant Geoff Jeffries, gunner; and Flight Sergeant
Peewee Williams, wireless operator

9 Squadron Ventura aircraft on their way to a target, early in
1945, as seen from Keith Hall's aircraft

9 Squadron at Emirau in front of a Ventura, January 1945. Keith Hall is at the extreme left-hand end of the third row from the front

An attack on Rabaul in 1945. In the dark area to the left is an active volcano.

Another attack in 1945 on Rabaul in New Britain, Japan's main base in the islands, bomb bursts being clearly visible

Coastal attack, New Ireland, 1945. An above water target bridge can be clearly seen. The Japanese often built their military bridges under the water level to avoid detection from the air

An attack on a beachside target in 1945

NEW ZEALAND'S P[...]

Guadalcanal — Solomon I[...]

THE IMPORTANCE OF THE CAMPAIGN

More than 800 New Zealanders were killed in the Guadalcanal-Solomon Islands campaign fighting to protect our freedom and independence. The significant part played by the New Zealand Armed Forces in the campaign was an important expression of our commitment to the defence of our country and the South Pacific region as a whole.

THE THREAT TO NEW ZEALAND

December 1941-August 1942

The Japanese advance through South East Asia and the Pacific which followed the attack on Pearl Harbour in December 1941 was the most serious military threat New Zealand has ever faced. New Zealand mobilised its forces to resist any Japanese attack. American troops were also sent to defend New Zealand. The United States Navy's victories in the battles of the Coral Sea and Midway in mid-1942, however, halted the Japanese advance.

School air-raid shelter, Devonport, Auckland

WHY NEW ZEALAND FOUGHT

American forces launched their first ground offensive against Japan by landing on Guadalcanal and Tulagi in the Solomon Islands about 2300 kilometres north of New Zealand on 7 August 1942. New Zealand was keen to assist in the campaign because driving the Japanese out of the Solomons would reduce the chances of a renewed threat to our area of the South Pacific.

A New Zealander leads a Fijian Commando patrol behind Japanese lines. Watercolour by Russell Clark.

HMNZS KIWI

THE STRUGGLE FOR GUADALCANAL

August 1942-February 1943

The struggle for Guadalcanal led to heavy fighting on land, sea and air, before the Japanese forces were forced to withdraw from the island in February 1943. The RNZN's light cruisers and minesweepers were active off Guadalcanal. In January 1943, for instance, HMNZS KIWI and HMNZS MOA destroyed a large Japanese submarine. The RNZAF, which began operating from Guadalcanal in November 1942, played a significant part in the air war over the island.

Many New Zealand officers and NCOs also served in the Fijian units which took part in the campaign.

Key

✕ 3 NZ Division operation   ⚓ RNZN engagement   ⚓ RNZN base   ✈ Major RNZAF base

Post war publication of the islands subject to wartime Air Force operations

Samedo and a convoy leaving Torokina Bay, Bougainville. Watercolour by Russell Clark.

THE ISOLATION OF RABAUL
DECEMBER 1943-SEPTEMBER 1944

The principal Allied objective in the latter stages of the campaign was to isolate and neutralise Rabaul. Japan's main stronghold in the area. Allied air forces carried out a concentrated campaign of air attacks on Rabaul which continued until the end of the war. RNZAF units played a major role in these attacks, which eliminated the ability of the substantial Japanese forces at Rabaul to influence the course of the war. The RNZAF also supported American and later Australian forces on Bougainville. The RNZN's minesweepers continued to operate in the Solomons area until the end of the war, and were mined in March 1944 by tactical patrol searches.

NEW ZEALAND ARMY OPERATIONS
September 1943-February 1944

The 3 New Zealand Division began its operations in the Solomons in September 1943 by clearing the island of Vella Lavella. The following month it made the first opposed landing by New Zealand troops since Gallipoli when it seized the Treasury Islands from Japanese forces. In February 1944, the division defeated the Japanese forces occupying the Green Islands. The New Zealand forces fought several fierce short actions during these engagements. Following the Green Islands operation the division was disbanded because of a shortage of manpower.

Stuartville Beach, in the Treasury Islands, morning of 2 November 1943. Water colour by Russell Clark.

THROUGH THE SOLOMONS
February–December 1943

During 1943 Allied forces advanced northwards through the Solomon Islands, landing on Bougainville the northernmost island in the group in November 1943. All three branches of the New Zealand Armed Forces made a significant contribution to the offensive. The RNZAF, in particular, increased in strength in the area. New Zealand fighters continued to take heavy toll of enemy aircraft making a major contribution to the destruction of Japanese airpower in the Solomons.

A Hudson escorting Kittyhawks en route to the Solomon Islands.

Escort Catalina over a Liberty ship near Guadalcanal. Watercolour by Russell Clark.

CONDITIONS IN THE ISLANDS

The New Zealand personnel involved in the campaign toward the hot, humid climate of the Solomons very trying. Malaria and a range of other tropical diseases were a constant concern. Accommodation for troops was generally very basic and recreational facilities limited. All the Allied forces organised sports and other activities to combat boredom.

New Zealand troops inspect an abandoned Japanese boat on Vella Lavella.

A captured Japanese Zero fighter on Bougainville,1945, flown by Wing Commander Koeford from Kara Airfield, Bougainville, shortly after it had fallen into allied hands. As an official war prize for New Zealand it is now an exhibit in the Auckland Memorial War Museum

Keith Hall and a beached Japanese transport on Guadalcanal, 1945. Note the shell hole in the bows of the ship near the water line

Dakota aircrew on Kokum Beach, Guadalcanal, 1945. L-R: Flight Sergeant John Green, engineer; Pilot Officer Trevor Adams, co-pilot; Flying Officer Bill Marshall, navigator (standing); Warrant Officer Greg Gregory, wireless operator; and Flying Officer Keith Hall, pilot

Japanese prisoners from Truk Island, awaiting confinement in Bougainville

Chapter 4.

First Time Unlucky

Bill Heslop

First Time Unlucky

Wartime military flying for me proved to be an experience wedged in between my lifetime of farming. It is difficult to imagine any two occupations of a greater contrasting nature. Yet there was – and if similar circumstances came along today there would still be – an underlying logic to the juxtaposition of farming and fighting. The peaceful pursuit of farming is essentially static. If predators threaten the integrity of the farming community there must be a defensive response. And this is exactly what happened at the end of 1941. The Japanese attack on Pearl Harbour on 7 December of that year simultaneously threatened the existing geo-political arrangements in the Pacific, and in particular precipitated the need for a defensive posture by New Zealand, whose war effort to that date had been entirely focused on sending trained manpower to the three armed services operating in Europe, the Mediterranean, and the waters of the northern hemisphere.

Farming in those days played a proportionately larger part in the economy of New Zealand, in terms of manpower directly employed, than it does today. So it was simply a question of abandoning the plough share and taking up the sword. In common with large numbers of my contemporaries, I volunteered to fight. As I had been born on 4 September 1923, I was sixteen and a day old when war was declared on 3 September 1939. On approaching my eighteenth birthday I asked my parents to give their permission for me to join the Air Force as I had my eye on learning to fly. But my mother refused. She thought it would be too dangerous to fly, but consented to my joining the Army. At first sight it could be argued that her view was irrational. The losses of men during the First World War had been horrendous. Small communities throughout New Zealand suffered the death of disproportionate numbers of their populations as did those in England and France, to say nothing of those who remained maimed for life. My own father was wounded twice on the Western Front in the New Zealand Army. Yet by September 1941, as I reached my eighteenth birthday, the proportionate losses of aircrew members – particularly in Bomber Command - had already reached significant rates, and fully engulfed its New Zealand members. Information about this was evidently not lost on my mother. So to the Army I went for over a year until I was able to persuade her to change her mind.

I had been born into farming. My father farmed cereals and sheep in the Brookside country area near Leeston to the south of Christchurch City. I was the oldest of three children and attended the local country primary school, where my teacher wanted me to go on to secondary education – an option that was inimitable to the family farming which I was expected to join as soon as possible. She used to tell me that I could "do better than go into farming." At that time of course farming was depressed with the general economic stagnation. I have often wondered if she would have offered the same advice in the post-war boom times which New Zealand farming enjoyed. In the event, instead of leaving school at thirteen, I went to the Christchurch Technical College for three years of secondary schooling. It was a long way to go to school. I had to leave home very early in the morning to bike three miles to the little railway station for the branch line train to Christchurch, and then take a walk from the station to College. When classes for the day ended, those of us who came in from the country had to remain in the school to complete our homework. Quite soon I learned of the prejudice against the country boys. My teacher said to me, "Train boys won't make it in this class. But we'll see what happens." I was never lower in class performance level than fourth and achieved a sufficient result in the matriculation to be accepted without pre-recruitment study requirements by the Air Force for pilot training. Perhaps my interest in the air provided the motivation to overcome the long days needed to go to school, and the teacher's apparent lack of expectation.

Leaving school at sixteen I joined my father in farming until my enforced choice of Army service at the instigation of my mother. The day came, however, in 1943 when I transferred from the Army to the Air Force. The pilot training which I coveted began at the Elementary Flying Training School at Ashburton in the South

Island and not all that far from home, where I was introduced to the Tiger Moth. After seven hours and ten minutes of flying with an instructor, I went solo, completing eighty-one flights in sixty hours and forty-five minutes altogether, and passing out with an average rating.

Having been allocated to fighter aircraft, my posting from Ashburton was to the Number 2 Advanced Flying Training School at Woodbourne to fly the Harvard. Again, I experienced no real difficulty in passing the course. I went solo after four hours and five minutes with the instructor, completing a total of 168 hours and forty-five minutes in 205 flights, with an average rating, and without any identified faults.

The next step for me as an intending fighter pilot was to the Number 4 Operational Training Unit at Ardmore. This base was a mecca for the fighter squadrons of the New Zealand Air Force. As well as its function as an operational training facility, Ardmore was home to front-line squadrons which were resting between tours.

The aircraft in use was the Kittyhawk. Over 3,000 of these fighter aircraft were delivered to the Royal Air Force and Commonwealth Air Forces during the war for use in the Mediterranean and the Pacific. It was also widely used by the American Air Force in the Pacific. Many squadrons of the Royal New Zealand Air Force were equipped with the Kittyhawk, which had served as its main fighter since combat missions began in 1942. It was still being used operationally when I joined the service but was being replaced by the more powerful Corsair.

Of the 292 Kittyhawks supplied to the New Zealand Air Force, twenty were shot down in combat, but 192 were lost in accidents of one kind or another. Many of these were lost in the process of being used as training aircraft. I was fortunately able to pass the course without mishap, being rated average as a pilot but above average for gunnery. My latter acumen may have been the result of a natural desire to make sure of a good result. I found during air to ground gunnery training, when we were paired to attack the target as we would in a combat mission, that the other trainee pilot usually fired too soon, probably overcome by eagerness and excitement. I used to delay until the last possible moment before pressing the firing button. Each aircraft fired bullets with differently coloured coatings so that individual performances could be ascertained. I completed ninety-five hours and fifty minutes flying in the Kittyhawk in 104 flights.

On completing my operational training I was posted without leaving the base to 22 Squadron which had recently returned from a combat tour for a rest period at Ardmore. It was customary to replace a squadron's pilot losses through enemy action, sickness, accidents, or postings, during its rest period at Ardmore. From 23 June 1944 to 28 July 1944 I was trained into 22 Squadron, being assigned to a Section and Flight, learning how to formate in small and large combinations of aircraft for combat purposes, and practicing every kind of manoeuvre, as well as gunnery. During this period I converted to the Corsair and took a few flights in it. For its forthcoming tour the Squadron would be flying the Corsair, the first squadron to do so.

I then became converse with the complexities by which squadrons were moved to and from combat postings across huge distances to provide aircrew members with relief from the enemy and the rigors of jungle postings. From 6 August to 23 August 1944 the Squadron moved to Espiritu Santo for further training, including a clutch of new pilots, myself among them, in tropical conditions. It then moved on to Guadalcanal for the period 28 August to 16 September 1944 for final training before becoming operational from 20 September to 2 November 1944 at Torokina on Bougainville, to which we were ferried in Dakota aircraft, to begin what was for me my first tour.

On 20 November 1944 my section of four Corsairs was ordered to conduct a sweep. This was at last the combat mission for which I had volunteered and trained for a seemingly endless amount of time, but which in fact was thirteen months, as I had actually joined the Air Force on 18 October 1943. Perhaps it was a touch of exuberance at the achievement of it, or maybe professional overconfidence that governed that first combat mission, but whatever the explanation - be it to my credit or otherwise - it

94

proved to be the one and only time that I nearly became a victim of the enemy.

The mission was to carry out a sweep for targets of opportunity to Duke of York on Cape Lambert. We spotted a Jap Army position that represented a really worthwhile target. The Section Leader ordered us into a line astern formation for a diving strafing attack on the Japanese force. Being one of the new pilots to the Squadron, as was customary for line astern attacks - as opposed to the finger four formation which was copied from the Luftwaffe, but did not become well established in the allied Air Forces until late in the war - I was the fourth aircraft in line. The danger for the last aircraft in line was always its vulnerability to a stern attack on the formation by enemy aircraft, but also from ground fire in low level attacks. Even the short time that elapsed between being alerted by the first incoming aircraft could be enough to allow gun crews to be better able to deal with any following aircraft.

On this occasion we each completed our intended strafing run. When I had finished my own attack, at a very low level, in common with the others, I knew I had ammunition left and that there was a target still worthy of attack. With very little forethought – it seems to have been something of an automatic response – I made a tight turn and came in at a low level to strafe the target again by myself. I was already firing my guns when I felt small shudders to the aircraft and simultaneously powerful, stinging blows to my legs.

It all happened so quickly. I realized I had been hit and could see blood running out of me onto the floor of the cockpit, but I could not assess the level of severity of the wounds. I immediately called the Section Leader to tell him I had been hit. He then asked, "Who has?" I had forgotten to identify myself. After a cursory attempt to assess the situation, he decided in favour of caution. He ordered all of us to form up and follow him to Green Island, an allied base that was considerably nearer than our own base at Torokina.

On approaching Green Island air base, we found that a large aircraft was already in the circuit getting ready to land. The

Section Leader asked for priority for the four of us and was given it. At that point I found that the aircraft's flaps were not working. The Japanese ground fire had damaged the controls. Consequently I had to land at near full speed and rely on the aircraft's brakes to bring the Corsair to rest. A fire engine and ambulance appeared simultaneously. The medical staff helped me out of the cockpit and whisked me off to the base hospital for examination and treatment.

As soon as the Section Leader arrived, he took one look at me and exclaimed, "Shit, is that all, I thought your guts were on the floor." It was a good attempt at consolation. In fact, I had been lucky. The ground fire had struck the aircraft from forward and underneath. Of the bullets that entered the cockpit, eight of them were deflected from injuring me by two tins that were carried – one to each leg - in pockets of my flying suit, low down between my knees and ankles. One tin contained a First Aid Travel Kit. This tin stopped two bullets. Two other bullets passed straight through it and hit me in the leg with greatly diminished force. The other tin for sunglasses stopped four bullets to my other leg, two of which completely penetrated the tin but did not exit. The fact that I still have two legs today and that they have served me for so long is almost certainly owing to these two tins, although I have always had a few twinges in my legs to remind me of what might have been.

The injuries from the bullets that reached my legs through one of the tins and directly through my flying suit, were not serious enough to warrant more than immediate treatment and a rest. Later the same day I flew back to my own base in Bougainville in a Dakota. Five days later I took to the air again for a test flight.

After this inauspicious start to my contribution in combat to 22 Squadron, I took part in its various operations until the end of the tour. These typically consisted of carrying a 1,000 or two 500 pound bombs, or incendiary bombs, for attacks on Japanese jungle locations. It was usual to follow up the bombing run with a return run for strafing purposes. We made numerous sweeps for targets of opportunity as well as attacks on targets subject to a specific briefing. We maintained dawn patrols and occasionally took part in a search for missing aircraft.

With the end of its tour, the Squadron returned to Ardmore for the short period 28 November to 8 December 1944 before once again moving to Espiritu Santo from 12 December 1944 to 6 January 1945 for Squadron practice purposes, and the incorporation of new pilots.

From 8 January to 2 March 1945 I completed my second tour with 22 Squadron operating from Emirau Island. The missions consisted of regular patrols and the everlasting strikes against Japanese ground forces wherever they could be found. During this tour I was also detailed to escort Catalina flying boats on their ceaseless patrols for the observation of enemy shipping and the rescue of allied airmen from the ocean. Since they flew at a very slow speed it was a tedious task to keep station on such escort duty. I had to throttle back so much that it sometimes became difficult to maintain an easy control of the aircraft.

My third and final tour followed a sojourn at Ardmore from 3 April to 18 April 1945. The war effort against the Japanese was still in full swing. As far as I was concerned at that time, in common with others, the end of the war in the Pacific still seemed to be a long way off. The thought of all that would have to be done to bring Japan finally to defeat was forbidding. We had of course no inkling of the existence of the atomic bomb that was destined to precipitate the end, the avoidance of a long and costly process of rooting the Japanese out of all the remaining territories still in their hands, and the actual invasion of Japan itself.

The Squadron once more embarked on another combat tour. This lasted from 24 April to 8 July 1945, based again on Bougainville. The tasks of 22 Squadron for this tour included a full range of strikes against ground targets, one of which was a Japanese Army Headquarters, and several searches for downed aircraft and pilots. One day we received notice from the American Army that one of their landing crafts would be coming ashore at a certain point to discharge an assault force to destroy two large Japanese guns that had been causing a great deal of trouble. There seemed to be a slight touch of cavalier spirit about their assurance that they would succeed where apparently other previous attempts to silence the guns had failed. Presumably there was an implication that our fighter-bomber efforts were wanting. Unfortunately for the landing craft in question, however, it was hit by the very guns it was coming to destroy. It had to be beached in a damaged condition but which remained a means of protection for the troops it carried. My Section of four Corsairs was sent off to silence the two guns, a task which we successfully accomplished – to the embarrassed gratitude of the task force.

I came out of the Air Force on 8 July 1945, having served about twenty-one months and completed the three tours which entitled a pilot to a stand down status. During my Air Force career I made 623 flights taking a total of 683 hours and thirty-five minutes. Of these, 240 hours and fifty minutes were flown for 126 missions. I finished with the rank of Flight Sergeant. Three other pilots and I were recommended for commissions at one point but at that time too many ex-Army officers were being trained as pilots with retained ranks, so we lost out. There was a certain amount of ill-feeling about the policy. In practice it could lead to anomalies. On one occasion our Flight of twelve aircraft was airborne when the Flight Commander, who also happened to be the Leader of the Section of four which I was in, and for which I was Deputy Commander, had to turn back with mechanical trouble. He handed over command of the Flight to me – a duty which I successfully discharged. On return to base, however, caustic and questioning comments were raised about his decision to depute me as Leader, being of Flight Sergeant rank – experienced albeit as I was – when among the other ten pilots involved were a number of commissioned Officers, including several who had transferred from the Army with retained commissioned ranks.

By taking advantage of the government's resettlement scheme, I was able to purchase a farm of my own in the same vicinity where I had been born and raised. I farmed sheep and cereals like my father. Eventually one of my sons took it over, but he later sold it for health reasons. My wife died sixteen years ago but our family of four children remain in close touch with me.

Bill Heslop flew as pilot in the following aircraft, listed in experiential order.

~~~

Tiger Moth
Harvard
Kittyhawk
Corsair

Photographs and the specifications of these aircraft may be found in Part 2, listed in alphabetical order.

**Bill Heslop in the Army in 1941
at Burnham Camp, New Zealand**

**A Royal New Zealand Air Force Kittyhawk of 15 Squadron over
the ocean in 1944**

Bill Heslop, third from the left, and the fellow pilots of his section in 1944. The Section Leader, on the extreme right, was one of the Squadron's two Flight Commanders

Bill Heslop's jungle accommodation. Non-Commissioned Officers lived four to a tent

22 Squadron pilots in a jungle setting in 1944. Bill Heslop is in the front row, third from the left

Pilot jungle living quarters. L-R: Harry Walker, Ken Bush, Bill Heslop, and Dick Ashton

A pilot climbing into a Corsair for a mission in 1944. It was not the easiest aircraft to get into and out of in full survival equipment

A Royal New Zealand Air Force Corsair taking off on a mission in 1944

Corsairs from several Royal New Zealand Air Force units in flight over the ocean in 1945

Devastated jungle after an allied air attack. Results were often difficult to see by the attacking aircrews themselves. Note the skull on the tree trunk

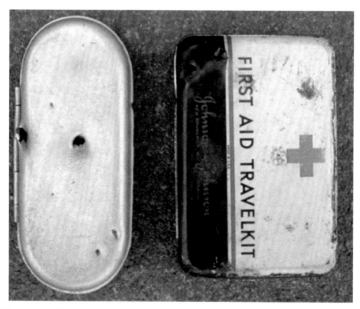

The two tins, one for First Aid and one for sunglasses, which arrested or stopped some of the bullets from ground fire that injured Bill Heslop on his first combat mission in 1944

Chapter 5.

Surviving to Serve

Frank Holmes

Surviving to Serve

I was born in Oamaru on 8 September 1924. When I was about four years old, my mother became ill with tuberculosis — a not uncommon illness in those days when the antibiotics and other remedies that we now take for granted were unknown. She had to go to Dunedin to a sanatorium for treatment. My father worked for a stock and station agency in Oamaru, reflecting the preponderance of farming in the economy of New Zealand at that time. During the long drawn out decline in her health, he must have incurred considerable expense in travelling frequently to Dunedin to see her. Until I was nine years old, I was looked after mostly by my maternal grandmother in Dunedin.

My father and mother were born in New Zealand, but both my paternal and maternal grandparents were immigrants. Grandpa Holmes was born in England, but he migrated to Australia and then to New Zealand. Grandma Holmes was born in Scotland, moved to Invercargill with her family when she was young, and then migrated to Australia, where she met and married Grandpa in 1891. The couple moved to Dunedin a year later.

Grandad Bagley was born in Australia. His parents had migrated there from England, and later went on to New Zealand. He followed in his father's profession as a pharmacist. Gran Bagley's father was of German origin and was a music teacher. When their marriage broke up in 1875, Gran's mother moved to Dunedin with her younger children.

This family background explains why my father, like many of his generation born in New Zealand, still referred to Britain as 'home'. It also illustrates the substantial movement of people both ways across the Tasman that occurred in his parents' generation, as people tried to find an Australasian location that best suited them.

I moved back to Oamaru at the age of nine to board with my father, who re-married in the following year..As a result of my family circumstances, I was a pupil at four different primary schools before attending Waitaki Junior High School in 1935 and 1936, and King's High School in Dunedin from 1937 to 1941. I was dux in the latter two schools.

My father had fought in the New Zealand Army at Gallipoli and was then wounded on the Somme, although he rarely spoke of his experiences. However, at school and at ceremonies on Anzac Day we were regularly made aware of the terrible conflict that had ended so recently, and the huge toll it had taken of New Zealand's young men.

The Rectors of both Waitaki and King's were very interested in British Empire, Commonwealth, and international affairs. Morning prayers usually made reference to the inflammatory events in Europe that were leading up to and finally culminated in the Second World War. The British Broadcasting Corporation was the main source of radio news, providing constant updates on those developments.

At the time, the New Zealand government was reflecting the views of the majority of the New Zealand people in asserting that, "Where Britain goes, we go", and promptly declaring war on 3 September 1939. There was no shortage of volunteers for the three armed services, a response given even more impetus by Japan's entry into the war with its attack on Pearl Harbor on 7 December 1941 – an aggression posing a direct threat to the territorial integrity and sovereignty of New Zealand.,

I was about to turn fifteen when the war broke out and completed my secondary school education at the end of 1941. I was still too young to join the armed services, so I spent a year at Otago University, studying English, Latin, French, and Greek. I wanted to join the armed services as soon as I turned eighteen, with a preference for enlisting in the Royal New Zealand Air Force, having taken part in the Air Training Corps during my year at university. I knew that I didn't want to be a sailor, and I didn't fancy the Army.

As I was still under twenty-one, I had to obtain my father's consent for overseas service, which was readily given. I was called up on 19 December 1942, and surprised when the Air Force sent me first to the other end of New Zealand, to Onerahi just outside Whangarei in the North Island. At the same time, I was excited, because apart from one visit to Christchurch, I had never been away from Otago and Southland before. I had become an Aircraftman Second Class (AC2), with the service number NZ 4217072. I was given a khaki battledress to wear with my Air Force hat and became a member of the Aerodrome Defence Unit (ADU).

The Japanese attack on Pearl Harbour was by then a year old. The spectacular territorial gains made by the enemy throughout the Pacific made us fear that there might be a Japanese landing on New Zealand's shores. The aircraft at our front line defences in Onerahi were Hawker Hinds. Further north, there were Vickers Vincents and Vickers Vildebeests. All these aircraft types were obsolescent biplanes from the 1930s. In the event of a Japanese invasion, they would have been no match for the Japanese Zero in air combat and an easy target for competent ground gunners.

I was required to guard the air fields with many others at Onerahi, Gisborne, and New Plymouth. We took overnight guard duties in turn. The day was reserved for elementary military training, physical training, and fatigues - the common elements in the induction of people into the armed services everywhere in those days, designed as they were to turn civilian boys into responsible fighting men.

After several months of this routine of guard duties and military training, we were all relieved to be posted on 1 May 1943 to the Initial Aircrew Training Wing at Rotorua. I was promoted to the rank of Leading Aircraftman (LAC), wearing a white flash in my hat to signify that I was an aircrew member in training. For eight weeks, I undertook a range of elementary aeronautical studies in the classroom and went through a series of aptitude tests, including tests of coordination based on the fundamental parameters of flying an aircraft. For the first part of the course, I was billeted in a hut on a site known as Jungle Town. We had many

111

reservations about the quality of this accommodation, but at that point we could not know that by comparison with what we would later have to experience in a true jungle setting, it was in fact quite respectable. Later in the course, some of us were transferred to a hotel in the town, enabling us to finish the course in style.

I was delighted at the end of this course to be told that I had been selected for pilot training, and that I would be posted to Taieri, near my home town, for the purpose. It was a great relief at last to climb into the front seat of a Tiger Moth initial training aircraft. My designated instructor, Flying Officer Paddy Fenton, in the rear seat, took me up on my first ever flight. This was the beginning of numerous flights designed to introduce the trainee pilot progressively to all the controls of the aircraft and their functions, and to every flying manoeuvre of which the aircraft was capable.

It was very cold in the open cockpit in wintertime at Taieri. The main handicap I had to overcome was recurrent air sickness. This persisted disconcertingly. With the combined connivance of my instructor and my own determination to overcome it, I was able to continue with the course without interruption. The sickness disappeared once I started to fly solo. I coped with all the demands of the flying training, but had some difficulty in judging my height above the ground on coming in to land. This was an important handicap, since it would be disastrous to stall at a considerable height above the ground. As a result, I had to complete almost twelve hours with the instructor before he felt it was safe to let me fly solo — a figure several hours greater than the average.

Having satisfactorily completed the initial training, I was posted to Woodbourne, near Blenheim, near the top of the South Island, where a good climate permitted almost continual flying in the Harvard aircraft which were used for advanced flying training. The course was in two parts, each of two months' duration. The first was used to teach us to fly a more powerful and mechanically more sophisticated aircraft than the Tiger Moth. The second focused on using an aircraft as an instrument of war. It was designed to ensure that, if we became fighter pilots in particular, we had reached such automatic mastery of flying the aircraft that we could concentrate on using it as a weapon of attack on enemy targets. Classroom studies, parades, and drill, formed part of the daily routine as well.

Our course included bombing and gunnery practice at Grasmere, emergency landings at Delta and dogfights with each other. Cine recordings of the dogfights were analysed to demonstrate how effective our efforts had been. At the end of the course, I was given an average assessment for general flying, aerobatics, night flying, bombing, and aerial gunnery, but was rated above average as a pilot/navigator.

At a ceremony in front of one of the hangars, all those who had passed the course were awarded their wings. I was commissioned as a Pilot Officer and posted to Omaka, a small Air Force station nearby, with others recently commissioned, to learn the duties of an Officer and Gentleman. At the time, this seemed another unnecessary interruption to what we wanted to do. Much of the information seemed irrelevant to the tasks we expected were lying ahead of us.

Most of us had expected to be assigned to a fighter Squadron. Instead, I found myself posted to Gisborne, with some of the others, to be part of a brand-new Squadron, flying the Grumman Avenger. 30 Squadron had already been formed with this aircraft and were away in the Pacific Islands. They had been given a period of further training in tropical conditions, complete with ground crew, prior to going into action. The Avenger had been designed and built by the United States as a torpedo bomber, operating from aircraft carriers — the use to which the United States Navy itself had widely committed the aircraft. Since the naval battle of the Coral Sea, the first major reversal for Japanese arms since their campaigns opened, the Royal New Zealand Air Force had decided that their Avengers should be used in a capacity for which they were not designed, namely as a dive bomber alongside its few Dauntless dive bombers, in association with American naval units in the Solomon Islands.

The Avenger was a robust, mechanically reliable aircraft. Its huge engine and airframe combined to make it probably the largest single-engine aircraft in the allied air fleets. It adapted well to being a land plane on jungle airstrips. One of its principal features was its capacity to fold its wings into a vertical position so that it could be easily transported on the lift down from the landing deck of aircraft carriers and economically parked in the ship's storage decks. As far as we were concerned, this was a redundant feature, although Fred Ladd, one of the characters of 31 Squadron, did make use of this facility on one celebrated occasion at Ohakea. To the consternation of ground crews working on other aircraft, and other people watching, he taxied rapidly after landing towards a lane reserved for motor vehicles between two rows of parked aircraft. At the last moment, he operated the mechanism that folded the wings, allowing his aircraft to pass along the narrow space safely.

Intensive training followed during the early months of 1944. Harold Kelsey was assigned to me as navigator, and Arch Alexander as wireless operator/air gunner. Both of them had returned from Canada after completing their training there. We had to become familiar with our respective workstations in the aircraft and the various tasks we would have to perform on operations in the Pacific. We had the use of elementary radar as an aid to improve our performance in navigation and target finding. As the construction and use of the mechanism were still close secrets, Harold held a detonating device with which to destroy it, should our aircraft be forced to land intact in enemy territory.

On one occasion, we were returning from a routine patrol off the Gisborne Coast, when Harold's observations on the radar led us to an object in the sea , which we could actually see below the surface. It disappeared into the depths on our approach. It might have been a whale, but it is possible that it could have been a submarine. Records show that Japanese submarines did operate around New Zealand. We reported the incident, but nothing came of it. During the same week, the crew of the inter-island ferry *Rangatira* reported that a torpedo had passed the stern of their ship. The Prime Minister explained to the nation that ferry sailings had been suspended and the ports closed for a short period because of the possibility that sea travel could be hazardous.

Unexpectedly, in early April 1944, the three of us were ordered to take leave prior to travelling directly to Bougainville as a reinforcement crew for 30 Squadron, which was in action there. Not only would our training in New Zealand be truncated, but we would also not enjoy the period of adaptation to living and flying in tropical conditions that those we were joining in 30 Squadron had had. Before we left on leave, our training in the use of the Avenger as a dive bomber was stepped up, both flying individually and in a formation of three aircraft.

Our flight in a transport aircraft began on 22 April, and was completed in three stages. The first day took us via Norfolk Island to Espiritu Santo, the second to Cactus in Guadalcanal, and the third to the Torokina airstrip on Bougainville, where we arrived on 24 April 1944.

Our precipitous dispatch was specifically to replace a crew whose pilot had been repatriated for medical reasons - a fact reflecting the wear and tear on aircrew members as a result of tropical diseases or physical and mental effects of the Squadron's particular operational duties and methods, notably ear disabilities arising from frequent high speed diving from 14,000 feet to sea level. On arrival I was soon introduced to the ways and means by which the Squadron conducted its domestic arrangements, together with some useful - perhaps vital - tips for the preservation of health and well being, such as ensuring my flying boots were free of scorpions before putting them on my feet. Our airstrip, in common with others, was an enclave on Bougainville Island which was still mainly occupied by the Japanese Army. From time to time the strip came under fire from enemy artillery located in the surrounding hills, and suffered the potential threat of a ground attack, at least one of which had already been attempted before our arrival.

The war having moved northwards by April, 1944, the strategic task was to keep the large Japanese Army in the area quiescent and isolated. Rabaul had previously been a major stronghold and base for Japan's conquest of the adjacent Pacific Islands. It was one of the finest natural harbours in the Pacific, providing splendid anchorage facilities for the establishment of a supplies centre. It was protected by a ring of five airfields and extensive anti-aircraft defences.

Rabaul was the regular target for Squadrons of the Royal New Zealand Air Force throughout its campaign against the Japanese. It remained a dangerous target, even after the Allies had achieved command of the air. The vast bulk of operations against Rabaul were conducted in daylight - notably early in the morning. Since there was the constant worry of tropical storms, particularly during afternoons, morning missions were the preferred option. The high winds and torrential rain in storms could have a devastating effect on navigational calculations. With visibility reduced to nothing, it was possible for crews to become disoriented and lost. Consequently, once a target was successfully reached and attacked, it was good policy to head for home base at the earliest opportunity.

My first operational mission from the airstrip at Piva was a strike on the Japanese airstrip at Vunakanau in New Britain, carrying 500 pound bombs. We were part of a force of eighty aircraft tasked to mount the attack. Forty-eight Dauntless dive bombers headed the armada. Their job was to immobilize the anti-aircraft guns which ringed the airstrip, clearing the way for twelve Avengers from the United States Navy and twelve from 30 Squadron to pulverize the airstrip itself.

We approached the target on the east coast of New Britain, making a right hand turn at 13,500 feet, then a high speed descent to turn left and peel off at 9,000 feet for a dive down to between 3,000 and 1,500 feet to release our bombs on the south-east end of the runway. Anti-aircraft fire was offering us our first baptism of battle. My own fearful preoccupation was to open the bomb bay and ensure that our bombs were on target, but I was conscious of the exploding shells around us. I caught a glimpse of a flash lower down and to my left. On return it was confirmed that the Squadron had lost its first aircraft and crew to enemy action. The aircraft of

116

my own Section Leader, Snow Gardner, had been hit. The aircraft, with substantial sections of both wings shot away, turned over and dived steeply onto the south eastern end of the runway, where it exploded and burst into flames. I had joined Snow's hut, and he had been especially helpful to me as a new boy, so I was particularly upset to learn of his loss.

On the basis of good psychological principles for dealing with the effects of such a disaster on inexperienced aircrews, the Squadron sent us up again to attack a less dangerous target on the afternoon of the same day. Our target was a group of naval guns at the Buka Passage on Bougainville itself. We dropped three bombs in the target area and strafed some buildings along the coast. The fourth bomb, however, refused to leave the bomb bay, so we had to jettison it by manual means over the sea.

A number of missions for the rest of April and early May followed this first day of combat, most of them being directed at targets in the Rabaul area. One of our missions at the south-east tip of Bougainville was notable in that we dropped a single 2,000 pound bomb on the target. On 10 May we lost another aircraft to enemy anti-aircraft fire during an attack on the Lakunai airstrip. It crashed into the harbour and sank immediately. Four other Avengers were damaged by the intense flak offered during this attack.

My own brush with disaster came on 14 May 1944. We took off at 0840 hours for a strike against Vunakanau airstrip in the Rabaul area, climbing to arrive over the target at 14,000 feet. At this height we were very cold and oxygen-starved. The accompanying Dauntless dive bombers were routinely tasked to silence the ground defences, but the Japanese gunners, appraised by our oft-repeated tactics, frequently let them pass to preserve the secrecy of their concealed positions, ready to open up on the following Avengers. I knew that we had been hit during the dive, but when I tried the intercom after taking the customary evasive action at tree top level and heading out to sea, I got no response from my colleagues. We had been hit by a 40 mm anti-aircraft shell that had exploded, tearing a large hole in the area beneath the navigator's compartment, destroying the radar, damaging the windows, the intercom and the navigator's parachute and survival kit, and buckling the tail plane.

Luckily, Harold had taken up a position to operate the sting gun at the rear of the plane. If he had been observing from the side window, he would have been unlikely to survive the explosion. Contrary to instructions, but for practical reasons, he had not been wearing his chest parachute and jungle survival pack. He had left these in his normal position. Consequently, they were full of holes and threatening to burst into flames from the hot shrapnel trapped inside them. However, an immediate solution presented itself. Urination came to his aid. Prevented by the armour plate behind me from communicating directly with the crew, I was naturally very relieved when Harold managed to pass a note to advise me that he had put out a fire by unorthodox means and that both he and Arch had escaped unscathed.

The damage to the tail plane caused some control problems but we were able to arrive back in good time, thankful that the Avenger was robust enough to take such punishment. The ground crew soon repaired the damage at a rate in accord with the proud record of 30 Squadron's Service Unit's achievement in keeping an average of 91 % of its aircraft daily available for service. One of them mounted a piece of shrapnel from the shell on perspex, as a permanent means for me to ponder a lucky escape.

Harold told me after the war that he felt safer in the Avenger than he did in the Ventura to which both he and Arch were later transferred in different crews. Arch died of severe burns received as a result of an accident on landing in a Ventura near Whenuapai later in the war.

We subsequently found that one or more bombs on several occasions failed to exit the bomb bay on command. This was a common experience among Avenger crews, who resorted to a variety of solutions. Some pilots shook their aircraft while operating the manual release. Some American pilots adopted the practice of flying close enough over other Avengers for a report on the state of their bomb bays by their pilots, who seemingly remained inured to the implicit danger they faced from any recalcitrant bombs that they were being asked to identify.

By the middle of May, many aircrews were feeling the strain of the tour, which had to be extended by two weeks when the arrival of 31 Squadron as our replacement was postponed. A full tour averaged thirty-three missions. The losses during May did nothing to relieve the tension as the end of the tour approached. The final departure of crews took place on 25 May 1944, leaving those of us who had been sent as reinforcements, but who had not completed a full tour, to rejoin 31 Squadron with which we had originally trained.

I was still only nineteen years old, but presumably because of my experience in action over Rabaul, I was asked to lead 31 Squadron's first strike on 26 May. It had to be abandoned, however, owing to bad weather, but the next day I led the Squadron's attack on gun positions on Hospital Ridge at Rabaul. Cloud prevented us from observing the results, but all aircraft returned safely. Thereafter, missions were led by the Squadron Commander or one of the Flight Commanders.

Only two days later, the Squadron lost its first Avenger when Mel Greenslade, one of the Flight Commanders, and his crew were shot down. On 31 May, a second aircraft was lost, and on 14 June, Gordon Prior, the other Flight Commander, and his crew, failed to return from a strike on Vunapope. A further Avenger was shot down on 1 July over Rabaul, after I had returned to New Zealand. Its pilot, Murray Aitchison, baled out successfully and spent two days - during which he hid from the Japanese - and a night in enemy territory. He used his one-man dinghy to drift down a river to the open sea, where he spent three nights and two days before being rescued by a United States torpedo boat. By any standards he made an epic escape.

The three of us finally completed thirty-six operational missions in the Avenger. Quite soon after the initial missions flown by 31 Squadron, we were used less frequently on the regular strike missions and made responsible for a programme designed to spoil the Japanese Army's crops discovered in plantations in the northern part of Bougainville. The Americans had been experimenting with an apparatus to spray the crops with diesel oil but it had proved faulty in use. When the difficulties had been finally overcome, two of the Squadron's Avengers were fitted with the spraying system that worked effectively in action. We made a few flights with the Americans to observe the methods used before undertaking many missions during the rest of May and the early days of June. On one of the early sorties with the Americans we acted as escort for the spraying operation. But we carried ten 100 pound bombs in case we came across a target of opportunity and used them to destroy a wharf which I spotted jutting out from the jungle to the sea.

I was never really happy in principle with what we called 'the potato hop' although I appreciated its possible value in helping to accelerate the collapse of the Japanese hold on Bougainville. The spraying required a low level, low speed approach which exposed us to a lot of small arms fire. Fortunately, the Japanese had concentrated all their anti-aircraft guns around their military installations, overlooking the potential of their crops as a serious target. Apart from a few holes in the aircraft, we completed the assignment without incident.

On one of our sorties during the tour, the pitch control of our engine developed a fault after completing the mission. I decided to head for Green Island, located nearer than our base at Piva, and was pleased to see that a Catalina, flying at sea level, had picked us up as a possible candidate for a sea rescue, but saw us safely down on Green Island.

With our tour of duty completed, we were posted back to New Zealand, leaving on 20 June 1944 for the three stage flight home and some leave. The return led to my separation from Harold Kelsey and Arch Alexander, with whom I had shared a baptism of fire and many experiences that tested our personal qualities and trust in each other, and our ability to co-operate for effective military action and survival.

I was promoted to the rank of Flying Officer and sent for eleven days to fly drogue towing aircraft used to train potential fighter pilots in aerial gunnery, before being posted to a conversion course at Ohakea to fly fighter aircraft.

The Kittyhawk was used as a training aircraft at that stage of the war, having been replaced as a front line fighter, and after giving notable service, by the Corsair. It had a high stalling speed and therefore a high landing speed. It was a very different aircraft from the Avenger. On one occasion when night flying, I lost control of the Kittyhawk on coming in to land, ending up by executing a 180° turn on the runway - to the consternation of the pilot following me in to a landing. The course was quite intensive, requiring up to six flights on some days. There were, of course, a large number of aspects to fighter operations. Major training experience was included for all the usual dimensions of flying the aircraft itself, formation flying in various numbers of aircraft, aerobatics, gunnery, and combat tactics.

After further leave I went to Ardmore on 21 September 1944 for a week's conversion course to fly the Corsair. Actual flying experience was preceded by careful ground instructions. The Corsair, as one of the outstanding fighters of the Second World War, was a very powerful aircraft, complete with its own foibles. It was difficult for the pilot to climb into the cockpit. It could somersault if the brakes were injudiciously applied on landing. It was likely to shed its elevators if the official maximum speed were exceeded in a dive. And it was not a straightforward matter if you needed to bale out - owing to the short distance between the cockpit and the aircraft's tail.

On 26 September I was adjudged above average on the conversion course and posted to the newly forming 24 Squadron, led by Squadron Leader M T Vanderpump, and destined for combat service in the Pacific Islands. About twenty seven pilots made up the Squadron strength, eleven of whom had had previous experience in Numbers 14 and 19 Squadrons. Alex George and Ron Bush were the two Flight Commanders. I was assigned to the latter.

For a whole month the Squadron practised formation flying in various numbers, learning to keep close stations and strictly trusting the leader of a formation through all the twists and turns of the aerobatics that could be involved in combat with enemy fighters or used in the process of ground attacks. When all had been prepared, we set off on the long flight in a transport aircraft on 29 October, bound for Espiritu Santo. We spent one night on Norfolk Island en route before moving on to this interim base the next day.

Espiritu Santo was a major supply and operations base for all branches of the United States military forces in the islands, including extensive naval repair and docking facilities, and well surfaced runways for the several airstrips used by the American Army Air Force and Marine Corps. We shared the airfield at Pallikulo with the Americans for most of our stay there. We had the pleasure of being able to shop in PX stores for goods that had disappeared from the shops in wartime New Zealand, some of which we could send back to our families and girl friends. Film and stage shows were regular diversions, the latter featuring world famous stars of the time.

Very soon I was involved in the experimental use of instantaneously fused depth charges for clearing ground undergrowth, without causing craters, to ease the passage of Australian troops advancing through jungle areas. One of our aircraft was lost during the experiment but its pilot, my friend Jim Hay, survived a crash into the sea by an epic swim. Meanwhile we were acclimatizing to the living and operational conditions while undertaking practice bombing and formation flying with various numbers of aircraft. As a diversion from this, I was one of twelve pilots commissioned to ferry aircraft to Guadalcanal on 9 November, returning in a Dakota transport.

On 12 December the Squadron moved to Bougainville. Again, I travelled in a Dakota back to the airstrip at Piva on the western side of the middle of Bougainville Island, where I had spent my previous combat time in 30 and 31 Squadrons. Under the shadow of the nearby smoking volcano, we operated there from 13 December 1944 until 24 January 1945. Missions to the Rabaul area in northern New Britain remained important in our programme, but we also carried out many strikes or sweeps to various parts of

Bougainville itself. Australian troops were replacing American forces, charged with clearing out the substantial numbers of Japanese still on the Island, who remained capable of disrupting allied shipping, and, of course, of conducting offensive operations against allied airstrips. On 31 December I took part in a combined operation involving Australian infantry, the United States Navy, and our Squadron, in the south of Bougainville. The Japanese were resourceful and ingenious in their use of camouflage, other forms of concealment, and the movement of their variegated assets, despite all our efforts to destroy or frustrate them.

The jungle was a beautiful environment in terms of its flora and fauna but a forbidding place in which to fight. Apart from the normal diet of death and wounds from the enemy's weapons, a soldier had to avoid the dangers posed by leeches, centipedes, scorpions, and snakes, to say nothing of the wide array of debilitating and lethal diseases that could be contracted. In the air, we were exposed to a different set of risks. Apart from the customary threat from anti-aircraft fire and enemy fighters, we were well aware that to fall into the hands of the enemy could result in ill-treatment and/or summary execution. In contrast, to survive a crash landing in the sea carried its own hazards of dehydration, severe effects from exposure to the sun, sharks, and weather that could be fatal for a dinghy. The possibility of a rescue by the ubiquitous Catalina flying boats, which maintained constant coastal patrols, was a safeguard we all appreciated and a few had to use.

24 Squadron lost no aircraft during this tour, in spite of taking part in the large-scale attack on the Japanese base at Rabaul on 15 January 1945 which proved so costly for both Number 14 and Number 16 Squadrons that were also involved. We had been the first to go into the attack, and having been delayed due to the late arrival of the squadrons from Green Island, we needed to return promptly to Bougainville. A number of the aircraft of the following squadrons suffered damage, one having to crash into the sea. During the prolonged but unsuccessful attempts to protect and rescue the pilot - who succeeded against all the odds by remaining afloat for many hours - seven aircraft were lost on being overtaken

by a tropical storm as they tried to return to their base on Green Island. The aircraft losses for that day were the highest suffered in one day by the Royal New Zealand Air Force in the Pacific in the entire war.

On my return to the islands for my second tour with 24 Squadron under the command of Alex George, I was based on Green Island from 23 March to 23 May 1945, having previously spent three weeks of tropical acclimatization and Squadron training at Henderson Field on Guadalcanal. The runway surface of coral there made a quiet and smooth alternative to the metal surface we had become accustomed to on Bougainville.

For my second tour I flew about half of my operational flights to the Rabaul area, often looking for targets of opportunity as well as for strikes against predetermined targets. I also flew to the Duke of York Islands and New Ireland against barges and road traffic. But the most demanding sorties were in support of the Australian infantry on Bougainville itself. As a Section leader, I often led my section in small scale bombing operations against Japanese positions ahead of the Australians. Since these were usually very close to the advancing Australians, pin-point accuracy had to be achieved. Anti-aircraft ground fire for these operations was typically muted. The Squadron by that time was deliberately avoiding targets that were known to be heavily defended, although we suffered the one loss to the Squadron on this second tour from unexpected ground fire.

We had to leave our Corsairs at Jacquinot Bay, in the south of New Britain, at the end of our tour, to be taken over by a replacement squadron to use in support of the Australian Army which was preparing for a major attack on Rabaul itself. I was one of the two pilots who first landed at the new airstrip there. It had been constructed by the Australians. It had a rough surface with a bump in the middle, and lacked a landing control system other than an Australian soldier standing near the runway with a radio and a microphone. A United States Catalina flew me back to Piva from which, during the following few days, the whole Squadron returned to New Zealand.

After leave, I joined Number 26 Squadron in the making at Ardmore, to serve, it was believed, as a Mustang Squadron in Borneo. Squadron exercises were in progress when the decision was made to disband the Squadron in face of the diminishing need. The end of the war came in August. I had resolved to resume university studies and apply for a discharge. I was transferred to the Reserve of Air Force Officers on 28 September 1945. I had completed my service with the rank of Flying Officer and was notified on 22 March 1946 that I had been "Mentioned in Dispatches for outstanding services relating to the Pacific war." Flying had been my life in the service, the details of which were as follows, but I decided to give it up for a life on the ground.

	By Day Dual	By Day as Pilot	By Night Dual	By Night as Pilot
Total Hours	99.2	624.05	11.1	28.1

	As Passenger	On Instruments
Total Hours	131.1	38.2

Operational Flying	Days	Sorties	Hours
Bougainville 24 April - 22 June 1944 (in Avengers)	59	36	79.4
Bougainville 13 December 1944 - 23 Jenuary 1945 (in Corsairs)	41	28	54.3
Green Island 23 March - 8 May 1945 (in Corsairs)	46	20	51.55
Totals	146	84	185.25

During the war my friends and I had frequently discussed what we wanted to do when it was over. I was uncertain but at least decided that I should take advantage of the Government's generous rehabilitation scheme to continue full-time study at Otago University. I knew that I did not want to major in the languages that had dominated my first year in 1942. I pursued my new interests in psychology, anthropology, and history. My continuing interest in international affairs had been whetted by a desire to play some constructive part in working towards a more peaceful and prosperous world. Reflecting the very British outlook of New Zealand at the time, despite the declining importance of the British Empire, joining the colonial service was one possibility in my mind. I was advised that economics and political science would be useful as a background for that sort of career, so I ended up majoring in those two subjects in my Bachelor of Arts Degree.

For the first two years student politics and romance assumed rather more importance than academic study. Nola Ross and I became fellow students in the Economics 1 course, which she was taking as a final unit for her degree. She was elected Lady Vice President of the Students' Association and a few months later I was elected to replace the President, who had to stand down after making a speech which precipitated a crisis in the Association's relations with the university authorities. The demands of office facilitated the development of our burgeoning relationship and we married at the end of 1947.

I followed Nola to Auckland where she found employment in 1948. I made up for lost time on academic study, finishing my bachelor's degree there with an ex-serviceman's senior scholarship in economics. When Nola became pregnant in early 1949 with the first of our two sons, Ross and David, I needed to get a job. I was fortunate to be one of three appointed in April to the Prime Minister's and External Affairs Department as a diplomatic trainee. My main job was assisting Lloyd White in establishing an economic division in the Department. I learned a lot about New Zealand's external economic relationships from this experienced official and established constructive relationships with others both inside and outside the Department involved in international affairs, contacts which were mutually useful later in my career.

I had managed to complete a Master's Degree in economics with first class honors by part time study during my first year in the Department. The outgoing Professor of Economics at Victoria

University College suggested that I might like to apply for a lectureship which was becoming available in 1952. After much agonising I did so and was successful in my application. I was again very lucky in serving my apprenticeship as a university teacher under the leadership of Horace Belshaw, whom I regard as the greatest New Zealand applied economist of the 20th century. He gave me a very demanding set of courses to teach and there were times, in my first year particularly, when I wished I had not left External Affairs. However he could not have been more helpful in enabling me to cope with my crises of confidence. He was also extremely generous, given the staff shortage at the time, in permitting me to take up valuable opportunities for personal development outside the Department. .

Until my formal retirement in 1985, I held a number of positions at Victoria University of Wellington, including the Macarthy Chair of Economics 1959–67, the Chair of Money and Finance 1970–77, and Visiting Professor of Public Policy and convenor of the Master of Public Policy programme 1982-85. I have moved between the academy, business, and government during my career. Business commitments included a period in the early years with the Tasman Pulp and Paper Company, and in more recent years on the boards of State Insurance, Norwich Union Life Insurance, and the National Bank of New Zealand.

In the field of public policy I was an advisor to the Royal Commission on Money, Banking and Credit Systems in 1955, then chairman of the newly-established Monetary and Economic Council, a position I held for two periods before 1972, preparing a report, *New Zealand and an Enlarged EEC* (Monetary and Economic Council, 1970), on the implications for New Zealand if Britain were to join the European Economic Community. I was the first chairman of, and later honorary adviser to, Asia 2000 (now the Asia New Zealand Foundation). I convened the Advisory Committee on Educational Planning set up in association with the National Development Council, which became the Advisory Council on Educational Planning, and organised the Educational Development Conference after 1972.

In 1976 I was asked to chair the Task Force on Economic and Social Planning. On the basis of the Task Force Report, *New Zealand and the Turning Point,* the Muldoon Government set up the New Zealand Planning Council, for which I was chairman, a position I held from 1977 to 1982. During that time the Council published significant reports on a wide range of issues from *The Welfare State?* to *He Matapuna – some Maori perspectives.*

In the early 1980s it seemed clear that Prime Minister Robert Muldoon wanted to disestablish the Planning Council – but it lasted another ten years - and the Commission for the Future, which he achieved in 1982. In that context, Henry Lang (former Secretary to the Treasury) and I were among those moving to establish an institute for independent commentary and research on public policy that could not simply be closed by a Government. Victoria University set up the Institute of Policy Studies (IPS) in 1983. From 1989-91 I became its chairman, and have remained involved in its work in one capacity or another to the present day.

Since a great deal of the work I have done has been in collaboration with others, I count myself fortunate to have been honoured publicly for services by the Crown, universities, and business and professional associations. I often reflect that there is a great deal of luck in life. My survival as a combat pilot during the war gave me the opportunity to live a long, full, and interesting life afterwards. But I always remember that such an outcome was denied to so many others by the fortunes of war.

Reference has been made to *Jungle Bomber*, privately published by Sir Frank Holmes in 2004, and to Ladley, Andrew and John R Martin (eds) (2005) *The Visible Hand – The Changing Role of the State in New Zealand's Development.* Institute of Policy Studies of the Victoria University of Wellington.

~ ~ ~

Frank Holmes flew as pilot in the following aircraft, listed in experiential order.

Tiger Moth
Harvard
Avenger
Kittyhawk
Corsair

Photographs and the specifications of these aircraft may be found in Part 2, listed in alphabetical order.

Frank Holmes and his two crew members of 30 Squadron with their Avenger, at Piva, Bougainville, in 1944. L-R: Holmes, Alexander, Kelsey

Frank Holmes and his two crew members of 30 Squadron with their Avenger, at Piva, Bougainville, in 1944. L-R: Holmes, Kelsey, Alexander

30 Squadron's camp in the jungle, Piva, Bougainville, in 1944

Frank Holmes at the controls of an Avenger over Gisborne,
1944

24 Squadron personnel during the Squadron's first tour,
Bougainville, 1944

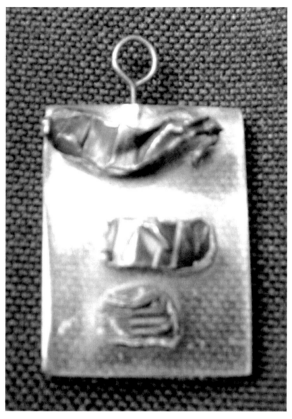

Shrapnel from a 40 mm anti-aircraft shell which scored a hit on the Avenger piloted by Frank Holmes during a bombing attack in the Rabaul area on 14 May 1944

24 Squadron personnel before the Squadron's second tour to Bougainville, 1944

Frank Holmes and Jim Hay in front of a Corsair, 1945

Dick Falconer and Frank Holmes with Corsair fighter bomber, 1945

The end of a 220 yards race on a jungle Sports Day, 1945. Frank Holmes is on the right

Frank Holmes in 1945

TOK BILOG GUVMAN

YU MAS LUKAUTIM GUT DISPELA MASTA. HAITIM
LONG OL JAPAN, NA B R I N I M LONG KIAP NA
SOLDIA BILOG YUMI. WOK BILOG GUVMAN
OLSEM, NA IGAT PE.

YU NOKAN SAKIM DISPELA TOK.

(TO BE READ TO NATIVES WHO CANNOT READ)

GOV'MENT E TALK YOU MUST LOOKOUT IM
ME. YOU NO CAN TALK IM JAPAN. WHERE
STOP KIAP ALL THE SAME SOLDIER BELONG
YOU-ME?
SHOWIM ME ROAD, NOW BEHIND YOU CATCHIM
PAY.

GOV'MENT E TALK

Pidgin English for the use of a downed airman

137

26 Squadron personnel, preparing to go to Borneo 1945. The Squadron was later disbanded without going into action

Chapter 6.

From One Extreme to Another

Arthur Hoskins

From One Extreme to Another

My mother was destined to have a large family of eight children. My older sister and I, being the first two to be born, were later able to help the midwife who made repeated visits to our house to supply her professional services. She was a dear soul, who encouraged us to help by boiling water and fetching and carrying, while she attended to my mother.

This midwife had a son who served pre-war in the Royal New Zealand Air Force. Flight Lieutenant Jack Watts was one of the pilots designated to go to England to prepare to fly a squadron of the newly produced Wellington bombers which the New Zealand government had purchased. In the event the departure of these aircraft was overtaken by the declaration of war on 3 September 1939. Thereupon, the New Zealand government offered the Wellingtons to the Royal Air Force. They became the basis for the formation of 75 Squadron, which served throughout the Second World War with great distinction, manned entirely by New Zealanders.

Following my older sister's birth in December, 1916, I was born on 11 May 1918, in Christchurch, and went to school there. Both parents were themselves born in New Zealand. On completing primary schooling, I attended Christchurch Technical College which provided a secondary curriculum but with some subject biases. Being a co-educational establishment, it offered building, engineering, and general knowledge for boys, the girls taking home science subjects. It was a very different regime from what is on offer today in the nation's high schools. The assumption was made that girls would become homemakers and mothers with large families.

My first job on leaving the Technical College was driving a horse and cart for a local grocer and hardware business. I went out alone on Mondays and Tuesdays on the shop's bicycle to visit numerous homes to collect their orders for the week. The husband and wife owners of the business, with their senior assistant, made up the orders which I then delivered over the rest of the week. But I always had my sights on other things. During my teen years I had been regaled by the midwife with stories of the Air Force and flying which subconsciously must have whetted my appetite for a place in the still relatively new profession of flying and the exciting form of transport that it offered.

Consequently, when the time and opportunity were ripe, before the declaration of war in 1939, I applied for a short term commission in the Royal Air Force. I received a note in reply to say that I would be sent details regarding a medical examination and other enlistment procedures. Meantime, the New Zealand authorities sent me another letter to say that as war had broken out I could join the Royal New Zealand Air Force. I did so in June 1940, with the early service number 402659. My service however seemed far from warlike when I reported to the base at Wigram. I helped to clean the aircraft there and the Education Officer gave me a book of assignments to improve my knowledge across a range of subjects cognate with flying. Being designated Aircraftman 2nd Class GD gave me much satisfaction as the letters GD, standing for General Duties, indicated that I was destined for aircrew training. My stay at Wigram was confined to perfunctory duties and induction procedures, which I both endured and enjoyed before being posted to Levin for aircrew training, where Squadron Leader Ron Sinclair was my Commanding Officer, with Warrant Officer Arch Beadle in charge, and Sergeant Robinson as the immediate disciplinarian.

My girl friend and I had been going out together since I was sixteen. While I was at Levin for elementary aircrew studies in the classroom, I learned of the likelihood of my being sent to Canada for wireless, bombing, and gunnery training, and that it was customary for an airman to be posted direct to England on completing his training there. In view of this probable outcome, we talked about our future, and decided to apply to be married. At the time it was necessary for an intending aircrew member to apply to the Air Force for permission to marry. It was believed that this requirement stemmed from the consideration that a high casualty rate among aircrew members would impose a liability on the government to look after the widows. Conversely, of course, for the couple concerned it was worth marrying for that very reason. I approached the Warrant Officer and had an interview with the Commanding Officer. A few weeks later, I was informed that permission to marry had been granted.

We duly married on 26 October 1940 in Christchurch, after seven hectic days of preparations. My best man was Jim Lloyd, an engineer in the Royal New Zealand Air Force, and close friend. My groomsman was Gordon Bonham, who later flew as a pilot in a Mosquito squadron in England. He was killed in action but his body was never found, his name being inscribed on the Runnymede Memorial for that reason. After spending our honeymoon from 26 October until 5 November, I returned to complete initial aircrew training at Levin and was posted to Canada.

I travelled to Canada in a beautiful ship called the *Awatea* that was sunk by a U-boat later in the war, disembarking in Vancouver, from where I went by train to Calgary. Of the group sent from New Zealand, half remained in Calgary, including me, the other half being sent on to Montreal. During my time at Calgary I had the distinction of learning to play ice hockey and representing a New Zealand team to play an Australian team. I completed three months in Calgary at the Number 2 Wireless School, using Norseman aircraft with Canadian Air Force pilots, followed by another three months' training at the Number 3 Bombing and Gunnery School at Macdonald, flying in Battle aircraft.

By this time I was experiencing the rigors of a Canadian winter, with temperatures that exceeded my imagination for their severity. It was interesting to see the adaptations that Air Force personnel had developed to keep a station operational in such incredibly low temperatures. This applied particularly to maintaining the aircraft for flying duties. It also applied to flying itself. If an aircraft's engine failed, it was possible for the pilot to make a landing almost everywhere it seemed on the ice.

As expected, I was posted to Halifax to await a convey to the United Kingdom. The year 1941 saw a steep rise in the loss of ships across the Atlantic Ocean. It was assuming such proportions that the U-boat warfare against allied shipping eventually became known as the Battle of the Atlantic. In its own right, the Atlantic was a theatre of war. It was a battle front in the west, together with that of Bomber Command's offensive, that simply had to be continued and won. But at the time of my crossing, the losses were part of the adverse characteristics of the entire war for Great Britain. Our own convoy, consisting of about twenty-five ships, was attacked by U-boats, losing six or seven ships. We were attacked by day and night. I saw the huge plumes of smoke from burning ships that stayed afloat awhile before sinking in the distance as the convoy ploughed on. It was a sobering experience for all of us to see the choreography of war for the first time, to be participants in it – albeit unwilling and passive - and to be an audience for the sights and sounds that it produced, and above all, to be assailed by concern for all those passengers, military and civilian, and crew members, who faced injury and death in explosions, fire, and drowning – to say nothing about the precious cargoes of food and war materials that were being sent to the bottom. All the time one kept thinking, "How soon will it be our turn?"

The Commodore in command of the convoy was on board the *Ausonia*, the ship on which I was sailing. It was designated AMC for Armed Merchant Cruiser. It had anti-aircraft guns, a heavier gun for engaging an enemy submarine or surface ship, and a stock of depth charges to use in the event that the ship found itself over a submerged U-boat. He gave orders that no ship should stop to rescue seamen from stricken vessels. The convoy was escorted by an inadequate number of corvettes. They had their work cut out in attacking the U-boats but could pick up survivors when there was opportunity and when they considered it safe to do so. A stationary vessel presented an easy target for a U-boat.

The convoy's surviving ships were ordered on a diversionary course to Iceland to regroup and await fresh escorts. We put into the harbour at Reykjavík, where we waited for two weeks for more escorts to arrive to shepherd the convoy to the Clyde at Gourock. Two days after leaving Reykjavik we were greatly heartened to see the arrival of a Sunderland flying boat of Coastal Command. It was able to offer better protection for the convoy by patrolling ahead to detect U-boats lying in wait for it. I left Reykjavik in a different ship, a Dutch liner called the *Volendam*. I soon found that a few British Army soldiers were patrolling the ship, armed with rifles and fixed bayonets. They had apparently been taken on board in Reykjavik as guards for a group of German U-boat crewmen who had been taken prisoner when they survived the destruction of their U-boats. They were kept below decks in captivity under strict guard. There was always the chance that they might contemplate taking over the ship. The Captain of the *Volendam* said that if we were torpedoed they would have to go down with the ship. We made our way to Scotland uneventfully, save for the odd depth charge that escorts dropped on suspected U-boat locations.

We put into Gourock in the middle of night, the following morning disembarking to entrain for Bournemouth, on the south coast of England, the clearing centre for newly arrived aircrew members from overseas, to await a posting. The journey was interrupted at Southampton, only twenty miles short of Bournemouth – a large raid on the city by the Luftwaffe had smashed the railway lines. Our train was obliged to wait for twenty-four hours for emergency repairs to be completed, before going on to Bournemouth, where we were housed in excellent accommodation and fed by a nearby hotel.

Waiting in expectation for a posting to a squadron, I was a little surprised to be sent for yet further training, to no less a place than Cranwell College in Lincolnshire, the Staff College and home of the Royal Air Force – or at least to the air base that was part of the total complex there. The reason for it was the need to be updated on the current radio equipment in use. We had apparently trained on obsolete radios in Canada. I had the experience of flying in the obsolescent Heyford bomber that had been relegated to training duties since 1937. I learned to use the new Marconi radio, which produced such clear signals.

At the conclusion of my radio updating I was finally posted to an Operational Training Unit at Chipping Warden in Northamptonshire, to fly Wellington bombers. We had to become familiar with the Wellington aircraft and our own work stations and work in it. When this had been accomplished, it was customary to give new crews initial operational experience by sending them on leaflet dropping raids over the coastal regions of enemy occupied territory in Northern Europe. Our crew was duly assigned to such a raid. We encountered some anti-aircraft fire but met no night fighters. At that early stage of the bombing campaign, the losses were incurred mostly as a result of the heavy barrage that the German gunners mounted against the Wellington, Hampton, and Whitley aircraft. The performance characteristics of these aircraft made them more vulnerable to ground gunnery than it did subsequently to their successors, the Stirling, Halifax, and Lancaster aircraft. It took time for the Germans to develop the night fighter force which wrought such havoc among the latter bombers in the second half of the war.

Newly formed crews usually stayed together for a posting to an operational squadron, but in my case I received a call to replace a wireless operator in an established crew of Number 12 Squadron flying Wellingtons at Binbrook, near Market Rasen, in Lincolnshire, north-east of Lincoln and south-west of Grimsby, where I arrived in December 1941. My first flight was a training flight by night. For some reason the rear gunner was unavailable so the pilot asked me to sit in the rear gun turret as it was not permitted to fly with it unmanned.

At the time of my arrival in 1941, no one could leave the station without a permit. However, the enemy caused a change in the prevailing strict regime. German fighter bombers such as the Junkers 88 began to take advantage of the Wellingtons on their return to base. The exhaust of the Wellington used to glow red, providing a ready beacon that an enemy aircraft could follow closely when the aircraft was approaching its home Station.

Since every returning friendly aircraft had to identify itself by using an apparatus with a special code called IFF, an enemy aircraft by keeping close behind an incoming Wellington could escape detection. It was thereby able to penetrate the airfield's defences, drop bombs on the runway and shoot up the hangars, crew quarters, and other buildings, before escaping into the night.

One night, when I was not operational, I was in bed when exploding bombs nearby woke me violently from sleep. A German aircraft had followed one of our Wellingtons in and attacked the station. As we did not have a hard runway, the bombs exploded harmlessly across the grass airfield. One of our Wellingtons in the process of landing had a lucky escape. This incident caused the Station Commander to arrange for the accommodation of aircrews off base. I had a permanent leave pass to live in Swinhope Hall, a large mansion for aircrew members a couple of miles away, which he obtained for the use of the base. This was a welcome concession, not least because when we were able to take time off we frequented the local Marquis of Granby pub.

In the event I completed a full tour of thirty operational missions in 12 Squadron from Market Rasen, involving over 300 combat flying hours, a short trip taking six or seven hours, a long trip ten or eleven hours return. I stayed with the same crew the whole time. We were an international crew, consisting of an English pilot, two Canadians, and two New Zealanders. The Squadron's losses were heavy in 1942, particularly against two singular targets. When the *Scharnhorst, Gneisenau,* and *Prinz Eigen* made their dramatic break through the English Channel from Brest to Germany in February 1942, the Squadron lost several aircraft to the weather as part of the futile attempts to arrest their passage, the weather turning against us dramatically after taking off. The other target was the German heavy water plant at Peenamunde. It was heavily defended, costing us several aircraft. My other missions included Hamburg three times, the Rhur a number of times, and targets in France, Belgium, and The Netherlands.

We were never attacked by a night fighter but were constantly met with intense anti-aircraft fire, especially at all the targets in German territory. We never suffered severe damage but often picked up a few holes. Our biggest enemy was searchlights. If one searchlight found us, others quickly joined the first to form a cone of illumination, giving the ground gunners a clear target. My job on an operational mission was to maintain contact with base. This was often difficult to do, such was the volume of radio traffic. Signal lights were changed every half hour, so I was constantly busy waiting for calls about the changes. I also had to keep the pilot informed with up to date information. I had to work in conjunction with the navigator, since I was in receipt of call signs and radio signals for navigational purposes. The Wellington was equipped with a loop aerial. When I picked up a station I could turn the loop until the signal became optimum, and take a reading off the dial in degrees to pinpoint our position. The tail gunner was responsible for a small apparatus called a drift recorder to measure the wind direction and amount of drift that had to be taken into consideration.

During the tour I had a week's leave every six weeks. This took a lot of the pressure off me. London was always an attraction for overseas aircrew members on leave, but I found that the availability of accommodation - and sometimes its quality - were not good. On one occasion I obtained permission to stay at the Canadian Forces Club, a fine facility in Gower Street, and on another I managed to stay at a club in Westminster. I always remember the satisfaction I felt on walking down Fleet Street, as the home of publishing and printing that it then was, recalling the delights of boyhood. My mother bought me a comic paper each week which had its origins in London.

But I also used to travel by train to Bournemouth, where I could have free accommodation and good meals, courtesy of the Royal Air Force. When going on leave, it was necessary to inform the Station of one's address in case of the need for a recall. I was in Bournemouth at the end of my tour when I was called back to base to be told that I was posted. I was offered the choice of staying for a second tour with the same Squadron, a posting as an instructor to an Operational Training Unit, or a posting overseas. I opted for overseas and was sent to the Number 1 Departure Centre at West Kirby, near Liverpool. Those in charge there informed me that I would not know where I was going until I arrived there. I had to visit the clothing store to be fitted out with tropical gear.

I embarked on the *Llansteven Castle*, a cargo and passenger ship of the pre-war Union-Castle Line serving the route from the United Kingdom to South Africa. The passengers included over thirty aircrew New Zealanders, in the charge of Wing Commander W E A Stevens, and a few who had suffered injuries and burns. The ship sailed alone through the north Atlantic at a time of the very worst rate of losses to U-boats to date, protected by its high speed. It was an uneventful voyage to Halifax, Nova Scotia, from the point of view of enemy activity, but it was a stormy crossing.

Over the ship's loudspeaker system, all the New Zealanders were asked to report to the ship's lounge, where the Wing Commander greeted us with the words, "Well, gentlemen, this must never be repeated and in no way communicated with your family - you are going home to New Zealand to help form new Squadrons for the Pacific theatre of war." The announcement had an electrifying effect. Mixed thoughts raced through my mind. I had thought we could be destined for the Middle East where the war was in full swing and far from being decided. To be able to go home to see my wife was a sudden and totally unexpected possibility. To form the seed aircrew members for the creation of new squadrons sounded like a testimony to my service to date. To be involved in carrying the war to the Japanese who, after all, had posed a real threat to my own homeland, seemed like a worthwhile way to spend my war years in the future.

From Halifax we travelled by train to an air base at Lachine, Montreal, where the hospitality for our nearly three weeks' stay was amazing. Without prior warning we were told one day that the next day we would be on the train again to an unknown destination. It proved to be a journey to Chicago, and then San Francisco, where we were daily issued with chits for meals at restaurants, and where the accommodation was invariably good, for a sojourn of several days. The only restrictions on us were the hours fixed by the hotel and a prohibition to go into China Town in uniform. The latter impediment was easily circumvented by my friend Fred and I when American hosts loaned us civilian suits and took us there by car. During the visit, however, Fred disappeared, so I had to return to the hotel without him to meet the deadline hour. It so happened that we were informed to be ready to leave the following morning for embarkation. The next morning arrived but Fred still had not returned to the hotel, but at the last minute he arrived at the dock still dressed in civilian clothes and unable to remember where he had left his uniform. He had had a narrow escape from being classified as a deserter. We rustled around to find him a uniform.

Two years later Fred and I were in the same squadron in the Pacific, both with the rank of Warrant Officer. We were at a base with American forces. As it happened, in the United States Army, a Warrant Officer was entitled to use the regular Officers' Mess, a worthwhile privilege to have, since the meals and facilities of the American Mess were superior to those of our own Non-Commissioned Officers' Mess. One day in the American Mess, Fred suddenly looked up and said to me, "Do you recognize that bloke over there. He looks familiar." Fred walked over to him and asked, "Excuse me, but did you live in San Francisco and take two New Zealanders to China Town." "You two!" the other man interrupted. "Fred, I've had your uniform dry cleaned and pressed, and all your presents and souvenirs are still there. But where's my suit?"

To our great delight we were destined to sail on the premier ship of its day, the RMS *Queen Elizabeth* of the Cunard Line. It was a surprise to find the ship on the other side of the United States from the Atlantic where it had been operating for military purposes during the war so far - and with which it was always identified in the mind of the maritime world. I was assigned to

Room 15 on C Deck. Several of us were berthed in the same cabin, so we had to take turns for sleeping. We had the use of the First Class lounge, and the run of a beautiful ship. The New Zealanders received a drinks allowance of beer, brandy, whisky, and gin. We drew lots from a hat to decide what each man could have. If a man were lucky enough to draw a bottle of whisky, he could sell it to an American serviceman on board for as much as US$100.

On leaving San Francisco our ship sailed in the company of an American ship. We had no escort. Our defence was our speed. After a while the Captain declared that the other ship's speed was too slow, a danger to the *Queen Elizabeth* and the large number of military passengers and crew members on board. We were soon aware of the increased speed of our ship on seeing the other ship recede gradually into the distance until it was out of sight. Arriving near New Zealand, the Captain explained that as no port in New Zealand could harbour the ship, he had to proceed to Australia, where he anchored in Sydney harbour, the ship being unable to go under the famous bridge. I went ashore and was billeted at Manly, but without any contact with my family in New Zealand. We were issued with meal tickets for breaks, lunches, and dinners, but were showered with so many invitations to private houses and hosted by voluntary organizations, that we didn't use many of them. I was able to see a lot of Sydney before travelling by train to Brisbane, to embark on a ship for Auckland.

By this time it was the middle of 1942. If anything, it was the wrong time to return to New Zealand in the worst of its winter months. But the weather proved not to be a matter of concern. On arrival in Auckland, we entrained for Wellington, where, at a distance of some 200 yards from the station to catch the overnight ferry to Lyttelton, the Port of Christchurch, Fred and I were accosted by Air Force Police, who drew attention to shortcomings in our dress. We were wearing the battledress that we had always worn for operational flying, and had tucked our forage caps, which we should have been wearing, of course, through our shoulder lapels. Apparently we had been noticed by an Officer on duty when we disembarked. We were told that the Officer wanted to see us at once, because he considered that we were improperly dressed. We rejected the reproach and the request and moved on. After a second challenge, which we ignored, a troop arrived and arrested us.

The Flight Lieutenant on duty asked for our names and numbers, before castigating us for being a disgrace to the Air Force, pointing to our long hair among all the other faults. We then became roused enough to turn nasty. I called him an armchair walla. We told him we had completed an entire tour. But he seemed unimpressed, assuring us that details of our behaviour would be sent to the station to which we would next be posted. His final judgement on us was to say, "You are not in the United Kingdom now. You are in New Zealand and you have to behave as you are expected to."

Our train took us to Wellington where we caught the ferry to Lyttelton. I was reunited with my wife for a second honeymoon before the inevitable telegram arrived a few days later, ordering me to report to a base at Nelson, where the Commanding Officer turned out to be the same Officer who had been in charge of the Initial Training Unit at Levin when I originally joined up. Of all the recruits who had been through his hands at Levin, he happened to remember me as the man for whom he had obtained permission to get married. He called me in to his office to raise the subject of my misdemeanor, to tell me that he had received a message from the Air Department in Wellington about it. But he promptly - to my astonishment - told me to forget the whole incident, adding, "I'll see that you're commissioned within six months" in an effort to recognize my service. I was in fact commissioned in 1944.

Number 9 Squadron at Nelson was being formed to fly Hudsons. I clearly remember the impression made on me on being introduced for the first time to the relatively well appointed American aircraft – in such contrast to the Wellington. It even had door mats. When the Squadron had formed its crews and trained up to initial operational levels, we flew as a fleet via Ohakea to Tontouta in New Caledonia.

While in further Squadron training in New Caledonia, the Squadron Commander called me in one day to announce that he had some bad news for me. My wife had given birth to my son Peter but he was not expected to live, owing to an undiagnosed condition. This was indeed a savage blow to me, buoyed up as I was with the exciting expectation of being a father. But the good news, he told me, was that he had been able to arrange an immediate flight to New Zealand on a United States Transport Unit's Liberator. When I arrived in Christchurch, it was to find that the prognosis was gloomy if not entirely negative. My wife, however, had previously had a contact with a Hungarian lady doctor. As a last resort, she asked if this doctor could see the baby. She did so and made an accurate diagnosis at once. The baby's condition required an operation which led to the rapid recovery of my son Peter.

The Squadron left our base at Buttons on Espiritu Santo in the New Hebrides on 5 April 1943 for Henderson Airfield on Guadalcanal. My pilot was Flying Officer Roley Probert. After the recent heavy fighting there, the place stank of death, the stench arising from the burial sites of the Japanese dead in lightly covered graves. During the very first night the air raid alarm sounded. I dashed to the fox holes but went back to bed when nothing happened. I did not realize at the time that this alert was a harbinger of the continuous and troublesome interruptions to our sleep and threat to our lives that the Japanese Air Force was capable of mounting.

The Squadron's task was to maintain constant controls to report enemy shipping movements. We carried bombs and depth charges to attack any enemy submarines we happened to find. One of our aircraft successfully found and destroyed a Japanese ocean going submarine during my tour. At first our aircraft were short of maintenance facilities. They were subject to daily, weekly, and monthly inspections. The Hudson had to have an engine change every 240 hours, requiring a return to New Zealand, so for a while we had to save flying hours, but eventually workshops were built to avoid this necessity.

The following day I flew on my first operational mission with the Squadron, a patrol at fifty feet over Isabel, Choiseul, and through the Manning Straits, almost to Bougainville, before returning to base, all the while keeping a sharp look out for Zero land based and float fighters. At 2000 hours that night the air raid alarm went off accompanied by the firing of anti-aircraft guns. I caught sight of a Japanese aircraft trapped in the searchlights. Bombs fell around us but it was all over by 2030 hours. The next day about 1400 hours a report came in that seventy enemy aircraft were heading our way. A great air battle ensued above the clouds over our heads, resulting in the destruction of twenty-seven Japanese aircraft for the loss of six American fighters. The New Zealand ship *Moa,* and an American destroyer and tanker were lost. Bombs were also dropped on Tulagi and Koli.

I was due to fly at 0700 hours on 8 April but was awakened by two air raid alarms during the night. The patrol was uneventful except for the fact that all members of the crew were soaked by the heavy rain storms we ran into. The Hudson was a rather leaky aircraft. During the night I was awakened by terrible screams. I shot out of bed to investigate to find a man in flames after he had spilt some petrol on himself and accidentally set himself alight. On 10 April we had an official report that the enemy had lost fifty-one aircraft out of a total of 195 sent to attack Tulagi.

The poor food, disturbed nights, the flies and insects, and the incredible heat, were by this time beginning to take their toll. Sleepless nights could be exacerbated by being soaked to the skin by torrential rains which penetrated everywhere. It was a relief to go for a swim in the ocean. The beach was littered with wrecked barges and beached ships. Millions of dollars' worth of stores and equipment were scattered everywhere, lying where they had become the detritus of battle.

Just before I took off on 14 April, I watched one of our aircraft begin to weave as it approached flying speed before take off. It performed a ground loop, the undercarriage collapsing. We held our breath in expectation that it would burst into flames and cause the bomb load to explode. It didn't. The crew emerged from the crash, shaken, but uninjured. Two days later the Japanese hit one of our fuel dumps which went up in smoke and flames during the night but failed to hit the runway. The almost nightly attacks by enemy aircraft were very disturbing. On the night of 18 April I saw an enemy aircraft destroyed in a sheet of flame when it was caught in the searchlights.

In the morning of 19 April I was detailed to replace a wireless operator who had been injured the previous day. With temperatures in the Hudson at 100 feet rising to 107.6°F, and a sometimes chronic shortage of sleep owing to Japanese air raids, a patrol could be a very tiring experience. To make matters worse, and my job more difficult, my hands had sustained multiple mosquito bites during the time spent in the foxholes.

Our flying was almost exclusively by day. We saw a number of Japanese aircraft during our patrols. If they didn't attempt to interfere with us it was policy not to interfere with them, as the Hudson's fire power and manoeuvrability were normally no match for enemy fighters, although we stood a good chance of outdistancing them if we had the benefit of a good start, particularly in the case of the Zero float fighter. During a patrol on 12 April when passing near Pendara Island and Simbo Island we encountered a Zero float fighter at about 800 feet above us at a distance of 1000 yards. We made good our escape as quickly as possible back to base. On 25 April it was reported that ten Japanese bombers and twenty fighters were on their way to Guadalcanal, a day on which I was due to fly a patrol to Russells, Rendova, and Simbo Islands.

When enemy aircraft were detected well in advance it was customary to take as many of our aircraft into the air as possible away from their intended flight path. On this particular day on the way to our patrol station, I spotted a Zero float fighter, which turned and chased us. We increased speed and managed to evade this aircraft, only to be dived on by another, similar aircraft, which chased us for ten miles at a range of 1,500 yards. But we managed to leave him behind, only to fall foul of two land based Zeros which had the upper hand on us as far as performance was concerned. We opened up full power and skimmed at sea level. They chased us for seven minutes, closing to 800 yards without opening fire. Eventually we were able to take advantage of low cloud to escape from them. On returning to base the alarm went off. About forty enemy aircraft on their way to attack Guadalcanal were met by chance by four American fighters on their way back from a patrol. The Americans dived into the formation and broke it up. In the dog fight which followed, seven Zeros were shot down for the loss of two of the American fighters. The surviving two returned to base absolutely riddled with bullet holes. They were lucky.

The operational missions of the whole tour took place between 6 April and 23 May 1943. Completing a whole tour between these dates implied a patrol at least every other day on average. Patrols were organized in different patterns with their code names, Oboe, Item, Charlie, Fox, George, How, and Jig, all of them of around four hours in duration. On 8 May we did a George patrol with two Warhawk fighters as escort, as the day before one of our Hudsons had been attacked by a Zero float fighter but had managed to shoot it down. When bad weather set in, the Warhawks turned back. We had to carry on alone through atrocious storms. I was glad to return to base. This patrol was our twentieth, leaving ten more to do in what turned out to be only fifteen days.

I watched a big aerial dog fight on 13 May. A force of twenty-five Japanese aircraft came over. Our fighter aircraft shot down sixteen of the enemy for a loss of five, two of the pilots of which were saved. We then took off ourselves for an Item patrol and were passing through the Manning Strait when I spotted an enemy aircraft about 6,000 yards away. We turned towards him and he turned towards us. On closing to 800 yards, we identified it as a land based Zero, so we dived to sea level on full power. He tailed us for half an hour but we were able to lose him by turning out to sea. Returning to base we were greeted only a few hours later by a cascade of enemy bombs, some of them landing very close to our foxholes. The attack seemed to go unmolested for over two hours on our Island and nearby Tulagi.

In a singular departure from our practice of flying by day, we took off to make a weather report from Vella La Vella at the request of the United States Admiral. A red alert cropped up just before we were due to take off but the flare path was still switched on for us. No sooner had we became airborne, however, than the searchlights and anti-aircraft defences went into action against the incoming enemy, so we had to move away from the area smartly. Returning to base after completing our mission at 2300 hours, we could see the battle was still in full swing when we were thirty miles away. While we veered off, I called up for instructions. They promised to switch on the flare path as we made our final approach. As soon as we touched down everything was immediately plunged into darkness again. Twenty minutes later the 'All Clear' was sounded. Eleven enemy planes had been sent over during a period of two and a half hours.

With only two trips remaining for us to do to complete the tour, our return to base on 19 May 1943 was nearly our undoing, as the aircraft blew a main tyre on landing. It was our lucky day, since such a mishap usually led to a crash. The fire engine and ambulance appeared but were not needed. Soon afterwards, at 2030 hours, Japanese bombers came over but our fighters could not catch any of them. They returned at 2200 hours but this time we saw one of our fighters pursue an enemy aircraft low across the airfield before bringing it down in a ball of fire to the delirious cheers of everyone. Just after midnight a third alert was sounded only a few minutes after we had scrambled back into bed, and again we watched a fighter destroy one of the intruders. The 'All Clear' sounded at 0230 hours but within fifteen minutes the alarm was sounded for the fourth time and lasted for ninety minutes during which more bombs rained down. At 0500 hours yet another attack arrived, this time catching personnel napping quite literally. Eight were killed and twenty injured. For the next four days repeated attacks by day and night were delivered. It was a trying and nerve-wracking time.

On completing our tour, and with a Wing Commander as our passenger, we set off for the long flight to New Zealand via the usual stages. It was a relief to go home, but it was still not the end of the war for me. I was required to report to Ohakea after my leave to convert to Ventura aircraft. This aircraft was the Hudson's successor with a marked superior performance. I was duly posted for another tour with Number 2 Squadron in the Pacific Islands. The Squadron's task with the Ventura was also to maintain maritime patrols but in addition to carry out strikes against land targets, notably on Bougainville.

One morning, on a normal patrol, I was standing with the skipper scanning the ocean ahead, when I saw wisps of smoke rising from the water. Our closer inspection revealed six yellow jackets in the water, fuel burning amongst them. An American aircraft had been shot down. I called up base to advice them of the situation, requesting a Dumbo – the name by which the Catalina flying boat on sea rescue service was known. We maintained station to guide the Catalina to the spot. It arrived surprisingly quickly, accompanied by four Lightning fighters from Munda, which attacked the guns on nearby Ballale Island, off the south of Bougainville, that were firing on the survivors, and threatening the flying boat while it was helpless on the sea for the rescue. Our job done, we went on to finish the patrol. Two weeks later our pilot was called to the Squadron Commander's office to be told that he had been awarded the United States Air Medal for making the rescue possible.

My second tour in the Pacific with the Ventura finished late in 1944. I then returned to New Zealand with the rest of the crew. Whilst on leave I received a telegram to see the Officer in charge of postings, based in Wellington. Previously, I had been commissioned and promoted by then to the rank of Flying Officer. My wife was reluctant for me to continue in the service, but this Officer told me the Air Force was reluctant to release me, as it needed to make further use of my knowledge and experience. I compromised by refusing another tour, as any aircrew member was entitled to do after having completing one tour, let alone three. He offered me a choice of two jobs. One was to take charge of signals training for wireless operators at the Operational Training Unit at Ohakea, the other being a post as aircraft controller on the East Coast at Gisborne. I opted for the former and stayed for over a year in the job, taking some flights in obsolescent Vincent aircraft for instructional purposes, before finally being demobilized in 1946. I had completed three operational tours, one in Europe and two in the Pacific, amassing an overall total of over 2,500 flying hours, mostly on operations.

My wife Doreen and I were able to buy our own home by taking advantage of the state's financial advance scheme for returning servicemen. After a while Doreen wanted to take a job on the other side of the city which provided accommodation with it. We therefore decided to rent our house and applied for permission to do so. The bureaucracy flatly refused to allow it. Being rather incensed over their intransigence, I took the bold step of writing personally to the Prime Minister, reminding him of my war service. He actually wrote back to me to say that we could rent the house for as long as we chose. The next thing we knew was that the officials complained to me about going over their heads. But the deed was accomplished. We rented the house with impunity.

In civilian life I worked for the Wine and Spirit Merchant, Frank A Cooks, in charge of customer services, for two years. Then a company called Trents asked me to work for them, either as a traveller around the South Island or to take charge of their warehouse. As their warehouse was in the City and meant regular hours, I took that job for quite a while. At one point I approached the Air Force to return to Air Force life but by that time there was no vacancy for me. I had several jobs connected with agriculture, before finally becoming a tally clerk at the Port of Lyttelton, a post I retained until formal retirement, but feeling too young to retire, I worked full time for five years more for a firm of tax consultants.

In retirement since then I have been a voluntary guide at the Air Force Museum at Wigram for twelve years. I retained my aircrew associations through my life membership of the Christchurch Branch of the Brevet Club, becoming its President for two terms of office.

~~~

Arthur Hoskins flew as wireless operator in the following aircraft, listed in experiential order.

Oxford
Norseman
Battle
Heyford
Wellington
Hudson
Ventura
Vincent

Photographs and the specifications of these aircraft may be found in Part 2, listed in alphabetical order.

Alert!

by Warrant Officer Arthur Hoskins, 3 Squadron,
Guadalcanal, May 1943

I'm lying in bed dreaming of home and my native land,
When my dreams are interrupted by a banging on a pan.
So I awake from my slumber and hurry out of bed,
For the banging was a signal, 'Enemy aircraft overhead!'

I yell a loud, "Let's go boys, Tojo's gang is here again."
Then I scream the same thing louder, I have to wake the men.
Meanwhile I'm hunting for my helmet and my pants and shoes,
I have to make it snappy because there's not much time to lose.

In a year it seems I find them and strain to get them on.
Right shoe, left foot, pants inside out, the whole damn mess is wrong.
But I curse and swear and struggle, then towards the trench I dive,
As do the others who want to stay alive.

So we're lying in our foxhole with our heads below the ground,
Our ears are straining for the bomber motor's sound.
A lump comes up within my throat and chills run down my spine,
As I listen for that motor's roar and bombs to whistle down.

But everything's so quiet, not a damn thing's happened yet,
I am filled with concern, on my brow a clammy sweat.
I wish to God they'd drop some, it's waiting in the night
That drives a fellow screwy, and fills the heart with fright.

You wonder if they're up there, what the target's going to be,
Or if it's just a recce flight to see what they can see.
The Army takes no chances so they banged 'condition red',
At this ungodly hour they got us out of bed.

All we've done is sitting here as tired as you can bet,
Thinking of home, our girls, and longing for a cigarette.
Yes, we've been in here an hour, no motor did we hear,
Ah! there it goes, that banging signals 'all is clear'.

Arthur Hoskins, at the extreme left, in an ice hockey team to play an Australian team at Number 2 Wireless School, Calgary, 1941

Norseman aircraft used to train wireless operators, Calgary, in 1941

The Calgary School of Technology used as the Number 2 Wireless School by the Royal Air Force

Members of Flight 8R of 2 Squadron at the Number 2 Wireless School, Calgary

Trainees at the Number 3 Bombing and Gunnery School at MacDonald, 25 May 1941. Arthur Hoskins is third from the right in the front row.

Battle aircraft used for bombing and gunnery training at
MacDonald, 1941

Arthur Hoskins
arriving in Iceland
on AMS Ausonia.
Note the depth
charges to the left of
the photograph

AMS Ausonia, later torpedoed and sunk, with AMS Maloja at
anchor in Iceland after the attack on the convoy they were
escorting

Convoy escorts at anchor in Iceland after the attack on the
convoy they were escorting

**Arthur Hoskins, left, Norman Lavin, and Walter Douglas in
Bournemouth on leave, 1942**

Arthur Hoskins' accommodation while temporarily in Iceland

Arthur Hoskins with his wife Doreen and their sons Peter and Robert. A daughter was subsequently born.

Arthur Hoskins' Identity Card as at 21 August 1944 on his promotion to Pilot Officer. He was subsequently promoted to the rank of Flying Officer

№ 10973

Description :—
Height : 5' 10½   Build : Medium
Colour of eyes : Blue   Colour of hair : Fair
Date of birth : 11th May, 1918

Signature of holder : A.G. Hoskins

Signature of issuing officer : [signature]

Rank : S/Ldr   Station : NELSON

IDENTITY CARD FOR R.N.Z.A.F. AND W.A.A.F. PERSONNEL (All Ranks).

This is to certify that No. NZ 402679
F/Sgt. Hoskins Arthur George
(Rank and full name.)

whose description is contained herein, is serving in the Royal New Zealand Air Force stationed at NELSON

Changes of rank or station are to be certified below.

Date.	Rank.	Station.	Signature and Rank of Officer certifying.
4/8/43	F/Sgt	No 9 Sq	[signature]
6.4.44	F/Sgt.	C.A.C.T.U.	[signature]
26.7.43			[signature]
15.4.44	W/O		[signature]
21/8/44	P/O		[signature]

169

Chapter 7.

Leader in Black

Bill Newfield

Leader in Black

Since both my parents were born in New Zealand, my pedigree as a New Zealander was already well established when I came into the world on 23 September 1923 in Lyttelton, the port of Christchurch in South Island. My father was a tally clerk on the railway which had a busy branch line from Christchurch city to serve the passenger and freight traffic of the port. I was one of eight children, four of whom are deceased. The first two years of my early schooling, in common with the rest of my brothers and sisters, were completed in Lyttelton but I had to transfer to the Waltham Primary School in Christchurch itself for the rest of it. I never went into secondary education, leaving school for ever at the age of twelve and taking a job as an assistant to a man who ran a door-to-door fish delivery business. His entrepreneurial endeavours were evidently successful enough to enable him to open a shop for the sale of fish. In parallel, my own acumen as an employee in my first job must have been sufficiently acceptable to him, inasmuch that he retained my youthful services in the shop, where my interaction with customers and the experience of business activities were well worth having.

My parents, however, were alert to the fact that I would need something more substantial as an occupation in the future than experience as a fish shop assistant. I think also that after having had a few months of working with fish I realised that it was time for a new initiative. Consequently moves were made for me to undertake a formal apprenticeship in fitting and turning as it was then called. The projected time to complete it was five years. In the middle of it, however, the storm clouds were gathering over Europe, New Zealand finding itself embroiled in the war that finally ensued.

When I reached the age of eighteen in 1941, I was more than willing to suspend my apprenticeship in favour of answering the call to arms. My parents had to consent to my voluntary application to join the Air Force. Perhaps the social climate was persuasive enough for them to view the abandonment of my apprenticeship and volunteering for aircrew duties as meritorious and justifiable steps to take. As far as I was concerned, however, I could only see a glorious windfall opportunity to fly. Since leaving school I had developed a hobby of making and flying model aircraft. Nothing appealed to me more than to fulfil my desire to fly in a real aircraft.

In volunteering for the Air Force in 1941, I had no inkling, of course, as to where the fortuitous and imminent events of the war would cause me to be. No one was prepared for the precipitous attack by the Japanese on Pearl harbour on 7 December 1941. This event had an unexpected outcome for me personally. The shock waves sent through the Pacific by this attack led to hasty preparations for home defence in New Zealand itself. Instead of going into the Air Force for which I had volunteered, I found myself being sent into the Army Defence Force early in 1942. It momentarily seemed to me that taking to the air would totally elude me. But unexpectedly I took at least a step towards my goal when I was posted to an Air Defence Unit, which in reality meant airfield defence. I became a member of the Air Force but wearing Army uniform. The airfield in question was home to a squadron flying obsolescent Vickers Vildebeest aircraft which were being used for anti-submarine patrols in coastal waters, and training purposes.

As the threat of a Japanese invasion waned, resources were re-allocated accordingly. At last I was posted to an Air Force base at Rotorua where, among other volunteers for aircrew duties, I was initiated into the Air Force and undertook studies in elementary aviation subjects, including Morse Code and navigation, to supplement the part time studies I had been instructed to take during the whole time since my original application, and which I had managed to accomplish whilst being in a variety of locations. I think that my long standing interest in model aircraft and my unfinished apprenticeship years in fitting and turning helped my understanding of many aviation concepts and mechanisms, so these studies proved interesting to me and on the whole presented me with no sleepless nights.

At the end of the course I took my turn to go before the selection board which turned out to be three officers, who interviewed me and sent me to the Elementary Flying Training School at Harewood in Christchurch to learn to fly the Tiger Moth. After flying with the instructor for a few hours the great day came to go solo for the first time. I suppose my trepidations on that day were no different from those experienced by any other trainee on facing his first solo flight. The tension and excitement gave way to satisfaction that I was to be trusted to fly by myself. My dominant thought on leaving the ground on that first occasion was, "Now I am up, how do I get down again?" I can remember how cold it could be in those open cockpits and how often the ground crew had to turn out to grab the wings of a Tiger Moth on landing on windy days. Those aircraft had no brakes and could quite easily scrape a wing along the ground on landing. Ironically, an instructor I flew with at Harewood used to take me along the wide Waimakariri dried river valley, hunting rabbits. Unbelievably, he tried to catch them with a wing tip. He might have been an excellent flier but he never caught one to my knowledge, although he might have killed me in the process.

On completing the Tiger Moth course, trainee pilots were sent either to Canada, if they were destined for multi-engined aircraft, or to Woodbourne near Blenheim, if they had been earmarked for single-engine aircraft. I was posted to Woodbourne to fly Harvards, first at the Initial Flying Training School for two months, then for a further two months at the Advanced Flying Training School, at the end of which I received my wings with an above average rating, and was commissioned as a Pilot Officer. There followed a short course of ten days on the duties, responsibilities and conduct of a Commissioned Officer, including instruction on how to behave in company and the etiquette required for the meal table and proceedings in an Officers' Mess.

My sense of elation on reaching this critical point in my flying career was marred by disappointment on finding I had been posted to a flying instructors' training course at Tauranga on Tiger Moths. The move did not appeal to me at all. I had greatly enjoyed flying the Harvard and looked forward to flying a fighter aircraft.

The war had presented me with a heaven sent opportunity to fly. That was how I looked at it at that young age. The fact that a home posting as an instructor could be considered a valuable contribution to the war effort whilst preserving me from exposure to the enemy, injury and death, did not enter the reckoning. All the danger and negative aspects of wartime combat flying were unknown to me and never really taxed my imagination for a single moment of time. That was how so many of us were at that stage of our service life. Nevertheless, I had a heightened feeling of relief and freedom, having achieved my wings and received a commission. As a young man I had a sense of occupational status for the first time in my life.

In the event it took two months of determined effort to escape from that posting but meanwhile I had to meet the demands of the course, the extra flying for which gave me extended initial flying experience which proved of great value later on for operational flying. At Woodbourne I had fallen in with a fellow trainee whom I had known at the age of eight at school. He also graduated well enough to be sent for training as a flying instructor – a vocation to which he was as vehemently opposed as I. To escape from it we realised that only two likely courses were open to us. We could formally ask for a posting, but we decided that such a request could incur a long delay. After all, the Air Force would want a return on the investment of resources they had made in us.

But we also hit upon the idea that we could fail the course. As we were already both competent fliers, the other main dimension to the course open to failure was the handling of the lexicon of steps and accompanying instructions with which the instructor tutored the trainee pilot. It was possible to have a deficient memory and deliberately to have poor levels of accuracy and precision. It was the one way open to us and we took it. Eventually I was carpeted in the Squadron Commander's office. "Newfield", he said, "we know what you are up to, so we are going to move you to the drones." He was referring to the Vickers Vincent aircraft that were used to tow the drones as targets for trainee air gunners at another base. It was ubiquitously regarded as a thoroughly boring job.

But he was pulling my leg. I had evidently made my position clear without evoking his wrath or invoking a breach of discipline, although I have often wondered since if such conduct did not constitute a mild form of malingering. To my great satisfaction I was posted to Ohakea and the Fighter Operational Training Unit there to learn to fly the Kittyhawk which was prominently used by the Royal New Zealand Air Force in its operations in the Pacific. During my stay there I briefly flew the de Havilland Moth Minor, a low wing monoplane which was available on the station for communication uses. Once again I enjoyed a smooth passage through the course to be posted at long last to an operational squadron.

Based at Ardmore, 16 Squadron had returned for a rest period after its customary two months' tour of duty on operations. The regular pattern for fighter squadrons consisted of home rest periods interspersing these operational tours. I joined it as it was about to return for its third tour. During a home period, an opportunity might be taken to spawn a new squadron from an existing squadron, as additional aircraft and personnel became available, by capitalizing on the latter squadron's operational experience. Some of the pilots and other staff could be used as the nucleus for the new squadron, its full complement being made up from new pilots and other personnel. Gaps in the existing squadron had to be met from newly trained personnel.

I found morale in 16 Squadron to be at a high level. Its work in the combat zone had evidently been effective and thoroughly appreciated by the allied troops it supported. On 3 August 1943, Major Berton Burns of the Twenty-Third Bombardment Squadron of the United States Army Air Corps had written to the Squadron as follows:

"My combat crews and I sincerely appreciate the excellent coverage your P-40s gave our B-17s yesterday. Our target was an extremely small beach area flanked by our own troops. To be absolutely sure that my bombs would fall in the designated spot it was necessary for me to make two runs on the target. This would have been impossible without your flawless coverage."

The Squadron's morale had been further heightened when it had shot down its first Japanese aircraft. One Section was unexpectedly scrambled on the previous tour when a report was received of Japanese aircraft approaching the Squadron's area. The four aircraft flew towards Rendova Island through heavy cloud whilst trying to gain height. It was reported that the Japanese aircraft were above the cloud. But the Section suddenly burst out of cloud onto thirty Zero fighter aircraft making their way back to base. The Section had no option but to attack before fleeing. One Zero was seen to burst into flames and fall away.

When the important day arrived to leave New Zealand for the combat zone, the Squadron's twenty-four aircraft were flown off to rendezvous with two Lockheed Hudson medium bombers which acted as our navigators. They were divided into 'A' Flight and 'B' Flight, each of twelve aircraft, each Flight flying with a Hudson. A third Hudson had been tasked to carry our baggage but became unserviceable at the last moment. Consequently we were without our personal effects for several days until we arrived at Espiritu Santo. I flew one of the Kittyhawks as a member of 'A' Flight, with my thoughts fixed firmly on the prospect of going to the war for which I had originally volunteered, albeit by way of my passion to fly. We flew in stages commensurate with the fuel capacity and flying time available to the Kittyhawk. After landing first at a base in the north of the North Island of New Zealand to top up our fuel, we flew to Norfolk Island, then New Caledonia, and on to Espiritu Santo Island in the New Hebrides, before landing at our final pre-combat destination at Guadalcanal in the Solomon Islands.

The Squadron spent two weeks at Guadalcanal for acclimatization and training purposes. The training programme was in three phases. We first practised as a Section of four aircraft. I was in Red Section of 'A' Flight with the Squadron's Commander, Squadron Leader Sievers, as the Section Leader, who had Flight Sergeant Reynolds as his wingman, the other two aircraft being flown respectively by Flying Officer Woodhead, with me as his wingman. Then the three sections of each Flight learned to fly together. Finally the whole Squadron took to the air to learn to fly as a complete formation. All three stages were important, as a mission could involve either of the three formations, according to the nature of the target.

On this occasion a very important tactical formation change was introduced into the Squadron. Until that date aircraft flew in V-formations to their operational zone, changing to line astern for an actual attack, with the unit's Commander in the lead, followed by the most experienced pilots, newly trained pilots bringing up the rear positions. This had been the classic formations adopted for fighter and fighter-bomber operations in the European theatre of war and followed at first in the Pacific. The Luftwaffe, however, had in the interim developed a 'finger four' formation for offensive operations, particularly for low level fighter-bomber missions. Eventually, the Royal Air Force emulated this practice after clinging to line astern formations for far too long, and with repeatedly disastrous results, the Luftwaffe learning to attack the aircraft that were last in the line where the most inexperienced pilots were placed. We had to change our formations to echelons to port or starboard. Our Squadron soon discovered the advantages of the different formation but at first found difficulty in executing 180° turns with them in an orderly fashion.

We practised air to air gunnery on a drogue which was temperamental in nature and constantly frustrated our practices. It had to be towed by a Kittyhawk that was the only aircraft available. This was not a suitable towing aircraft for it. It soon became unserviceable, putting an end to our training. Air to ground gunnery and bombing practice, however, continued without remit.

On 26 and 27 March 1944 the Squadron moved on to Torokina, in Bougainville, in the Solomon Islands, for combat operations. At the time of our arrival there, American troops had seized and secured an area of only 8.000 by 5,000 yards from the Japanese. The Japanese were in force on the island and constantly made their presence felt.

The Squadron's precarious strip on this limited area was under intermittent fire from Japanese artillery, usually by day but also at night. If the shelling became sustained, as many aircraft as were serviceable were flown off for safety. Foxholes had to be dug for all personnel. The shelling interfered with the routine maintenance and repair of aircraft at times but the ground crews produced a remarkable level of service. However, the landing strip itself did not turn into mud after rain as was usually the case for island emergency landing strips. It was mercifully free from mosquitoes and offered a delightful beach for swimming and surfing, creating a feeling of being far from the prevailing warfare. Unfortunately, Japanese infantry were able to deploy their lighter weapons to fire on us every time we took off. But gradually the Americans pushed the perimeter outwards. Later on we had the use of two relatively safe strips to use for our missions, which were primarily flown to destroy Japanese aircraft on the ground, and shipping.

On a day early in this location, the Squadron found itself undertaking a task for which its aircraft were originally not intended. We variously carried incendiaries, depth charges, and 500 pound or 1,000 pound bombs in response to a report from American pilots that a force of seventeen Japanese submarines had been sighted between Duke of York Island and Cape Gurry, New Ireland. In retrospect it seemed most unlikely that the Japanese Navy could concentrate such a force at that location at that time of the war. Nothing was found, but anti-submarine patrols were maintained.

At least 90% of our operations were flown over water. In the Pacific the area of land in relation to that of water was infinitesimal. Being island based, it was the case that as soon as I took off I found myself over water. Targets were never far inland, consisting mostly of coastal Japanese military installations, troop concentrations, air strips, and moored shipping. It was very near impossible to detect potential targets in jungle areas inland, protected as they were by the endless canopy of tees. All our attacks were carried out in daylight against these coastal targets which were heavily defended. The Squadron operated in support of the United States Army. As one island was cleared the Army moved on to the next, an island hopping process which we had to emulate.

At first, our missions consisted of fighter patrols but they gave way to dive bombing attacks. The Kittyhawk was able to carry up to 1,000 pounds of bombs, usually of various calibres. In our case they were always carried centreline, although Kittyhawks elsewhere were fitted to carry one 250 pound bomb under each wing, and a 500 pound bomb centreline. We improvised armaments for jungle fighting that the aircraft's manufacturers never envisaged. We used to fill the 44 gallon drop tanks with any ignitable fuel that we could lay our hands on and attach a normal small incendiary bomb or other ignition device. When we dropped these tanks on jungle targets the effect was similar to that of napalm weapons used with notoriety by the Americans during the Vietnam War.

One of the major regular targets for the Squadron from Bougainville was the strategic base of the Japanese at Rabaul in New Britain, a round trip of some 300 miles which we managed by refuelling on Green Island. On some occasions our interim stop at Green Island had to be prolonged when the weather was too bad for flying the next leg of the mission towards the target or back to base. After the first enforced experience of this we all used to carry a few personal items in case of an overnight stop there. On one of the early trips to Rabaul the Squadron arranged to form up again off Cape Gazelle but the effort to do so did not reflect well on our previous Squadron practice, ending in an embarrassing disarray.

Bombing targets were always specified but after dropping our bombs we were free to seek targets of opportunity for strafing runs with the aircraft's six .5 inch machine guns. For these operational purposes, either 'A' Flight or 'B' Flight would usually be assigned to a particular mission, flying in three sections of four aircraft, each section under the command of its Section Leader. If the whole Flight were engaged in a mission, the Flight Commander gave orders on the method and sequencing of attack to the three sections under his command. Section Leaders had discretion over the more detailed tactics to be employed. A Section always flew in the 'finger four' formation, as developed by the Luftwaffe in Europe. It had taken the Allied Air Forces far too

181

long to realise and value the advantages of this attack formation, especially for low level operations, but by 1943 it had been firmly adopted by us. For dive bombing a Section was usually split into two pairs.

I returned from my first tour with 16 (F) Squadron by numerous stages and some delays on Sunday 21 May 1944. We reached New Zealand with seventeen aircraft. Eight had been lost or abandoned during this tour.. One had crashed into the sea with a defective motor on take-off from the strip. Several had to be abandoned en route at the staging posts, but none had been lost directly as a result of enemy action.

After leave, the Squadron re-assembled at Ardmore from 12 June to 7 July. Eleven of its pilots were posted to instructors' courses and other squadrons – this number included the Commanding Officer who was posted to the Gunnery School at Gisborne - and thirteen new pilots were added to its strength.

Enthusiasm and enterprise pervaded the unit, as can be judged by the escapade of two of its pilots who had completed the recent tour with the Squadron. With foolhardy audacity they flew low down the main street of a suburb of Auckland during an evening training flight in the dark with their landing lights on. New Zealand towns were subject to blackout regulations, so the fright and outrage caused by the noise and suddenness of their action in the dark led to a complaint being lodged with the Commanding Officer. A chain of events erupted from it, the final result of which was that when the Squadron left for a further combat tour, the two valued and experienced pilots involved had to be left behind. In retrospect this result seems to have been of a disproportionate nature. A bitter and costly war was being waged. The two pilots, for all their want of discretion, were risking their lives in defence of the complainants.

Good as a fighter aircraft the Kittyhawk had been, during the last two years of the war the Corsair was introduced as its replacement. When the Squadron's turn came to be re-equipped with the Corsair, it was introduced to the new aircraft at Espiritu Santo, en route for a further Squadron – and my second – tour. The

Squadron moved on to Cactus for the period 25 July to 28 August where I was assigned to Green Section of 'A' Flight, with Flight Lieutenant Tucker as the Section leader, Flight Sergeant Lyons as his wingman, and Sergeant Bates as my wingman. Intensive training then followed on the Corsair – take-offs and landings, formation flying in Sections, flying with the other two Sections as a Flight, and as a whole Squadron. There was air to air and air to ground gunnery, and bombing practice. The opinion was formed that the Corsair's electrical bomb release and better visibility offered the chance of greater accuracy than could be achieved in the Kittyhawk. Finally, it was decided to undertake some night flying.

In taking my share of becoming familiar with flying the new aircraft, I was returning to base from a late evening training flight alone after nightfall, when the engine cut out without warning, at 2,000 feet. I had already begun preparations to come into land at a distance of about three miles off-shore. My first reaction was to apply the standard checks and routines for such an eventuality. But as it was all to no avail, I was suddenly confronted with the probability, if not the certainty at that precise moment, that I would have to bale out – a fate dreaded by every pilot, especially when it was a precedent, as it was for me.

I managed to call the base to give my position. By that time the aircraft was down to 800 feet and running out of height at which it would be safe for me to bale out. As a crash landing into the sea did not appeal to me, I chose the lesser risk to bale out. In a Kittyhawk the routine to evacuate the aircraft was to slide the cockpit canopy fully open, pull the stick back, wind the trim forward, then push the control stick forward. As the aircraft plunged forward and down, the pilot could bale out. But this routine could not be followed in the Corsair. The distance between the cockpit and the tail was short. As the tail itself was large there was virtually a certainty that a pilot following the Kittyhawk routine in a Corsair would be struck by the latter's tail. Oddly enough, in the Squadron we had been discussing the issue only hours before I found myself testing the validity of the argument.

To abandon the Corsair, therefore, the way out was simply over the side, hopefully with the aircraft in reasonably level flight. The angle of descent of my aircraft was sufficiently shallow to enable me to escape. On pulling the rip cord I was as relieved as so many other aviators had been before me to see the parachute open. It was providential for me that my parachute was one of the newly introduced nylon kind which opened more quickly than those made of silk. I did not have far to fall and braced myself for the heavy plunge into the ocean. I was of course falling in the same direction as the flight of the aircraft at the point of my departure from it, in the absence of any wind currents. Furthermore, I was still swinging severely, having had too little time in descent to steady the fall, but fortunately I hit the ocean on a reverse swing which lessened the impact with the water as compared with the impact suffered on a forward swing. My inflatable dinghy had duly followed me out of the aircraft attached to my flying suit. It inflated and I was able to scramble thankfully into it.

I could have unstrapped my parachute and abandoned it to the sea but instead I hauled it into the dinghy. The strange thought passed through my mind that the precious material that had just saved my life could come in handy for some other purpose.

The sea was calm. The night had been dark but it was soon illuminated by my aircraft which crashed into the water between me and the shore and burst into flame at a distance of 600 yards. Since such a high proportion of our flying time was spent over water, a remarkable patrol and rescue service had been established around inshore areas of the islands and along the flight paths which squadrons took on their operational missions. One of these was provided by Catalina flying boats which were capable of remaining on station for extended periods of time for this purpose. If a Catalina landed to rescue downed airmen, it might sometimes be necessary for its crew to tow an airman's dinghy with the airman still in it away from enemy fire from ship or shore until it was safe to take him aboard. The other means of rescue was the Air-Sea Rescue launches which operated in-shore. Three of these vessels came out to find me. The blazing aircraft gave their crews a general idea as to where I had ditched in the sea but after that the boats gyrated around trying to find me. One of them passed so close without seeing me that its wake almost sank my frail craft. I was soon found, however, having spent half an hour in the water.

A day or two later on returning to base, I handed in my rescued parachute to the parachute section with the request that I could have it back. It was not permitted to take possession of government property as simply as that, however, so they cut it in half. They retained half as proof of usage for the purpose intended and made a pillow of the other half. I guarded this pillow throughout the rest of the war. After the war my pillow was transformed into a beautiful wedding gown for the girl I married.

The Squadron moved on to stay at Torokina from 29 August to 21 September 1944. The first mission it was called upon to discharge involved the whole Squadron of twenty-four aircraft led by Wing Commander Quill for an attack on Shahili, which was largely frustrated by heavy cloud, but which did not prevent the aircraft all meeting up at the appointed rendezvous after the attack. A succession of targets around Bougainville and New Britain followed. The tour, however, ended in disaster. On the 15 September, Sergeant Rowlands from our Squadron, and Bill Jardine of 21 Squadron, collided over the strip, both being killed. Only six days later, on the very last day of the tour, 21 September, three aircraft piloted respectively by Keith Stannes, David Ellison, and David Maclean, collided when returning from a raid on New Britain, all three being killed. The next day in sober mood the Squadron returned to New Zealand, arriving on 22 September 1944.

We assembled again at Ardmore for the period 16 October to 21 November 1944 for what was to be the Squadron's fifth – and my third and last - tour. Our Squadron Commander, Squadron Leader Jones, was posted to be the Commanding Officer of 4 Operational Training Unit at Ohakea. Eight other pilots were also posted. The new Squadron Commander was Squadron Leader Green who was returning to operations for his fourth tour. Our reinforcements were fourteen new pilots, plus Flight Lieutenant Avery who was returning to the Squadron after completing an instructor's posting. Before leaving Ardmore, we suffered the loss of Pilot Officer Barstow who went missing over the Alps in bad weather during a cross country flight with other aircraft, all of which had to make an emergency landing at Westport. One of these other pilots, Pilot Officer Robert Reynolds had to miss the imminent tour in being detained for the Board of Enquiry. The Squadron was subsequently brought up to strength en route with the arrival of two replacements.

Several weeks were spent at Guadalcanal but one of the Dakotas employed to ferry the Squadron to it had to return to Norfolk Island with engine trouble. The Squadron operated in gruelling conditions. Some time was spent under the Commanding Officer's direction in analysing the variations of bombing procedure followed by every pilot. From the aggregated data a best method was fashioned and adopted by the Squadron, leading to improved operational results.

The first operation of the tour, however, was the unusual hunt for a lost United States Piper Cub reconnaissance aircraft. One Section was despatched to find it – a mission that was successfully concluded with the discovery of the Piper Cub in a jungle clearing.

The Squadron moved on to Green Island to prepare for operations in earnest, consisting mainly of patrols to Rabaul, either of four hours' duration using extra tanks, or for shorter durations carrying bombs. We also escorted Catalinas, which could be a tedious task as they were slow flying aircraft. Sometimes we flew alongside them but sometimes we adopted a weaving pattern above them, which proved to be stressful for the Corsair pilot. The third task was to maintain dawn and dusk coastal patrols, attacking targets of opportunity with bombs and strafing runs. I became Section Leader of Black Section, of the six Sections formed.

A combined operation with 14 Squadron on 15 January proved to be an epic but disastrous day. The attack was against the wharves at Taboi in the morning. Flight Lieutenant Frank Keefe of 14 Squadron was hit by ack-ack and forced to bale out in Simpson Harbour. On landing successfully in the water he struck out for the open sea, hoping to be picked up by one of the

American-piloted Catalinas that were patrolling for that very purpose. He was evidently a strong swimmer and managed to survive for several hours in a providentially placid sea.

Late on the same morning, I was on patrol in the Rabaul area, the mission taking two hours and fifty-five minutes, when I received a call to say that a pilot was believed to be down in Simpson Harbour. When I reached this location I quickly spotted Frank Keefe swimming strongly towards the sea. I flew low between him and the land at just about the range of Japanese land based small arms and machine gun fire, which I could see disturbing the water like a shoal of flying fish beneath me. He was already out of range of the enemy fire.

I returned to base to report his whereabouts. Fifteen aircraft from 14 and 16 Squadrons led by Squadron Leader Green, the Commander of 16 Squadron, were scrambled to escort a Ventura bomber carrying life rafts. Apparently, when a raft was dropped about 100 yards from Frank Keefe it was perceived that he made no effort to swim to it. Meanwhile a Catalina flying boat had arrived in the vicinity, the American pilot expressing his willingness to come inshore and put down on the water for a rescue. He was explicitly forbidden to do this as his aircraft would have made a sitting target for Japanese guns.

As it was feared that Frank Keefe had drowned, this formation set course for base but soon ran into a severe front that extended all the way to Green Island. Only eight Corsairs survived to reach their base, 14 Squadron losing four aircraft and 16 Squadron three. All were lost as a result of the atrocious weather. At least one pair of aircraft collided, and it was believed others hit the sea while trying to fly below the heavy cloud that descended almost to sea level.

I had seen Frank Keefe swimming strongly when I first found him during his frightful hours in the sea. I concluded that he had not been wounded by the ack-ack that had brought his Corsair down. At a later date, however, the Japanese authorities reported his immediate survival but subsequent death from gangrene as a result of wounds sustained. The truth of the nature of his ultimate fate will never be known, but I have always had the distinct suspicion that if he had actually lived to reach the shore by his own efforts, or had been rescued by the Japanese, he was subsequently shot by the enemy. I went back to Simpson Harbour the following morning during a routine patrol but could see no sign of the previous day's events.

Soon after that, 16 Squadron reached the end of its fifth tour. Having completed three of those tours with the Squadron, I was posted to the Central Flying School at Woodbourne for two weeks' training to be a pilot instructor at the Operational Training Unit at Ohakea on Kittyhawks and Corsairs, a job I held until VJ Day on 14 August 1945. During this time I took a single flight in an Avenger. My military flying record, in hours and minutes, was as follows, omitting the minor time flying the Moth Minor and the Avenger.

	With Instructor	Solo	Total
Tiger Moth	55.30	66.40	122.10
Harvard	77.20	253.35	330.55
Oxford	3.30	2.25	5.55
Kittyhawk		226.50	226.50
Corsair		228.10	228.10

My total military flying time was 914 hours. Of these, 193 hours and five minutes were occupied in combat flying on 92 missions – thirty-nine on the first tour, twenty-nine on the second, and twenty-four on the third.

My return to civilian life was comparatively straightforward. With my apprenticeship background I secured employment with a firm which manufactured large heavy clay products – such as bricks and pipes – but also tableware. In the post war period of rising population, extensive house building, and expanding trade opportunities, boom conditions for this industry prevailed. At one time the company had seven plants operating in the South Island.

My occupation was on the engineering side of the firm. I became first the manager of one of the factories, then general manager with oversight of the existing seven plants. But by that time, the boom conditions had passed. Foreign products captured our markets with cheaper products made of different material. With the downturn in sight I had the painful and stressful job of closing down four of the factories.

In advanced retirement I still retain an interest in heavy clay. I employ my engineering skills as a hobby in working with friends who like to make huge pots for garden decoration. It has been a joy for me to follow the careers of my six sons, three of whom have emigrated to Canada. Two of them have followed my own interest in flying. One of them, Theo, with his team mate David Speight, took line honours in the United States Sports Class Gliding Championships at Parowan, Utah, in 2005, and holds the world glider speed record for a 300 kilometres triangular course. My sons have not been called upon to do what I had to do in the 1940s, but I remain firm in my belief that they in their time, and others of the oncoming generations who are so often maligned, would rise to the occasion as faithfully as we did in our day, should the need arise.

~~~

Bill Newfield flew as pilot in the following aircraft, listed in experiential order.

> Tiger Moth
> Harvard
> Kittyhawk
> Moth Minor
> Corsair
> Avenger

Photographs and the specifications of these aircraft may be found in Part 2, listed in alphabetical order.

Learning to fly. Bill Newfield in the rear seat of a Tiger Moth in 1943 at Harewood

Bill Newfield on being commissioned as a Pilot Officer in 1943

Bill Newfield and his
Corsair in a jungle setting,
1944

A United States P40 Kittyhawk fighter on its nose,
Guadalcanal, 1944

191

Guadalcanal, 1944. The sign reads: Guadalcanal Mosquito
Bowl. It was used for entertainments

Fighter air strips on Guadalcanal, 1944

Bill Newfield's fellow pilots with local children on Guadalcanal,
1944

Dauntless and Corsair aircraft at dispersal in jungle station,
Guadalcanal, 1944

Allied air strip on Guadalcanal, 1944. Note the United States Airacobra aircraft to the right

A native village on Guadalcanal, 1944

Bill Newfield flying a Corsair on combat mission, 1944

A wrecked Corsair, the result of a bad landing, Guadalcanal,
1944.

**16 Squadron pilots in front of a P40 Kittyhawk. Bill Newfield is
at the extreme right hand end of the middle row**

Bill Newfield with Corsair at Wigram, Christchurch in 2005

16 Squadron fighter pilots' reunion 1998. Bill Newfield is second
from the right in the middle row

Chapter 8.

To Save a Friend

Artie Shaw

To Save a Friend

My father was a soldier in the First World War. At the end of it he had the opportunity to go to England with the Army for a short while – a visit for him that was to prove as significant in the same way as my own connection with the Army was to prove for me. Whilst in England he met the lady of his life and married her. She duly emigrated to New Zealand and raised my elder brother and me in Christchurch City. They raised us in difficult economic times. I was born on 2 February 1923 and went to the local primary and secondary schools.

I had no other thought in my mind than to leave school as soon as I could do so to find employment, which happened in 1938 at the age of fifteen. Jobs were not easy to come by but I managed to be taken on at a warehouse dealing in automotive parts. Car ownership at that time was on a small scale. Cars had to be imported and the roads were generally of poor quality outside of the city. Consequently, the motor trades were at a low level of activity, their difficulties being exacerbated by the absence of a dynamic economy. The immediate pre-Second World War conditions contrasted sharply with those of the post-war years, presenting a miserable business picture by contemporary standards.

Within three years of taking this job it became obvious that the cost of employing me, modest though it might have seemed to others, was proving too onerous for the firm to carry under the prevailing business circumstances. At the same time, as I had reached the call-up age, it was expected that I would inevitably be lost to the firm anyway. The boss called me in one day to tell me that I could no longer be employed.

Quite soon after that, in 1941, I reached my eighteenth birthday. I was ordered to report to the Army at Trentham Barracks in the North Island for initial training, after which I was posted to the 1st Canterbury Regiment. Although recruitment into the armed forces had been brisk from the very start of the Second World War, the need for it was given fresh impetus by the Japanese attack on Pearl Harbour on 7 December 1941 as a prelude to Japan's subsequent spectacular conquests around the Pacific. The event sent shock waves of apprehension through countries that might be next subjected to attack. New Zealand was electrified by this possibility - to the extent of initiating a programme of building coastal batteries and maintaining regular air patrols. The country's supply of recruits for the Army and Air Force for the first time was no longer exclusively destined for the conflict in Europe and the Middle East. Part of it was committed to home defence and the preparations to engage in offensive operations against the enemy.

The 1st Canterbury Regiment was an infantry unit that later became part of a force despatched to Italy where it fought in the protracted battle of Monte Casino in the early months of 1944. I had been in this unit for eleven months, when a surprise appeal was made for volunteers to serve as aircrew members in the Royal New Zealand Air Force. By that time I had learned to hate Army life, so I felt it was a God-sent opportunity to escape from it with honour and dignity. The one abiding benefit that the Army bestowed on me – albeit indirectly – was that I formed a firm friendship with a fellow infantryman. Just after the war I ran into him again by chance in the street in Christchurch City. He promptly invited me to a party that night where I met his sister Nancy, whom I married in 1951.

The extraordinary outcome of this appeal for aircrew members was the incredible lack of response. Only three of us soldiers actually left the large Burnham barracks, where my Regiment was stationed, to go to the Air Force. This surprising result in my mind at the time begged an explanation. Perhaps it was the case that the great majority enjoyed Army life, although, judging by the constant negatives of the barrack room it was sometimes hard to countenance such an explanation. Perhaps it was believed that Army life offered a safer war than that of the Air Force. Maybe inertia generated by a reluctance to embrace the unfamiliar accounted for the outcome. A plausible factor may have been that some would-be volunteers were unable to obtain parental permission – a requirement if a volunteer for aircrew was under twenty-one years of age. Perhaps I was one of the few who obtained it.

I was posted to Masterton for an induction to Air Force life. The volunteers on the course were from a variety of Army units, including a number of Officers who were allowed to transfer their commissions. We Army volunteers mingled with those who had made applications for aircrew service direct from civilian life. Most of the time at this place was spent in classroom studies in a range of elementary aviation subjects, which in turn were followed by a further course at Rotorua, mainly for the study of navigation, lasting four months.

In October 1943, I was sent to the Number 3 Elementary Flying Training School at Harewood, in Christchurch, to begin to learn to fly. During the three months remaining until the end of the year, I flew in the Tiger Moth for a total of thirty-seven hours and ten minutes with an instructor, and twenty-three hours and thirty minutes solo.

My instructor was Frank Keefe whose name has become remembered in the annals of the Air Force for the tragic fate that overtook him later in the war. On 15 January 1945 he was shot down during a major attack on the strategic Japanese base at Rabaul in New Britain. It was the day that the Air Force lost eight aircraft altogether – the worst loss it suffered in one day during the entire war in the Pacific. He was a Corsair pilot operating from Green Island and was seen to go down near the Beehive Rocks in Simpson Harbour. Fellow Corsair pilots who flew around to protect him saw that he was trying to swim out of the harbour towards the open sea, where he could expect to be rescued. It was customary for a Catalina flying boat to patrol off-shore in support of bombing and strafing attacks on Japanese facilities, supplies, and positions, in case any attacking aircraft were shot down. The Catalina itself usually had a fighter escort for such close in-shore work. In spite of valiant efforts to rescue him, however, Frank Keefe was swept back towards the shore and was later reported to have died of wounds, after having survived for nine hours in the sea.

Towards the end of the course at Harewood, when I was mostly flying solo, Frank Keefe said to me one day, "You have done very well. Your landings are particularly good. If you ever have any difficulty on coming in to land, don't try to change it, just open up and go round again." One day when coming in to land, it was quite windy. I had just touched down when my port wing dipped and scraped the ground. In an instinctive reaction I over-corrected the aircraft's attitude and caused the other wing to touch the ground. Tardily, on remembering my instructor's advice, I tried to open up but by that time I had insufficient flying speed. The starboard wing sliced into the ground causing the aircraft's nose to bury itself in the earth. The tail rose high up in the air before settling back. All in an instant I thought the aircraft was about to flip over onto its back, with me underneath it. I was well strapped in but partly hanging out of the cockpit, suddenly fearing the aircraft might burst into flame. Almost before I could unstrap myself and descend from the wreckage, the ambulance and fire-engine arrived, the doctor immediately demanding, "Where's the other fellow?"

Apart from a small bump on my head I found I had escaped the mishap without injury. Nevertheless, the doctor took me back to the medical centre for a thorough check at the end of which he gave me a chit which declared that I was 'Fit to Fly'. I took it straight to my instructor who took one look at it and said, "That's what he thinks." I gathered from his remark that he would apply more stringent criteria to prove it as a fact. He immediately took me up in a Tiger Moth and put me through the hoop, testing everything he had taught me. His action was in the time honoured tradition of military flying. To preserve a pilot's confidence, it had always been recognized that after a mishap it was essential to take to the air again as soon as possible. Any delay in doing so allowed time for doubts and fears to multiply to the point of a pilot's loss of nerve.

I was never reprimanded for the accident. It was the only time that an aircraft in my hands suffered damage in my military flying service as a result of my own action. In fact, whilst I was still at Harewood flying the Tiger Moth, I had the opportunity to vindicate myself. On returning one evening after a solo night flight, I approached the airfield in the normal way according to my knowledge of the prevailing conditions, only to find that the aircraft was unmistakably drifting to the left. The movement suddenly became potentially serious when I saw three men throw themselves to the ground. I immediately took corrective measures and landed safely, if a little shaken by this last minute and unexpected event. A short while later I was joined by one of the three men who had apparently been suddenly overcome with concerns for their own safety on my landing. He turned out to be Frank Keefe, my instructor. I was suddenly overcome with embarrassment when he demanded, "What have I done to deserve that?" But his tone changed as soon as he had asked the question, his face breaking into a smile with the statement, "You made a good job of it, Shaw, the wind changed before the flares could be re-positioned. Well done."

On passing the course I was posted to Woodbourne, where I remained until April 1944. I had previously expressed a preference to fly single-engine, rather than multi-engine, aircraft, which in practice meant going to war in fighter aircraft rather than bombers. Trainee pilots destined for bombers either went to Wigram to fly Oxford aircraft or went overseas to Canada for further training. By being posted to Woodbourne I knew that my preference had been fulfilled. This was particularly gratifying to me as I realised that my instructor at Harewood, in spite of my mishap, must have supported my application for fighter aircraft. Instructors were routinely consulted over their trainees' preferences. Their opinions were usually decisive.

At the Advanced Flying Training School at Woodbourne I found it a great experience to fly the Harvard. I had no troubles with it. In fact, I found it an easier aircraft to fly than the Tiger Moth, contrary to expectation and the opinion of many other trainees. I completed 106 hours and forty minutes dual flying with the instructor, and 107 hours and fifty minutes solo, resulting in an average rating when I completed the course and the award of my wings.

It was in May 1944 that I flew a Kittyhawk fighter aircraft for the first time. I had been posted to the Operational Training Unit for fighters at Ardmore. The Kittyhawk was a good aircraft to fly as I found throughout the sixty training hours I spent in a Kittyhawk cockpit. I was given an average rating as a pilot at the end of the course but an above average rating as an air gunner. Air gunnery was practised with the aid of a drogue, which was a large, sleeve-shaped contraption towed behind a larger and slower aircraft. Typically a section of four fighters took off for practice with the drogue aircraft. The ammunition in each fighter was coated with a distinctive colour so that on return to base, an examination of the drogue could reveal the relative degree of accuracy of each fighter pilot.

One day, three other pilots and I were flying with the drogue, accompanied by the air gunnery instructor, Flight Lieutenant de Willamoth DFC, a returned veteran from the European theatre of war. On this occasion he chose to join in the gunnery practice by firing in his turn at the drogue. When we returned to base and were assembled for our debriefing, he made a thorough inspection of the drogue, making a count of the respective number of hits scored by all five of us. At the end of his calculations, he looked up and said, "Who had green today?" "I did, sir", I replied, thinking I was just about to be the recipient of a deprecatory remark. Instead, to my surprise, he paused for a moment and then said, "You have scored the most hits today. You have scored more than me." "Unfortunately", he added by way of an explanation that he knew would not be taken at face value, but served as a means to avoid embarrassment, "only one of my guns was working." The Kittyhawk, when used as a training aircraft, was armed with two .5 inch guns, rather than its normal armament of six when used as a combat aircraft.

On 19 July 1944, before completing the course at Ardmore, I took to the air for the first time in a Corsair, which was to be the fighter that I would take to war. The Corsair had largely replaced the Kittyhawk for operational flying, good service though the

206

latter had given for over two years during the war in the Pacific. No one knew at that time for how long the conflict would continue, so re-equipment and the improvement of offensive capacity was an ongoing policy. It was expected that the Japanese would have to be painfully driven out from each little piece of conquered territory one at a time. These prospects were not encouraging – to say nothing of the anticipated ultimate need to invade the Japanese mainland itself. It had taken me some three years of military service in all to reach this point, although the actual flying training part of that service had been relatively speedy. The time had come for me to take part in the diverse endeavours of the Air Force to reverse the fortunes of war in the Pacific in favour of the Allies, a process that was well under way by this date.

On 6 August I was posted to 22 Squadron, a new Squadron being formed at Ardmore in preparation for its first tour. It was the first Squadron to convert to Corsairs in New Zealand, though others had done so overseas. All the twenty-seven pilots and other Squadron staff were flown in DC3 Dakotas to Espiritu Santo where Corsair aircraft were waiting for us. We spent the period 6-29 August 1944 in Squadron training with these aircraft before once again leaving them behind and flying by Dakota on 29 August to Guadalcanal, where another fleet of Corsairs was waiting for us to undertake more Squadron training, including formation flying, night flying, gunnery, and dive bombing.

From Guadalcanal we moved to Bougainville where the Squadron was based for the whole of its first tour which lasted from 18 September to 2 November 1944. On the completion of it we returned to Ardmore and took some leave. The Squadron re-assembled at Ardmore on 28 November 1944 to resume training flights, notably at night. During one night's flying, the weather conditions became atrocious, claiming the lives of two pilots. One was found. The other was a friend who was never found. I had been best man at his wedding three months earlier.

For its second tour, the Squadron was once more given an aerial lift by Dakota for a two-day trip via Espiritu Santo to Emirau, a small island on the Equator. This tour lasted from 5 January to 4 March 1945, at the conclusion of which we followed the regular routine of returning by Dakota to Ardmore and taking further leave. On 3 April 1945 the Squadron left Ardmore by Dakota for its third tour which it again discharged at Bougainville from 21 April to 10 July. During this time the gratifying news of Germany's unconditional surrender on 7 May gave new heart to those fighting in the allied forces in the Pacific. There still seemed to be, however, nothing less in prospect for the war against Japan than a systematic slog to root out their forces from every scrap of island territory that they had taken. The necessity finally to assault the Japanese mainland was looming ever closer as a daunting task. Who was to know that after a further three months of painstaking mopping up around the Pacific, a terrible weapon would be unleashed against the Japanese to avoid this enormous undertaking?

In the event the Squadron's third tour proved to be my third and last tour. My contribution to the work of the Squadron had been as follows.

	First Tour	Second Tour	Third Tour	Totals
Operational Hours	45.30	101.50	90.35	237.55
Number of Missions	25	33	66	124

From being given the rank of Sergeant when I qualified as a pilot, I was promoted to Flight Sergeant for my first tour. During that tour I was recommended for a commission and was interviewed by the legendary Sir Robert Clarke-Hall, famous for having served at a senior rank in all three armed services during the course of two World Wars. For my second tour I was promoted to Pilot Officer and for my third tour to Flying Officer.

It was a strange kind of war. Several pilots in the Squadron who had been on early tours were engaged in combat with Japanese fighters and had confirmed kills to their credit. The strategic balance had changed in the interim, however, to the point that we were on the offensive primarily in support of ground forces. I never saw a Japanese aircraft in the air, so never suffered an attack in the air by the enemy. One seldom saw the enemy on the ground, but we felt their presence. My aircraft suffered hits from ground fire on several occasions, but never fatally. The reason for rarely catching sight of the enemy on the ground was the endless jungle canopy. On every island the Japanese occupiers made every use of the natural vegetation as cover for their movements and stores. By far and away the majority of the fighter-bomber missions which I flew were directed against an unseen enemy lurking in the jungle. The bulk of our missions were in support of either the American or Australian troops engaged in trying to clear Japanese troops from first one island then another across Micronesia. I have since learned that there were 70,000 Japanese troops or more on Bougainville alone. Typically, from American or Australian Army Intelligence reports, when the presence of a concentration of Japanese troops or a supply dump was located, although such locations were often more approximate than pin-pointed, our Squadron was ordered to attack it.

Usually either 'A' Flight or 'B' Flight would be briefed to undertake the attack on the identified site, although a single Section or the whole Squadron might be used, according to the nature of the target. The twelve aircraft of the Flight detailed to carry out the attack took off in three Sections of four. Almost certainly any mission, in common with most of all the missions flown, required a long flight over the ocean to an island. Once over the island the aircraft came under attack from anti-aircraft fire from hidden positions under the canopy. Sometimes an aircraft from another squadron, as instructed by Intelligence, was tasked to mark the target area in the jungle for us. Sometimes we had to find the location for ourselves if the target was relatively visible. If we were delivering a fighter-bomber attack, we first carried out dive bombing, one Section at a time, diving in line astern, led by the Section Leader, after which we reformed as a Section in line abreast to return at low level over the target area for a strafing run. We opened fire when the Section Leader did and operated our rudders as we did so to make our aircraft swing left and right, thereby causing our shots to be spread as widely as possible on the hidden enemy. The other two Sections carried out the same manoeuvres in their turn.

A quite different task for the Squadron was to provide escort cover for Catalina flying boats. They were so slow flying that it could be tedious work to keep station with them. They maintained regular patrols along the flight paths and in the areas where allied aircraft were on combat missions to rescue any downed aircrew members from the sea. American medium bombers were frequently tasked to attack jungle – or sometimes coastal – Japanese Army locations in exactly the same kind of conditions that we ourselves faced. We also maintained routine patrols over the ocean and island coastal areas in the region of our base and at a distance, on the lookout for Japanese submarines, shipping and aircraft. All our missions were carried out in daylight. We flew them as far as Rabaul, the major Japanese base in New Britain.

It was on the return leg of one trip to Rabaul that an unusual incident nearly cost the life of one of my closest colleagues. Our Section was flying in line abreast in very bad weather with Dave Barr the Section Leader on the extreme left. To his right were his wingman Ron Bennett, then Owen Marshall and finally me as Owen's wingman. Well out over the ocean I suddenly sensed that Owen was sliding towards me. I waited for him to make an automatic correction but it failed to happen. As his aircraft edged still further towards me, I was compelled to move away. It was then that I suspected something was wrong. I called him on the radio only to hear incoherent mumblings.

At a greater distance from him I repeatedly spoke to him by radio in the belief that he was in some kind of trouble, hoping that my calls would be a stimulus to keep him going. We had been flying at 15,000 feet but by this time his incapacitation caused his aircraft to lose 8,000 feet. I followed him down. His head had been lolling to the side of the cockpit hood at first but as we descended he seemed to become more alert to the point that I was able to ask about his condition and tell him to check his oxygen supply. The

Section made a safe return to base where it was found that Owen's oxygen system had not been functioning properly. He had not connected its feed pipe to the oxygen bottle firmly enough. Many years later at a Pacific Fighter Pilots' Association reunion I met him again. One of the topics of conversation was that trip to Rabaul.

The Association in its heyday held a reunion of fighter pilots drawn from many countries. I served on its committee. It was interesting to find that about 80% of the members were wearing hearing aids. I myself have had residual hearing and other troubles from my war service, the cumulative effect meriting a full normal pension plus ten percent.

On the completion of my war service I returned to civilian life by way of an invitation from the boss of the motor accessories warehouse who had stood me down in early 1941 for want of sufficient business. In the post war period, returning servicemen and an active government immigration programme combined to lift the economy. Although cars at first were very difficult to obtain as they had to be imported in a world market where demand was not yet matched by supply, the prospects were good. I stayed with the firm for six years, becoming its sales representative. On leaving in 1951, I married Nancy and secured a job as branch manager of another company in the same line of business and stayed with it for seven years.

In 1959 I was approached by an Australian company called Wibroc which was keen to open a manufacturing plant for car accessories in New Zealand. I was its manager for thirteen years. In 1972 I bought a retail motor accessories business in Christchurch and sold it in 1982. By that time I had accumulated the interesting experience of having worked in each phase of motor accessories – manufacture, wholesale, and retail - and was at one stage President of the Canterbury Automotive Wholesalers' Association.

After formal retirement I served as manager for five years in charge of housing maintenance for mentally handicapped people who were enabled to live in the community in their own housing. I subsequently spent five years in the real estate business and after that doing clerical, warehouse, and delivery work for a former business friend for three years. My succession of retirements, however, still had one more phase to run. For five years I had a job re-locating hire cars for Budget Cars. Tourists commonly used to hire a car to tour the North Island after landing from abroad at Auckland Airport, then leave it at the ferry terminal, take the ferry to the South Island, hire another car at Picton and eventually leave that car in turn at Christchurch Airport to return home. Consequently I made 105 return trips to the ferry port at Picton from Christchurch with cars to be returned to Picton.

Finally I think I have retired but only in the sense of not having to go out to paid employment. I still play golf twice weekly at the club where I served once as its full time Secretary Manager, and enjoy the extended family life provided by my four sons and eight grandchildren.

~~~

Artie Shaw flew as pilot in the following aircraft, listed in experiential order.

Tiger Moth
Harvard
Kittyhawk
Corsair

Photographs and the specifications of these aircraft may be found in Part 2, listed in alphabetical order.

Pilots at a jungle strip being taken to their aircraft for an operation in 1944. Artie Shaw is the middle pilot of the three clinging to the step of the 15 cwt truck

Corsairs, with engines running, preparing for take-off at a jungle airstrip in 1944. Note the 1,000 pound bomb underneath the nearest aircraft, Number 338

22 Squadron pilots in 1944 at their jungle base. Artie Shaw is at the right hand end of the front row. The notice at the top of the photograph reads 22 (F) Squadron Headquarters. It is tented accommodation

22 Squadron pilots at Ardmore, New Zealand, on the eve of the
Squadron's third tour, 1945. Artie Shaw is third from the right
in the front row

Ernie Speedy, Artie Shaw, another pilot, and Reg Wellington
who formed one Section of 22 Squadron's 'A' Flight, standing in
front of Corsair 14 'Leslie', at a jungle strip in 1945

Dave Barr, Owen Marshall, Artie Shaw, and Ron Bennett. Artie
Shaw flew as wing man to Owen Marshall, and Ron Bennett to
Dave Barr, who was the Section Leader of 22 Squadron's 'A'
Flight in 1944 – photographed together at a 22 Squadron
Reunion in the 1970s. Only Artie Shaw survives

A Corsair aircraft by the late New Zealand tapestry artist Colin
Lester, from an original photograph of Corsair NZ 5462 taken
at Piva, Bougainville, in the Solomon Islands. It was
commissioned by his sons and given to Artie Shaw on his
seventieth birthday in 1993. On seeing the number of the
aircraft and consulting his wartime log book, Artie Shaw
discovered that he had flown this aircraft several times, the
first for an attack against Papas during his third tour on 11 May
1945.

Chapter 9.

Triumph of Judgement

Fred Thomas

Triumph of Judgement

Colonel Thomas was a British Officer serving in the Indian Army around 1850, when India was still firmly under British rule. He was stationed at Dehra Doon where he managed to involve himself in commercial activity by acquiring tea plantations. He exported tea to Britain but ultimately became bankrupt, which was a heinous state to fall into in those days. This use, or rather misuse of his position and influence apparently led finally to disfavour with his higher command and to what today might be termed his constructive dismissal. Instead of returning to the United Kingdom, however, he chose to venture southwards to New Zealand, which at the time was very much in an inchoate state of development. It seems that his familiarity with life in India had inured him to difficult, if not primitive, conditions, so he regarded the virtually virgin state of New Zealand as an opportunity rather than a dangerous risk. He was my great grandfather.

He came to the northern part of the South Island and bought 4,000 acres of land at Motueka to set himself up as a farmer with sheep and cattle. His son took over the farm on his father's death and successfully developed it, handing it on in turn to his own son who was to be my father. Unfortunately my father died in the early1930s when I was only thirteen, so the farm passed to his brother.

I was born in Motueka on 24 September 1918, just a couple of months before the end of the hostilities of the First World War which had claimed the lives of so many New Zealanders, the total casualties being incommensurate with its small population. My father married Ruth Marchant at St Mary's Church in Timaru on 6 September 1916. I had three sisters but no brothers. My childhood was not particularly happy. My record at Riwaka Primary School in Motueka, where the strap was freely used, and at Nelson College for four years of secondary schooling was undistinguished, but I enjoyed my time at Nelson College as a boarder, in spite of the bullying that went on there, sports being of great interest to me, especially cricket, rugby, and running.

There was no real incentive for me to spend further time in the education system as my attitude and expectations were geared to interests other than those represented by schooling. I left the Nelson College at seventeen without obtaining my matriculation, so there was no question of considering a continuation of study into higher education. Perhaps it is an overstatement to say that I had an aversion to schooling but it is not incorrect to say that as a young man I had an aversion to farming, although my first paid employment was on the family farm. I had been brought up in farming and thoroughly imbued with the knowledge that the Thomas family had farmed the same land for decades in the successive hands of my great grandfather, my grandfather, and my father. I suppose there must have been a moral obligation on me to have a passion for farming but truth to tell my passions were directed in very different directions.

When I was aged twelve I made a model of the first aircraft to cross the Tasman Sea between Australia and New Zealand. It was called the *Southern Cross* and landed at the Wigram air base in Christchurch on Tuesday 11 September 1928, piloted by Charles Kingsford-Smith, who was a Squadron Leader in the Royal Australian Air Force. This aircraft had three Pratt and Whitney engines of equal power. My model, however, had a large centrally mounted engine and two smaller engines, one on each wing. Someone with a sharp eye pointed this out to me but I was too proud of my achievement to be crestfallen over such an inaccuracy. I am not sure whether the attainment of completing this model gave rise to a lasting and growing interest in aviation, or whether such an interest was an antecedent which spurred me into making the model. The solid fact was that my desire to fly was no longer a passing fad. I saved and begged enough money to learn to fly at Motueka aerodrome, beginning when I was seventeen. It took two weeks' pay to buy one hour of flying with an instructor. I eventually went solo for the first time when I was eighteen in 1936 and qualified for an 'A' license with the Marlborough Aero Club. I continued to buy as much flying time as I could afford for the following two years and was accepted for a short service commission in the Royal Air Force in June 1939, an appointment, however, that I was unable to fulfil, owing to the declaration of war.

With the advent of war on 3 September 1939, by which time I was three weeks short of my twenty-first birthday, I was filled with a determination to take advantage of the flying opportunities which the Second World War seemed to be offering. I volunteered for the Royal New Zealand Air Force soon after the declaration of war but was immediately turned down on the grounds that I had not obtained my matriculation at school. Within a few months it must have been apparent to all and sundry that the demand for aircrew members would not be met unless a different attitude to prerequisite qualifications prevailed. The institution of study by correspondence and part-time attendance at evening classes later enabled hundreds of young men who had had modest or indifferent school careers to compensate for their scholastic deficiencies, and the chance to measure up to the requirements of knowledge and skills that provided the necessary grounding for pilot training.

After another abortive attempt to enlist for pilot training, I was finally admitted to the Air Force early in 1940, with service Number 40993, serving in it from 9 April that year to 21 December 1945. I was a relatively early recruit but later on an avalanche of volunteers for aircrew duties appeared as the war years progressed. I was privileged to be in the van. Training systems were still in their infancy, and the attitudes and expectations shown towards trainees bore the marks of peacetime practice. To meet the huge training demands that were expected to materialise in the war, many innovations and developments in training methods and locations, together with adaptive attitudes towards trainees, took place. The Air Force Act of 1937 created the Air Force as a separate service and provided for the foundation of new flying training bases at Ohakea, Whenuapai, and Woodbourne, plus a major expansion of the existing Wigram base. Not least of the developments which took place after war arrived was the installation of the huge Empire Flying Training Scheme in

221

Canada to which so many of New Zealand's volunteer aircrew members were subsequently sent. They were exposed there to a wide variety of training personnel from other nations and a consequent variety of attitudes and training methods.

As an early recruit my own training was wholly completed in New Zealand. The Air Force sent me first to the Elementary Flying Training School at Taieri near Dunedin, a base which was destined to expand its capacity to cope with a flood of trainee pilots for their very first experience of taking to the air. During the period 10 May to 21 June 1940 I completed the required number of hours of flying with an instructor and solo.

My experience at Taieri, however, was jaundiced. I had no difficulties in flying the Tiger Moth. After all, I had already learnt to fly, so potentially I was considerably ahead of my fellow recruits. All went well until the end of the course came in sight. It was standard practice for the Chief Instructor to take a newly trained pilot for a test flight before his course could be considered concluded. The Chief Instructor was none other than the man who had taught me to fly at Motueka aerodrome. As far as I was aware, my flight with the Chief Instructor was satisfactory, so it was to my astonishment and dismay after returning to base that he announced to me, "Your instructor has informed me that you are not suitable to be appointed as a pilot in the Royal New Zealand Air Force."

Whilst nursing my injured pride over this unexpected turn of events, my regular instructor came up to me exclaiming, "Whatever happened to you, you should have passed." On his saying this, I was truly taken aback. But how could I then tell him the thought that filled my mind? The implication was that the Chief Instructor had invented the basis for his declaration. On reflection I could only explain the anomaly to myself in personal terms. It may have been a matter of incompatibility. Perhaps at Motueka it was a case of the customer calling the tune, since I was paying for my tuition. As a young man of seventeen I remembered that I had not taken to him as my instructor. Maybe he sensed that and considered me a precocious upstart.

The prospect of being rejected at that stage, after my previous experience of failing to be accepted by the Air Force, through circumstances out of my control, was devastating. In the wake of it, however, it seems that my regular instructor managed to intervene on my behalf. I was given another final test and was passed as fit to be a pilot in the Air Force. As I couldn't possibly have changed my potential so quickly in the time, the incident left questions unanswered, but implied unsavoury conduct.

I was posted to the Advanced Initial Flying Training School at Wigram in Christchurch, where I had a few flights in the obsolescent, single-engine Fairey Gordon before flying the twin-engine Airspeed Oxford, which proved to be the standard initial training aircraft for pilots destined to fly bomber aircraft throughout the Second World War. This training lasted from 5 July to 19 October 1940 with a course membership of thirty-five of whom one failed. I was the youngest trainee but was able to assuage the bitter experience of previous rejections by coming top of the course and receiving my wings as an accepted member of the Royal New Zealand Air Force with the rank of Pilot Officer. I was twenty-two.

As if to compound the healing process of my self-esteem, I was posted to be trained as a flying instructor to the Flying Instructors' Training School at Hobsonville in Auckland for the period 16 November to 25 December 1940. Following my successful completion of this course I was appointed to the Advanced Flying Training School at Ohakea. At this station, between 30 December 1940 and 25 February 1942, I instructed trainee pilots variously using at first two obsolescent aircraft types that had been relegated to training duties - the Hawker Hind and the Fairey Gordon – and then the modern Harvard and Oxford aircraft. After their initial elementary flying training on the Tiger Moth, trainee pilots flew either the Harvard if they were destined to fly fighter aircraft, or the Oxford if they were destined to fly bomber aircraft. I seemed to specialise there in instructing trainees who had had an accident or had accumulated a record of faults, such as heavy landings, for re-assessment.

From 12 March to 21 May 1942, I was posted to Number 10 Operational Training Unit at Levin to be an instructor on the Lockheed Hudson bomber. My conversion to this job required three flights with Flight Lieutenant George Harvey as my instructor, and thirteen flights flying solo. Thereafter I flew a further twenty-four solo flights during the first ten days of June. Having made a long indirect contribution to the war effort by training others to fly, however, I knew it was time for me to make my own direct effort in an operational squadron. I had enjoyed my time as an instructor. There was a lot to learn on the technical side. In addition there was a lot to learn about myself in relation to the trainees. The experience was a maturing one for me. I soon discovered how easy it was to confuse a trainee to the point of actually inducing mistakes by being too precipitate in making an instruction, by intervening too quickly to correct a mistake, by being censorious over his efforts, and by using a tone of voice and words that were other than encouraging.

I left instructing for two and a half years of operational flying covering one tour in Hudsons and two tours in Venturas. A tour itself in an operational base in the islands in a bomber squadron lasted for six months. Some of the Hudson aircraft of 3 Squadron which I joined were accompanied en route to their war posting by Kittyhawk fighters that were on their own way to operational bases in the Pacific. The Hudsons provided the navigational facilities which the fighter aircraft lacked for flying long distances over the ocean. I was piloting one of these Hudsons when it ran into mechanical trouble before reaching Guadalcanal. One of its two engines seized up, causing a sudden loss of height - to the consternation of one of the accompanying fighters whose pilot, however, was quick enough to prevent a possible collision.

I had to complete the flight and also to land at Guadalcanal on one engine. Undoubtedly, my long experience as an instructor came fully to the fore. This mishap on my way to war for the first time, however, was soon followed by a second. The Hudson I flew from Guadalcanal to Espiritu Santo on a submarine search completed the flight itself in good order, but on landing its brakes immediately failed. We always used brakes when landing to keep the aircraft straight. At the moment I realised that they had failed, we were heading for the jungle surrounding the airstrip at 70 mph. Being unable to keep the aircraft straight I had five seconds to take action to slow the aircraft down. There was no option but to raise the undercarriage as the aircraft hurtled unchecked over the ground. When I did so the left wheel collapsed first. This caused the aircraft to slew round through 180^0. When we stopped we were facing the way we came in. Had I taken more than five seconds making the decision it would have been too late as we had two tons of explosive bombs on board. As it was, the Hudson was a write off.

Around June 1945 over one million pounds of bombs were dropped on Japanese positions in the Solomon and Bismarck Islands in a period of eight weeks by the Squadron operating from Green Island. For half of this period over ten tons were delivered daily, representing the most concentrated period of bombing by any Royal New Zealand Air Force bomber squadron during the entire war in the Pacific. 200 missions were flown by aircraft of the Squadron, eighty-three of which were against major targets. Night missions were flown against Rabaul, together with anti-submarine patrols, searches for downed aircrew survivors on land and water, weather observation, leaflet dropping, photographic missions, providing cover for shipping and troop movements, and routine reconnaissance. The Squadron successively operated first from Guadalcanal, then Bougainville. It was the first Ventura Squadron to operate from Emirau.

It fell to my lot one day to carry out a unique mission for the Squadron. The Australian Army asked for supplies to be dropped from the air at a mountain location where they were isolated in the face of Japanese troops. It was exacting work to ensure that the parachuted supplies fell on the Australians rather than the enemy. It was a worthwhile mission to accomplish successfully. The Squadron received a signal from the Australians to say that the drop had been accurate. It was signed by Sergeants English and Searle. With typically Australian humour they invited my crew and me to a party in the jungle but alas, it was neither an attractive nor feasible proposition, so we politely declined.

Another unusual assignment falling to me was a mission to a small round island on which New Zealand Air Force engineers had constructed a new airstrip. The Squadron Commander told me that I could land there to try it out if it seemed safe to do so. I found on landing that the curvature of the water's edge had been followed too closely, making the landing strip itself slightly more curved than straight. Taking off from it was easier than landing, however, provided the take off was in the direction which had the sea to starboard. Since the propellers of an aircraft turn anti-clockwise - from the pilot's point of view - in multi-engine aircraft in particular, this results in a pronounced pull to port on take-off, which must always be counteracted by the pilot. But in this case the slightly left-curving take-off strip nicely made the corrective for him.

In surviving my five tours in thirty months of operational flying in Hudsons and Venturas, I was fortunate to evade serious damage to my aircraft and mishap at the hands of the enemy, with a single exception. On 9 September 1944, a request was received from the American Army for an attack against one of the five or more airfields constructed by the Japanese as a defensive arc around their main supply depot and strategically important base at Rabaul in the north of New Britain. This particular one was at Karavat, about twelve miles to the south-west of the base. The mission required a return flight of approximately 540 miles, a distance within the normal range of our Ventura aircraft. The target however, had to be identified by the attacking aircraft crews themselves. As it was a direct assault on a fighter airfield of crucial importance to the enemy, the mission was potentially risky as well as difficult.

It was to his credit that the Squadron's Commanding Officer, Wing Commander Ian Morrison, chose to lead the mission of three aircraft himself, with respectively Flight Lieutenant Roye Stevens and me to pilot the other two aircraft needed for the attack. We took off at 05.30 am, a timing to enable us to reach the target as dawn broke and provide the visibility we needed.

On the way to the target we passed through heavy rain and thunderstorms. Although radar was being fitted to some aircraft,

226

my aircraft for this mission, NZ4522, was not one of them, so I had no option in those conditions but to time our flight to make a landfall at dawn. In trying to find the target I flew at heights varying from 2,000 feet above sea level down to only 100 feet between Cape Palliser and Karavat. In coping with the weather, I used an auto-rich mixture in the light rain but a full rich mixture and hot air in heavy rain, which reduced cylinder head temperatures down to 160°, but left the engines performing perfectly.

When I arrived at the target area I was gratified to make contact with the mission leader who had arrived before me. I was unaware at that point of the whereabouts of the third aircraft flown by Roye Stevens. I asked permission to make my attack and received an affirmative that all was clear. I adopted a shallow dive from 2,300 feet above ground level, releasing the bombs at 1,200 feet before climbing steeply to port. On feeling the explosions of the bombs, I turned sharply and dived low to carry out a strafing run against an object spotted at the north end of the airstrip. During this run all the guns of the aircraft were in action. Of the six bombs we carried, however, we found that two had failed to drop. Of the options open to us, I chose to go round again as it seemed a pity either to take them home again or waste them in the sea. I told the crew that we could never live it down if we returned with two bombs hung up in the bomb bays. As the anti-aircraft fire from the ground was sporadic, rather than heavy, the second bomb run seemed worth the risk. Our respect for Japanese ack-ack was not immense. We usually found that Japanese Army gunners fired directly at an attacking aircraft. They apparently did not fully grasp the need for deflection shots to allow for the delivery time of their munitions.

The Commanding Officer by this time, having executed his own bombing attack, was in the process of carrying out a strafing run, so I followed him in from 2,100 feet and pressed the bomb release button at 1,200 feet, Flying Officer Shanks activated an alternative release mechanism to ensure the bombs fell off. Again, I climbed steeply until I felt the bombs explode before repeating the manoeuvre to dive for a second low level strafing run, paying particular attention to a clump of trees that looked like suitable cover for parked aircraft. As the dive began, however, the starboard engine cut out without warning.

My first reaction was to look at the engine for vibration - perceiving none, but noticing that the airscrew was milling smoothly. All my instruments seemed to be performing normally except for the flow of fuel, fuel pressure, and cylinder temperature readings, which were falling. I trimmed the rudder and elevator, opened up 2,700 rpm and 45 inches of manifold pressure and closed the booster pump of the port engine. In realising that I could not make the return flight to base in the prevailing bad weather, nor climb over the mountains of New Ireland to land at the nearest allied airfield at Green Island, on one engine, I tried every means to re-start the starboard engine.

I tested all petrol tanks with and without booster pumps. At the moment that the starboard engine cut out, the aircraft had forty gallons of fuel left in each of the cabin tanks, in each of the two auxiliary tanks, and in each of the two rear main tanks, plus 100 gallons in each of the two front tanks, making an overall total of 440 gallons.

Meanwhile the wireless operator, Warrant Officer George Miller, was trying to contact the Flight Leader, Wing Commander Morrison, and the Catalina flying boat which we knew had been detailed to patrol the coast precisely for rescuing aircrew members caught in the kind of dilemma that we faced. His calls were unsuccessful, owing to the fact - it was believed - that the turret gunner had inadvertently shot the wireless aerial away, the automatic cut out mechanism to prevent such an eventuality having failed.

I flew out to the bay area to be over the water in case we had to make a forced landing, and to be out of the reach of ground fire. When I consulted them, all members of the crew agreed that our best course of action was to fly westwards around Cape Lambert and head for allied territory that had been wrested from the Japanese on the Willaumez Peninsula, near the middle of New Britain's north coast. If we flew reasonably close along the north coast of New Britain – up to ten miles out to sea – we stood a good chance of reaching the shore during the night in our dinghy if the aircraft had to be ditched.

During this delay and attempts to re-start the engine, the aircraft had lost valuable height down to 200 feet above sea level. I gave the order to prepare for ditching at 500 feet when the noise of the port engine began to sound unfamiliar, given the aircraft's speed and the engine's power setting. At 2,700 rpm and 45 inches of manifold pressure our speed was eighty knots at 200 feet. A down draught must have been responsible for this accelerated descent, as a little later the aircraft was back at 400 feet but at the same power settings that could only produce eighty to eighty-five knots.

On the order the crew jettisoned the door and canopy. Half an hour later the .5 turret gun and ammunition were thrown overboard, followed by everything else that was movable to lighten the tail of the aircraft, including our parachutes. During this action the navigator's maps were somehow sucked out of the aircraft to compound our problems.

At times the aircraft was very low on the water - at times as low as twenty feet above the water. The port engine's performance remained perfect. At the speed of eighty-five knots that we more or less maintained, I was able to open the cowl gills a little to help to keep the engine cool, but it required more oil than usual. We pumped in one gallon of oil at the time that the starboard engine cut out, and another gallon later on.

The course we set westwards varied between five and twenty miles off the coast. This variation was deliberately incurred to take advantage of the up-draughts that occur under cumulus clouds. By altering course slightly we managed to pass under two banks of cumulus. As we passed under the first our height above the sea was a near perilous 100 feet but after moving away from the cumulus area we had climbed to 900 feet. I used the new height to experiment with speeds up to 110 knots at 2,700 rpm and 45 inches of manifold pressure but found that height could only be maintained at speeds of 90 knots or less. The experimentation cost us 300 feet anyway. It seemed best to adopt a cruising speed of eighty to eighty-five knots at 2,400 rpm and 40 inches of manifold pressure, suffering the loss of a few feet per minute, whilst heading for another cumulus cloud formation about fifty miles away in the path of our general direction. For ten minutes before reaching this second bank of cumulus our speed was eighty-five knots at 2,600 rpm and 45 inches of manifold pressure, during which time I again gave the order to stand by for ditching as our height had fallen to 200 feet. In passing under the cumulus we gained height to 800 feet, permitting a reduction of power once more to 2,400 rpm and 40 inches of manifold pressure.

I was able to reduce the manifold pressure at times down to 35 inches, but all the time the aircraft was losing height at the rate of a few feet per minute. At 400 feet we passed through some light rain for twenty minutes, necessitating a few minutes of instrument flying, before emerging from the rain at 300 feet – a height at which we remained until we arrived in sight of the Willaumez Peninsula in the area of Talasea. The crew members remained at ditching stations in face of the fuel shortage and the likelihood that the one engine would finally cut out. Power was then at 2,500 rpm and 43 inches of manifold pressure, and our speed was still at eighty-five knots, with a distance of forty miles to cover to landfall.

When twenty miles offshore we were able to identify the Talasea Inlet and headed for it, passing Cape Hoskins on the port side at a distance of eight miles. We could discern roads and buildings there, with a long grass strip that looked as if it had been prepared as a landing field. However, we did not know if the American Army had yet taken it from the Japanese. We could see no signs to settle the issue at that distance. In deciding not to make the diversion to investigate it, promising though it seemed to be at first sight, we chose to conserve our fuel and take advantage of the continuing good performance of the port engine. It subsequently proved to have been a wise decision, as we discovered that the field was unused by aircraft except for a small part of it from which American Piper Cub short take-off and landing reconnaissance aircraft operated. The rest of it had not been cleared of the mines left by the enemy.

We arrived at the Talasea Inlet at 0915 hours, only five minutes short of two hours since the engine had cut out over the target area at Karavat. In a bay we could see small vessels carrying United States flags. At the same time on our port side we spotted a small muddy clearing in a swamp stretching across the Willaumez Peninsula, surrounded by high trees, at about thirty feet above sea level. It appeared to be available as a landing strip as we could see American flags and a B25 Mitchell aircraft under the trees – which we soon found had crash landed there. But as a space to land it was far too short for a Ventura. Furthermore, at each end of it there was a sharp drop to the beach. We had never heard of it before. It was not listed as an emergency landing ground and we could see that we would have to brush through some trees while executing a left hand turn to the ground.

However, on turning in the bay against the dead engine, we decided that it was our last chance at a reasonable landing, as our fuel supply was too low for further flying. I made a wide turn at 150 feet above the site. On my signal, the navigator, Flying Officer Geoffrey Shanks, lowered the undercarriage and operated the hand pump to lower the flaps. With a wind direction from port at five knots, I levelled out at eighty knots at the edge of the strip with 85% flap, making a slight side slip whilst levelling out to put the aircraft down, the tail wheel touching the ground seventy yards from the edge of the strip.

On hitting a rise in the ground whilst the necessary hard braking was being applied, the aircraft's tail rose high in the air, but the aircraft came to a standstill at 115 yards from the edge of the gully on the inland end of the strip. The soft ground was a factor aiding the successful landing in an area that we found later measured 1,800 feet long and 132 feet wide. Our fuel supply had held out. On landing there were twenty gallons in each cabin tank, twenty-three and twenty-eight gallons respectively in the two rear main tanks, and twenty and forty gallons respectively in the two auxiliary tanks. There had been little flying time left.

231

All the crew members had been magnificent. Not once did anyone make any negative or dispiriting remarks. We were a long standing team and together we pulled though. We jumped out and sat on mother earth for a while, fearing that the aircraft might catch fire, but glad to have survived. Very soon some American troops turned up and immediately invited us to a cinema show that night. We must have looked a trifle indifferent in our exhaustion. One huge trooper came over to where I was sitting in the mud and yanked me to my feet in one swift movement saying, "Up you get, Dad." I think their hearts were in the right place but their exuberance at that moment seemed a little too much to bear.

The wireless operator immediately repaired the damaged aerial so that we could notify someone of our survival. At first our signals met with no response but at 1630 hours we managed to contact Emirau and asked for the following message to be transmitted to our base.

"COMAIREMIRAU from 6B14

Thomas force landed at Talasea. Fuel line starboard motor shot away. All safe."

The local American Commander independently sent a message to his South-West Pacific Headquarters on 9 September, the day of the landing. It was relayed to Melbourne, then to Wellington, and back through the islands, eventually reaching our Squadron's base on 15 September – the day after we had actually returned to it.

Our aircraft's starboard engine had been hit by a 20mm shell. The shell had cut the main starboard fuel line between the fuselage and the starboard engine. Miraculously, it had not set the fuel alight, and had just missed the main spar, emerging from the wing to strike the fuselage at a point only twenty-five centimetres from the navigator who had been sitting alongside me. Otherwise, the Ventura was undamaged. It was towed off to a parking place under the trees nearby to a spot which proved to be its final resting place. Members of our Squadron flew over Talasea and reported seeing it still in the same position. The space available was insufficient for it to take off again. Its engines and instruments were later removed but I had no knowledge of the fate of the rest of the aircraft until 1979.

We had managed to land in territory won back from the Japanese by the American Army. The Colonel in charge of the local troops at Talasea sent further reports on his own account. During the following day of our enforced sojourn with the American Army we ran the port engine to recharge the batteries and tried calling a patrolling Catalina flying boat.

After two days, a United States Catalina landed in the sea near the shore to take us to its own base at Emirau Island, about 280 miles to the north. Two B25 Mitchell medium bombers were sent to escort the Catalina. Off New Ireland's south-west coast the three aircraft approached Dyaul Island, the Catalina's pilot taking his aircraft straight for high cumulus clouds that partly shrouded the hills of the off-shore and main islands. I remarked to the pilot that as there were hills of 500 feet on the Island it would be wise to climb, to which suggestion he agreed. He took the Catalina up through the cloud but when we emerged into clear air on the north-east side of New Ireland there was no sign of the second B25 Mitchell escorting us.

The other Mitchell and our aircraft searched the area and made radio calls for three hours unavailingly. We concluded that the escorting Mitchell had crashed into the hills in cloud. The Catalina's pilot invited me to sit next to him as we flew at the Catalina's modest speed of 100 knots at 900 feet above the sea, taking an indirect route across New Ireland, to the south of Kavieng, an airport held by the Japanese at the north point of New Ireland, before turning towards Emirau where we landed in a bay on the south side of the Island. We were then ferried back to our Squadron's base at Piva in a United States C47 Commander aircraft.

We learned later of the sustained efforts made by our own Squadron to search for us, in which most crews took part. For four days they searched all the areas between our base and Rabaul, looking for wreckage or a dinghy as evidence that we had crash landed. For example, one Ventura crew on 12 September searched the sea for nearly five hours, following it up the next day with a search of the southern part of New Ireland. For two nights this crew slept in the United States camp on Green Island, partly to carry out the routine patrol to report the weather over Rabaul, and partly to continue a search for us in their allotted area. At first the Squadron had no news of our survival. No trace was ever found of the third Ventura on the strike mission piloted by Roye Stevens. He and the other members of the crew together with their aircraft must have crashed into the sea or a remote jungle spot where the wreckage remained concealed from the air.

When we arrived back at our base the Commanding Officer asked me to write a report on the mission. I told him that my immediate preference was to take a flight with the crew and cruise around for a while on two engines. He stared at me for a moment and then assented.

I happened to be at an Air Force Base between tours when I was called to the telephone for a message from Air Force Headquarters, which informed me of the award of the Distinguished Flying Cross, the citation for which was as follows.

Citation 4 December 1944 DFC 3 Squadron RNZAF Ventura

"By his courage, skill and determination in the face of danger, this Captain nursed his severely damaged bomber for two hours and made a brilliant landing without further damage on an emergency strip only 1,800 feet long. Captain of one of three aircraft detailed to bomb Japanese supplies in the Bismarck area at dawn on 9 September 1944, Flight Lieutenant Thomas reached his target after flying through darkness, heavy rain, and thunderstorms. He immediately attacked with courage and determination. Two bombs hung up on his first run so he strafed his way round the target area and made a further run in the face of heavy enemy fire to release his remaining bombs. As they dropped on the target area, his starboard motor cut out, the main fuel line having been shot away by anti-aircraft fire. Flight Lieutenant Thomas was faced with exceptional difficulty. Extremely bad weather on the direct course to base made it undesirable to attempt the return on one motor, and the loss of power prevented a crossing of the highlands of New Ireland. Accordingly, he set course for an emergency strip at Talasea in New Britain. It was doubtful in the extreme if the aircraft would remain in the air, and it was only by the pilot's determination and skill in making use of up-currents below cumulus clouds that he kept sufficient altitude throughout a most hazardous flight of two hours' duration. His landing was an outstanding achievement particularly with only one engine and throughout he displayed the utmost coolness and courage. Flight Lieutenant Thomas has completed over 260 hours of operational flying in the Pacific in the past year."

I completed three operational tours, the first taking 149 hours of operational flying time in Hudson aircraft, the second in Ventura aircraft taking 218 hours, and the third tour also in the Ventura taking 115 flying hours. My Air Force total flying hours was 2,697 hours and twenty-five minutes.

After the war, aged twenty-nine, I returned to my fourth-generation family farm near Motueka and married the local hotel keeper's daughter. My aversion to farming had evaporated. With the capital I had amassed from my savings throughout my war service and a 3% rehabilitation government loan, I was able to buy a farm of my own and build a house on it, specializing in apples and tobacco. My wife died in 1978 but I have been fortunate in having three daughters and two sons who support me in retirement. In 1979, following my wife's death I arranged to re-visit Talasea by helicopter and was able to take photographs of my crash site from the air and land nearby. It was a nostalgic moment for me. I found the aircraft still sitting in its parking lot with grass up to a metre and a half high around it. I climbed on top of the remains of the aircraft that was almost covered by jungle growth, with a renewed sense of what might have been helping me to keep a positive perspective on life.

I kept in touch with my crew members and other pilots from the Squadron. In 1994 a reunion in memory of our landing at Talasea was organised. During a conversation with Geoffrey Shanks, the Ventura's navigator, I asked him how low he thought we really had reached at one point. He simply said, "Too bloody low." I believe we had actually been as low as only a few feet above the water at one point but I did not put this in my official report as it seemed so unbelievable. However, an American airman once told me that it was possible that the air pressures created by the remaining propeller and the engine exhaust could have been enough to strike the water and form a cushion, helping to sustain the aircraft in flight.

Fred Thomas flew as pilot in the following aircraft, listed in experiential order.

~~~

Tiger Moth
Gordon
Hind
Harvard
Oxford
Hudson
Ventura

Photographs and the specifications of these aircraft may be found in Part 2, listed in alphabetical order.

Some members of flying training course Number 18 at Wigram,
1940

Aircrew members Sergeant Tonkin, Sergeant Turner, Flying Officer Burgess, Flying Officer Thomas, and an American Marine Corps Lieutenant in front of a Hudson aircraft at a jungle base in May 1943

Flying Officer Thomas, Flying Officer Burgess, Sergeant Turner, a United States Marine Corps Lieutenant, and Sergeant Tonkin, pose at a jungle brew up in May 1943

An unusual - if not a unique - view of Ventura aircraft of 3 Squadron flying in line abreast formation over the Pacific on 18 April 1945, led by the Squadron's Commanding Officer, Wing Commander Ian Morrison. They were returning from a bombing strike against a Japanese gun position at Ebery's Lease plantation

Ventura aircraft on the left await their bombs from the bomb train at Ruiaka in 1943. Six of these 500 pound bombs were carried by each aircraft

Navigator at an operational pre-flight briefing in 1943, with
Fred Thomas looking on

Wing Commander Ian Morrison, Commander of 3 Squadron, in
the centre of the front row with the Squadron's Administration
Officers in 1944

The crew members of a Ventura aircraft in 1945. Left to right at the back are Warrant Officer George Miller, DFM, wireless operator; Sergeant Richard Budd, gunner; and Flight Sergeant Arch Gillies, gunner. In the front are Squadron Leader Fred Thomas, pilot; and Flying Officer Geoffrey Shanks, Mentioned in Dispatches, navigator

Fred Thomas and the wingless and canabalized Ventura in 1979, in its final jungle resting place

An aerial view of the Ventura still in the jungle in 1979

An aerial view, taken by Fred Thomas in 1979, of the Ventura
at the top of the photograph. A United States Air Force
Mitchell medium bomber in the foreground had crashed in the
same space before Fred Thomas arrived with the Ventura.
Note the paths to each aircraft worn by sightseers and trophy
hunters

An aerial view of the abandoned Ventura and Mitchell aircraft,
taken in 1979, with the sea visible at the top of the photograph

Chapter 10.

Diversities of War

Jim Tocker

Diversities of War

As a New Zealander my roots are pretty deep. Both my parents were born in New Zealand, my mother being the granddaughter of Archibald McCallum, an immigrant who founded the Invercargill Timber business McCallum and Company. They were both from Scottish stock, although my father had some Irish and English blood. My great great grandfather Tocker landed at Petone Beach in 1840. He and his wife had left the United Kingdom with six children, one dying and another being born on the way to New Zealand. I have often reflected on the intrepid character of my forebears. The risks and distances involved in their initiatives were of a high order. One can only suppose that conditions in their places of origin plus the promise of better circumstances in another land were powerful enough to overcome the trials, tribulations, and privations they had to suffer to reach it and then to survive there.

For a few months my great great grandfather worked as a dock labourer unloading ships at Petone. Unfortunately he fell into a seven foot hole and was drowned at the age of forty, leaving all those children fatherless and his wife without support. My great great grandmother, however, was not a woman to fall easily to the effects of misfortune. She started a school in Petone, teaching the local children as a means to survive and then to make her way in the world to give her own many offspring a start in life in their new country.

Jumping the generations to a later age I know that my grandfather on my father's side of the family was a blacksmith in Greytown – an occupation that owed its existence primarily to the ubiquitous use of the horse for work and leisure purposes. My father was expected to succeed to the ownership of the business and actually did work with his own father for a while, but found their relationship - and perhaps the demanding physical nature of the job - not to his liking. He mounted his bike and rode away to find another job at the age of twelve, but after a week or so his mother persuaded him to return home.

In complete contrast to the profession of blacksmith, my father eventually became a teacher, for which the precedent had already been set many years previously in the family. He was teaching in Lower Hutt when I was born on 30 November 1920, the first of three boys. Both my younger brothers survive, one having retired in New Zealand from a career as a civil engineer with Shell, the other marrying in New Zealand before moving to England forty years ago and living there ever since.

I was only one when my father took a job as lecturer and assistant to Jack Condliffe at the university in Christchurch, which was then called Canterbury University College. When Jack Condliffe left for England in 1926, my father succeeded him and became Professor of Economics, before assuming the position of Rector of the University College from 1938 to 1943.

Childhood spent with my two brothers was a happy time, and we were well looked after. When I was eight years old my father bought our first car. Cars generally then were rare. Everyone in Christchurch rode bicycles. Father used to ride his bike to the university - as I did later to school and to my first job.

After attending Elmwood Primary School, I went to Christ's College for four years of secondary education, leaving in 1937 to take a job in an accountant's office. I was fortunate in having every encouragement in the home to study and to set my sights on higher education. A university education in commerce at that time was undertaken by part time study. My mother suggested that I should study law, but accountancy proved to be my preference. So as an office boy in an accountant's office I went to the university in the evenings to begin the long road to be a qualified accountant. Part time studies lasted throughout most of the war. The Air Force allowed me to sit my final accountancy examinations during 1942 and 1943 but I continued to study for the rest of my war service, eventually obtaining a master's degree in commerce and a fellowship of the New Zealand Society of Accountants as it was then called.

In 1939 it became increasingly obvious that war was looming, the possibility of military service having to be factored into future plans. Some of my contemporaries at Christ's College volunteered immediately. I had been a member of the Cadet Force at Christ's College, a commitment expected of every fit boy, so I had already made an acquaintance with the Army. I think there was also a Navy group in the Cadets but none for the Air Force, reflecting past military conditions rather than the developments then taking place. But having earnestly embarked on accountancy studies, I was keen to make as much progress as possible before taking a break from them. I joined the Territorial Army, however, serving two years, 1938 and 1939, in the artillery, but in 1940, having completed three years of part time study towards qualifying as an accountant, I volunteered to join the Air Force at twenty years of age.

The act of volunteering for the Air Force in view of existing Army connections was probably precipitated by a single factor. Early in 1939, before the war started, my father told me that he had heard that a few people out at the Wigram Air Force base were teaching young men to fly free of charge, in view of the fact that war looked to be likely in Europe. The thought of being able to fly caught my imagination. I took my father's car out to Wigram to confirm that the offer existed and that I could be included in the flying training programme. It was clearly designed to interest young men in the Air Force. This opportunity certainly whetted my appetite for flying. I accumulated sixteen hours of flying – seven with an instructor and nine solo - in a Tiger Moth, by the time war was declared in September of that year. The free lessons then disappeared immediately as the instructors were all committed to the full time training of volunteers for war service.

This experience was curiously reminiscent of the precedent set in 1916 during the First World War, when, under Henry Wigram's inspired initiative, a few young men were given elementary flying training prior to their transfer to England to join the Royal Flying Corps for combat service on the Western Front in France. This enterprising event proved to be the beginning of military flying in New Zealand, the genesis of the Royal New

Zealand Air Force, and the foundation of what was to become the largest Air Force base in New Zealand, aptly named Wigram.

In May 1941 I reported to the base at Levin for six weeks of induction into the Air Force and some elementary studies regarding flying. I was then posted to the Elementary Flying Training School at Taieri near Dunedin, to renew my acquaintance with the Tiger Moth. We were billeted in two-man wooden huts. My companion was Bruce Wisely, with whom I lived for four months. He became a good friend. I was later saddened to learn that the Whitley bomber he was flying had disappeared in the Mediterranean in 1942.

The squad of twelve trainee pilots of which I was a member, elected me to be one of the two squad leaders whose job it was to pass on orders from above, to arrange week-end leave, and to march the squad between classes and around the base. The pay-off for undertaking this duty was exemption from fatigues, the endless attempt to keep the site clean and tidy – a task which fell partly to the lot of the trainees.

My pre-war flying experience enabled me to make rapid progress as a trainee. At Taieri I flew for forty-four hours in Tiger Moths – at the slow rate of less than six hours per week. It was winter flying and often bitterly cold. Snow first fell on 19 June, heralding icy weather and unusual flying conditions which fully justified our use of insulated flying suits.

At the end of the course we were divided into three groups, one destined for Canada for further flying training. The other two groups stayed in New Zealand, one to train as fighter pilots, the other as bomber pilots. I was posted to the Number 1 Flying Training School at Wigram for a course lasting twelve weeks to train as a bomber pilot. I trained on Airspeed Oxford aircraft, completing a total of ninety-two hours of flying as a pilot, either with an instructor or solo, and a further fifty hours in the same aircraft as either bomb aimer, turret gunner, or as passenger between Wigram and a temporary landing strip at the practice bombing range at Birdlings Flat. We dropped hundreds of practice bombs at this range, each bomb emitting a small puff of smoke on its impact with the ground to indicate the extent of our accuracy.

At the end of the course at Wigram we were awarded our wings. I was lucky to be included in about one quarter of those qualifying to be commissioned as Pilot Officers, the majority being promoted to the rank of Sergeant. Some 90% of the course members were then posted to England to join Bomber Command but I was not among them, having been given a posting to an instructors' course. At that point of the war in October 1941, no one knew that hostilities would soon break out in the Pacific, following Japan's premeditated and opportunistic but unheralded attack on Pearl Harbour two months later on 7 December. I watched many friends leave New Zealand with mixed feelings. Unknown to me, most of them were destined to join the squadrons of Wellingtons, Hamptons, and Whitleys that formed the strike force of the bombing offensive mounted from British bases – a campaign which proved a boon to British morale but of limited effectiveness, at the cost of heavy losses. Most of those who survived for the following two or three years converted to the next generation of heavy, four-engine bombers – Stirlings, Halifaxes , and Lancasters - but by the end of the war only about half of those of my course who made the trip to fight in Europe returned to New Zealand.

I was transferred to the flying instructors' course at the Central Flying School at Tauranga in the North Island, where the facilities were adequate but not luxurious, as it had been taken over as a centre for this purpose only three months previously. Each of us slept in a wooden floored one-man tent. But at least we were able to eat in comfort at the Officers' Mess, food being brought to our tables. The training, in being focused on how to teach others, involved not only learning the language and behavioural aspects of instruction, but the psychological dimensions of our own personal conduct in dealing with trainees. It was all a matter of eliciting a good performance from each trainee but safely within his capabilities. Flight Lieutenant George Harvey was my instructor. He was the best I ever had, exhibiting in his own teaching all the skills and virtues that were universally enjoined on instructors. Later in the war he flew Lancaster bombers from England, on one occasion bringing home a damaged aircraft from a mission to Berlin, earning the Distinguished Flying Cross, and being promoted to the rank of Squadron Leader.

I spent most of my time at Tauranga flying Tiger Moths, but had the opportunity to widen my experience by flying in Oxfords again, and two aircraft that were new to me - the Harvard and the Hawker Hind, the last named being an obsolescent biplane that had seen important service as a light bomber in the Royal Air Force during the later 1930s before the advent of the monoplanes, notably that of the Fairey Battle, which superseded it. The training course lasted for eight weeks. At its conclusion I was posted to Harewood at Christchurch in the South Island, my home territory. The training programme for each trainee pilot allotted to me was of a routine and inclusive nature – from aircraft familiarization, through take-offs and landings, stalling, and spinning, to aerobatics, cross-country flying, instrument and night flying, and dive bombing.

During the early months of 1942 Japanese forces swept all before them in a lightning conquest of vast territories of the Pacific. The clear threat to New Zealand led to hasty defence preparations, including the installation of coastal gun positions and the maintenance of coastal patrols. The alert even filtered down to our station at Harewood, requiring us to take turns at night to keep watch with rifles from the First World War, which would certainly have been of only limited use if the need had arisen.

After six months as an instructor, I had judged a trainee to be ready to undertake his first solo flight, and stood as usual on the edge of the landing field to watch him complete his first circuit. Unfortunately I had made insufficient allowance for a storm that was brewing from the south. During the trainee's flight it gathered very quickly and burst at the moment of his landing. He managed to put the aircraft down but it turned over on its back, fortunately without any injury to the pilot.

The Chief Instructor held me responsible for the mishap as a result of which I was posted to a bomber-reconnaissance squadron. As it happened I was not entirely unhappy to have a change of direction, although disconcerted by the circumstances giving rise to it. Instructing had begun to pall on me a little by this time. Life in the service to date had been a pleasurable experience, tantamount to having a normal job in many ways. But having originally volunteered to fight as an airman, to some extent I had always felt a twinge of unease about being removed from combat action for so long. The posting therefore was for me a new beginning and a fulfilment.

In July 1942 I was sent to Levin, where I had first reported for service in the Air Force. By this time a flying unit had been added to the base called Number 10 Bomber Operational Training Squadron. I had to take a course of eight weeks, learning to fly the Lockheed Hudson medium bomber. Every manoeuvre and function was practised to bring pilots undergoing their conversion to an unfamiliar aircraft up to an initial operational standard. This included navigational experience, gunnery, sea searches, and emergency procedures. Hudson aircraft played a prominent part in the Royal New Zealand Air Force during the war and immediate post-war years. A total of ninety-four were used between 1941 and 1948 variously for bombing and anti-submarine missions, ocean patrols, and transport and training purposes.

My posting from Levin was to Whenuapai, north-west of Auckland, a major base for conducting home defensive patrols and a point of departure and arrival respectively for outgoing and incoming squadrons during their tour postings to and from the war zone in the Pacific Islands. In October 1942 my promotion to Flying Officer brought a welcome increase in salary, representing a notable contrast to my modest pre-war weekly wage as a clerk in an accountant's office.

At first, I had no crew of my own. I was the spare pilot who was called on to discharge the odd jobs that cropped up, such as the delivery of important passengers, and ferrying personnel to other airfields. My first operational mission was on 8 October as second pilot in a Hudson captained by Flight Lieutenant Johnstone to escort a convoy off North Cape. It was an eight hour flight requiring a long-range cabin tank. The Hudson, in common with other bomber aircraft at this stage of the war, normally carried two pilots. Using two pilots was standard practice in the United Kingdom for the first years of the Second World War, a practice that was soon discontinued, however, in the face of heavy losses of aircraft. This change of policy was adopted later by other Air Forces. Our patrol itself was uneventful, but during the return trip, when we were off Northland's east coast, the weather closed in with heavy cloud and steady rain. For half an hour we had an anxious time until the Captain suddenly spotted a rugged hill on our starboard side and called out, "That's Cape Brett." This identification then permitted us to fly low over the sea with enough sight of the coastline to reach the nearest available airfield at Onerahi, where we spent the night before returning to our own base the following day.

At the time I had no real fear for our safety, but afterwards realized that without the Captain's local knowledge the outcome could have been very different. During the war, Hudsons were lost, as were other types of aircraft, on domestic flights as a result of bad weather. Hudson NZ 2034 from the Number 1 Operational Training Unit at Ohakea took off on 24 August 1943 on a training flight but crashed in poor weather into the sea without trace near the mouth of the River Rangitikei. All five members of the aircrew on board were killed. In April 2004, sixty-one years later, the fishing nets of a trawler out of Nelson snagged what turned out to be one of the Hudson's engines. It was recovered and is now on display in the Air Force Museum at Wigram.

On a subsequent occasion when flying out of Whenuapai, in November 1942, I was captain of one of four aircraft flying independently on exercises over the extreme north of New Zealand, when all four aircraft received notice that the weather had closed in over our base. We were ordered to land at an emergency station. Local people kindly offered us meals and we were accommodated in temporary huts overnight before returning to base the following day – a day, incidentally, on which I was due to take accountancy examinations in Auckland at the university at 10 am, an appointment I was able to keep by persuading my crew to rise very early in the morning. My performance was evidently up to the mark, as I was subsequently admitted to membership of the now Institute of Chartered Accountants of New Zealand on 24 February 1943.

Until late November 1942 I carried out routine flights. We had been taught how to identify ships of all kinds and how to report them. Our sea patrols also included a search for Japanese submarines, which failed, however, to put in an appearance. The suspicion that they might appear, and being alert to the possibility, were retrospectively found to have been well justified. Submarines I-21 and I-25 of the Japanese Navy actually cruised undetected in New Zealand waters in March and May 1942. Submarine I-25 sailed westwards submerged through Cook Strait between the main islands on 8 March, passing along the east coast of North Island to be off Auckland on 13 March before proceeding northwards between the New Hebrides and Fiji Islands. On the same route in a reverse direction, submarine I-21 reached the north of New Zealand on 24 May but after sailing along part of the east coast above Auckland turned westwards on 26 May and was off Sydney by 29 May.

At that particular time of course Japanese arms everywhere were in the ascendant. By the year, when I was on sea patrols, they had suffered reversals at sea and were generally being put into a more defensive posture by American arms with the support of Australia and New Zealand, although the strategic situation was not clear enough to prevent fears of a Japanese invasion of New Zealand. This prompted, among other measures, the hiding of aircraft and the establishment of patrols - albeit armed with antiquated and insufficient weapons - around the perimeter of the base at Whenuapai.

At the end of November I was posted to New Plymouth for a course of six weeks in astro-navigation, a welcome break from what had become a tedious round of duties at Whenuapai. It proved to be the most interesting course I took in my Air Force career. We practised the customary methods of navigation by dead reckoning and visual sightings, and could check our calculations in the air by using our loop aerial giving access to a radio beam. In addition we learned to use astronomy in the time honoured tradition of mariners the world over, facilitated by lectures from an American Naval Officer who had a compendious knowledge of the stars of the southern hemisphere. This course ended with a return to Whenuapai and a resumption of duties as a spare pilot for any job which came along.

Eventually a crew was assigned to me – Pilot Officer Ian McGechie, co-pilot, Sergeant Chum Gardner, navigator, and Sergeant Eric Eastwood and Sergeant Jack Mobbs, wireless operator/air gunners. It became evident that as an aircrew we were about to be dispatched to the war by ourselves. We were briefed to fly to Nausori, a village and airport about fifteen kilometers east of Suva, near the south-east corner of Viti Levu, the main island of the large collection that made up the Fiji Islands.

On 29 April 1943 we took off at 0700 hours with a long range cabin tank of petrol in addition to the normal full load in the four wing tanks. It was the longest flight by far that either the co-pilot or I had ever undertaken. The navigational demands for it gave us some concern. We flew endlessly over the sea, the co-pilot and I sharing the flying with the auto pilot. It was consequently with relief that at 1330 hours we saw land for the first time. This turned out to be Kandavu Island about sixty miles south of Suva, and only ten miles from our designated landing. We called up Nausori control tower for permission to land and brought our long flight to an end on the Marston matting - the interlocking, perforated steel plates used as a surface for landing strips where the natural surface of the ground was unsuitable for aircraft. We had arrived to join Number 4 Bomber Reconnaissance Squadron.

After this experience we soon became used to flying over the sea. Islands became familiar by sight. The weather was usually fine with little cumulus cloud to worry about – a favourable circumstance, as cumulus could be fatal. On at least one previous occasion aircraft flying in formation were lost when passing through cumulus, presumably by colliding with each other. It was wise to break formation on seeing unavoidable cumulus ahead.

Officers were each given a hut with a concrete floor, a light frame, and a thatched roof. Fortunately, local men were employed to do all our personal chores and look after the camp. They even cut the grass – with native knives in downward chopping strokes.

The task of the squadron we had joined was normally reconnaissance and convoy protection. We could offer cover for ships up to a limit of 350 miles from our base. The principal concern was to spot Japanese submarines lying in wait for a convoy. To carry out an attack on a convoy a Japanese submarine had to be in position ahead of it, a position it could usually reach only on the surface, since its underwater speed was inferior to the average speed of the convoy. Our Hudsons, therefore, ranged fanwise ahead of a convoy in a systematic sea search, carrying depth charges for an immediate attack against a submarine before it could dive to safety. As it happened I saw only one enemy submarine during these patrols but realized that the presence of our aircraft must have been a source of reassurance to the sometimes hundreds of crew members and passengers in the ships of the convoy. Japanese submarines achieved some success around the Pacific over the nearly four years of war there, but on a scale that bore little resemblance to the vast carnage and strategically important achievements of German U-boats in many theatres of the war elsewhere, particularly in the Atlantic.

On 1 July 1943 we were posted as a crew to the Number 9 Bomber Reconnaissance Squadron, based on the south-east corner of Espiritu Santo in the New Hebrides Islands. The island was fifty miles in length and thirty wide, with mountains rising to over 2,000 metres. Apart from clearances for native settlements and plantations, the Americans had created spaces for camps and built roads and airstrips. Otherwise, the island was covered in endless jungle. The flight involved in the transfer lasted four and a half hours, covering 600 sea miles. At Espiritu Santo our landing strip was made of crushed and densely packed coral - the universal material used in the islands for wartime airstrips and roads. It was fifty metres from the water's edge, but only three metres above the level of high tide. In common with all allied airfields in the Solomon Islands, New Hebrides, and New Caledonia war zone, it was American controlled. Our ground crews worked in the open. It was hot and often windy, and mosquitoes had to be avoided, but generally it was possible to be very healthy, with plenty of swimming to keep fit.

Operational flying consisted mostly of anti-submarine patrols and convoy escort work, interspersed with special tasks such as searching for a downed American torpedo bomber and a Japanese submarine that were reported in our area. An unusual mission, and a precedent for us, on 8 July 1943, was to act as navigation aircraft for six American P40 Kittyhawks and two light bomber aircraft to fly from Espiritu Santo to Guadalcanal. Whilst we held our course the fighters broke formation at times to fly around us, to ease the tedium of flying at the Hudson's cruising speed, which was slower than theirs, but taking care to keep in visual distance and radio contact.

Only ten days later, on 11 July 1943, my crew and I were given the task of taking a Hudson back to New Zealand for a major overhaul, flying it first to Nausori in Fiji. Our assignment, as a crew, may have been testimony to our previous record of long independent flights, or it may have been a question of selecting the odd man out. The next day, during our break there, I was offered the chance to take a short flight in a Catalina flying boat moored in Lauthala Bay, near Suva. To prepare the aircraft for a thirty minute test flight took three hours. This was a routine precursor for setting out on a patrol that could last for twenty hours. The procedures for flying and responsibilities of the eight crew members were so complex and in such contrast to flying the Hudson, that they raised my concerns and determination not to transfer to flying boats. On 13 July we flew the Hudson on to New Zealand and were granted three weeks' leave, a welcome respite in the middle of a tropical combat tour, albeit in the worst month of the winter season, which in fact gave me the opportunity to join some friends for a skiing trip to the Mount Cook area.

On 6 August 1943 I had to fly a renovated Hudson from Rukuhia, Hamilton, to Whenuapai, where our full crew mustered to fly the aircraft on a seven hour trip from New Zealand to Norfolk Island to refuel before going on to Tontouta in New Caledonia.

When we moved on to our base at Espiritu Santo on 10 August, we soon found ourselves back in the old routine of ocean patrols and convoy escort duties, relieved by gunnery and bombing practice, and some mock aerial combat with Royal New Zealand Air Force Kittyhawk fighters. On 23 August we searched for a downed American torpedo bomber, but without success. This effort involved a flying time of nine hours and forty-five minutes – the longest day I ever spent in the air as a pilot.

With my crew I experienced another transfer of squadron on 29 August 1943, when we joined Number 3 Squadron based on Guadalcanal in the Solomon Islands. The move involved a flight of three hours to the north-west and a closer contact with combat activities. 3 Squadron's main task was to maintain daily patrols of the sea and coast to the west and south-west of the Island, each aircraft being allotted an area 300 miles long outward from the coast, and twenty miles wide at that extreme distance. In this way, four aircraft with a visibility of ten miles could search a fan-shaped combined area the outward perimeter of which stretched for 160 miles.

It was on 4 September 1943, the day of our third patrol, that we sighted a Japanese medium bomber flying ahead of us on a south-easterly bearing, evidently on a similar mission to ours. We identified it as a Mitsubishi G4M, known in allied code as *Betty*. It was a large, twin-engine aircraft developed in the second half of 1937, outclassing its predecessor with regard to speed and range. Although it had a serious design fault in lacking self-sealing fuel tanks – a deficiency which made it vulnerable to combustion when attacked - it nevertheless became the most widely used bomber in the Japanese Air Force, a total of 2,446 being manufactured up to August 1945. The first prototype flew on 23 October 1939, the first mass-produced aircraft leaving the assembly lines in April 1941, well before Japan's attack on Pearl Harbour. In 1942 the G4M2 , a more powerful, better armed and protected version of the aircraft appeared. A total of 1,154 of these were produced. We were unable to distinguish which variant was crossing our path but we did know that both variants could outrun the Hudson. As soon as its crew saw us they turned north-west and retreated at high speed.

Eight days later in the same area we spotted a submarine sailing on the surface in a south-westerly direction. We had not been alerted to any known presence of a Japanese submarine at our briefing but we assumed it was Japanese and prepared to attack it. Its crew must have been keeping a sharp look-out, however. As soon as they spotted us they executed a crash dive quickly and successfully enough to make an attack ineffective. The next day, at a distance, we saw what might have been the same submarine in the same general area, but it dived before we could arrive at a point for attacking it.

On 24 September we were ordered to fly several passengers to Munda, an airstrip on New Georgia in the mid-Solomon Islands. It had been open for only six weeks since American troops captured the Island. We dropped one passenger and picked up four others for the return trip. Resuming our standing patrols, on 5 October we again spotted a G4M or G4M2 flying in a south-easterly direction. This time, however, its crew members were seemingly unaware of our approach until we were less than half a mile away and preparing to do battle. But their aircraft suddenly turned sharply to the north-west, making off at high speed which we could not match. It was disappointing to lack the speed to bring it to battle. In September we had witnessed the doom of two similar aircraft over our own base. They came over one evening at about 4,000 feet, pursued by two Lockheed Lightning fighters of the American Air Force, which caught up with them easily. Both Japanese aircraft burst into flame when attacked and crashed with loud explosions into the jungle. It was learned later that both aircraft were totally wrecked and that there had been no survivors. This particular incursion proved to be the last Japanese air raid on Guadalcanal in the Second World War.

There had been extensive fighting between American and Japanese forces for Guadalcanal between August 1942 and February 1943, with major losses of men and materials on both sides, in a campaign requiring substantial support from the sea and heavy naval losses. In off-duty time I was able to tour some of the recent battle areas where the material debris of war remained undisturbed, although the dead had been buried. In one little bay where I used to swim there were four wrecks left from an engagement between a Japanese force of fourteen warships escorting four troop transports, and an American naval task force, as a result of which the four troop transports were beached. When swimming around two of them I encountered two Americans sitting on a makeshift raft drinking small bottles of beer. They had clearly found them among the stores and equipment on the ships. On seeing more rotting cartons of these bottles, I went to the shore to find something to carry them in back to the base and was fortunate enough to rescue six empty sacks for the purpose. With a little help from a passing American truck, I was able to transport six laden sacks of beer to our tent – enough to last its occupants for a week or two that otherwise would have been dry. Of course my popularity rating soared in our tent at this time.

On 24 October 1943 I flew some passengers for the 500 miles trip to Espiritu Santo. Although our Squadron was in the process of moving back to New Zealand, I stayed on there for a month, resuming convoy escorts and occasionally a search for ships with which contact had been lost. Many vessels kept radio silence as a means of avoiding detection by enemy submarines or aircraft. Towards the end of November 1943, our hopes, as a crew, of returning to New Zealand for Christmas, were dashed when I was told that we were to remain while other crews one by one were returning home on the completion of the Squadron's tour. Our retention was probably due to the fact that previously we had had nearly four weeks of leave in the middle of the tour after taking an aircraft home for a major overhaul. We were assigned to passenger ferrying duties, the first of which was to take Wing Commander Tancred and a civilian to Vila, where we had eight hours off duty to explore the town, but there was little to see of interest.

We took Squadron Leader Grace to Guadalcanal on 13 December, staying overnight and returning the next day without passengers. Diverting a little on the return flight, we looked down with interest at a small coral island called Rennell Island, which was ringed with reefs. There was nothing to be seen from the air of the epic event a year or more earlier, when a squadron of American fighters made a navigation error, flying away from their base out to sea and running out of fuel. It was by the greatest of good fortune that they spotted this remote island in their path. All the pilots baled out or tried to crash land. Their previous radio messages had alerted their base to their plight and direction of flight, so a Catalina was able to rescue the survivors.

The following day we ferried American Navy Captains Greber and Erdman, and our own Squadron Intelligence Officer, Jasper Baldwin, to Nadi in western Fiji. As most of the Squadron had already departed for home, Jasper Baldwin had little work to do but welcomed the opportunity to see Fiji. One of the Americans asked me if he could smoke during the flight. I had no wish to offend him but I knew the risks of fire in an aircraft, so I simply said, "We don't." Fortunately, he abstained for the three hour flight. We later took them on to Nausori the same day, and after an overnight stay brought Captain Greber and Jasper back to Espiritu Santo.

About a week later, as Christmas approached without any remission in the war, we took Wing Commander Price and three other passengers to Ondonga Island in the mid-Solomon Islands, a non-stop flight of four and a half hours. We landed at an airstrip cut out of thick jungle by the Americans about five miles north of Munda, near the western tip of New Georgia. The Island had been recaptured from the Japanese four months before. The next day we returned our passengers to Guadalcanal for an overnight stay before taking them on to Espiritu Santo.

Our ferrying missions resumed on 28 December when we took the Area Commander of the Royal New Zealand Air Force, Air Commodore Buckley – a former Bomber Command pilot and the first Commander of 75 Squadron, the first all-New Zealand bomber squadron in the Royal Air Force - and two of his aides on a tour of some of the New Zealand and American camps in the South Pacific. We flew them to Guadalcanal and then to Ondonga. On leaving Guadalcanal we ran into a tropical storm front, of a kind that had proved fatal to many aircraft during the war. Looking ahead to the possibilities for passing through the storm, I saw one area which looked lighter than the rest and entered the cloud at about 300 metres above the sea, but flew into heavy rain that persisted and became so threatening that I felt obliged to say to the Air Commodore, who was in the co-pilot's seat, "Do you think we should turn back?" He very properly reminded me that, as captain of the aircraft, the decision rested with me. So I turned through 180° away from New Georgia, found a safer alternative route, and landed at Ondonga.

After taking another passenger to Guadalcanal on 4 January 1944 and delivering a Hudson to an American airstrip on Espiritu Santo for repairs, we were given leave to return to New Zealand – one of the last crews of our Squadron to do so. We flew two passengers to Tontouta on 9 January and returned to Whenuapai the following day for three weeks' leave, but mine could not be taken until the next day, after I had flown our Hudson to Rukuhia, Hamilton, for a major overhaul.

After my leave, I reported to Ohakea, where 3 Squadron was newly based, to resume my duties on 8 February 1944. One-man huts had been built for the Officers of the Squadron in a position exposed to the westerly winds, which could be very cold. At this point of the war the Royal New Zealand Air Force discontinued the use of two pilots in its bomber aircraft. I retained two of my former crew, Chum Gardner, the navigator/bomb aimer, and Stu Cullen, the wireless operator/air gunner. To complete the new crew, we three were joined by two air gunners, Harry Marks, and Keith Shivas. The next day we flew as part of a protective screen for the liner *Mariposa* that was on course for Wellington from Australia, taking off at 1630 hours and returning after 2000 hours. The flight was incident free but required a night landing, which had become unfamiliar to me during the preceding months.

The main purpose of our stay at Ohakea was for the Squadron to convert to Ventura aircraft. This newly arrived aircraft had been developed from the Hudson. It was commissioned by the Royal Air Force to embody improvements reflecting the operational experience gained in the Hudson during the latter's first two years of use in the Second World War in Coastal

Command work. Although its debut in Britain was subsequently disappointing, leading to its precipitate withdrawal from operational duties in the European theatre of war, the Ventura proved to be well suited to the conditions prevailing in the Pacific in the war against the Japanese.

The Ventura was a faster, more powerful, and better armed aircraft than the Hudson, and with a longer range. Consequently plenty of work was required for each crew member to become familiar with his work station, and the functions and characteristics of the aircraft. We practiced air to air, and air to ground gunnery, bombing on land and sea, and the full range of flying manoeuvres, which I hoped would ensure that my handling of the aircraft left nothing to be desired.

Duties with the Hudson, however, were not yet over. On 17 February we once more took to the skies by flying in two stages to the far north of the North Island of New Zealand to Kaikohe in the far north of the North Island of New Zealand, where we stayed overnight in a wooden hut. The next morning we flew out to sea to protect a large liner, the *Matsonia*, which was Auckland bound from northern waters, leaving at the early hour of 0410 hours and returning after a four hour patrol to Whenuapai. Sleeping there overnight, we took off again the following afternoon to escort the same liner which had by then docked in Auckland and had set sail again in an easterly direction. For three hours we escorted the ship out into the Pacific before returning to Whenuapai and then to Ohakea.

In a Hudson on 1 March I flew with six passengers and a reduced crew of only the navigator and wireless operator/airgunner as escort for three Grumman Avenger torpedo bombers to Guadalcanal. As with fighter aircraft, Avengers had insufficient navigational capability of their own to undertake long flights alone, so we were there to provide it. After three days in Guadalcanal and with some different passengers on board, we escorted the same Avengers to Norfolk Island, and to Tontouta the next day. Our return journey in several stages with more passengers involved an eight hour flying day from Espiritu Santo to Whenuapai, broken by two fuel stops.

After more passenger carrying in New Zealand I requested a transfer to England, where the war in the air was at its height. My request, however, was turned down. I was told that experienced pilots were still needed in the Pacific – a reply that I thought was intended as a reassuring gesture, but it did not satisfy me.

The Squadron was by now preparing for a combat tour with its new Ventura aircraft. It was at this time that I took my turn to fly a venerable Vincent aircraft as a drogue towing aircraft for practising air to air gunnery. On one day I lost two drogues, probably as a result of their tow lines having been cut by bullets. The training lasted until the end of April 1944, and included formation flying at each sub-unit level up to that of the full Squadron.

As a private initiative one day I put the Ventura through a barrel roll. It was not an authorized manoeuvre for the Ventura. Perhaps I overlooked the fact that although as the pilot I was strapped in, other members of the crew were not normally strapped in during training flights. They were thrown about by the manoeuvre and pinned to the floor at one stage of it. I discovered that the Ventura with plenty of power applied could perform the barrel roll very well. My crew members however voted unanimously that it should not be repeated while they were on board, a view that I respected. I never heard of any other Ventura being put through it, so I was possibly the only pilot - in the Royal New Zealand Air Force at least - ever to have performed it.

As a demonstration of national air strength and a boost to civilian morale, the Royal New Zealand Air Force marshalled over seventy aircraft of various types for a fly past over the city of Auckland in late March 1944. I flew as a passenger in one of the nine Venturas taking part. It seemed to me that I was still as far from taking a direct part in the war as ever. This feeling was modified a little within a few days, however, when I took part with other aircraft of the Squadron in the practice of finding and bombing a real submarine. A United States Navy submarine was made available for this purpose in Cook Strait. On 3 April, with about twenty others, I then went to sea in the same submarine while other Ventura crews searched for us and then bombed us.

We could hear the small practice bombs clanging on the hull. The submarine's Captain told us that he had carried out this practice mission for many allied Air Force units but had found the accuracy of the bombing by New Zealand crews to be of the best. In Fiji their bombing had damaged the vessel's main periscope, reducing them to using their reserve periscope.

I returned to Ohakea on 12 May 1944 to prepare our Ventura for the forthcoming tour, making four-hour test flights, and loading it with our personal gear. Seven days later we departed on a four hour flight to Norfolk Island, followed the next day by further flights to Tontouta and then Espiritu Santo, the familiar stages for getting to the Pacific war zone from New Zealand. On Espiritu Santo we spent over two months either at leisure, exploring the area, in flying training, or practicing our skills - particularly dropping practice bombs on another cooperative United States submarine.

At last, on 27 July, we flew with three passengers to Guadalcanal. We spent some time improving the site, where we were camping in the same quarters that we had used a year before. Some of our Squadron's aircraft had not yet arrived from Espiritu Santo. One of them, piloted by one of the Flight Commanders, Flight Lieutenant Frank Rolston, disappeared en route. Several months later the wreckage of his aircraft and bodies of all the crew were found on Malekula Island, about 100 miles south of Espiritu Santo. The aircraft had crashed in dense jungle well off course. It had probably flown into heavy rain and tried to divert to a safer flight path, but without success.

15 August 1944 was a red letter day. I had carried out many operational missions to date but had never come to direct grips with the enemy. But on that day, I carried the fire to the foe for the first time. We dropped six 100 pound bombs on a Japanese strongpoint on an island near New Georgia. As our target was located in thick jungle, the results of our attack were impossible to see – a frustrating experience shared with many other bomber aircrews in the Pacific.

Only two days later we carried three passengers on a 400 mile transfer flight in a north-west direction to Piva on Bougainville, the scene of large and bitter land battles between Japanese and United States forces between November 1943 and March 1944. We were stationed there for two months, only ninety minutes' flight time from Rabaul, Japan's main stronghold in the South Pacific, and the object of continuous allied attention from the air.

My crew and I flew as passengers - although I was able to stand in as co-pilot - in another Ventura on 31 August 1944 for a mission along the east coast of New Ireland, finding and demolishing a twelve metre bridge. After this, enough aircraft were available for us to undertake repeated patrols over Japanese-held territory in Bougainville and New Ireland, bombing and strafing targets of opportunity, plus some early morning weather reconnaissance missions over Rabaul itself, to report the prevailing conditions to our base.

On returning one day from a five-hour patrol, I landed the aircraft as usual but when I pushed the throttles forward to taxi to the end of the runway and our parking bay, the engines suddenly stopped. Almost at once I realized the reason - I had forgotten to switch the fuel supply from the extra tank carried in the fuselage for long flights to the normal wing tanks. It fortunately occurred on the ground. There could have been a disastrous outcome if it had happened during the landing approach.

The Squadron moved again. On 11 October 1944 we left Piva on a 500 mile flight north-west to Emirau, a normally uninhabited island in the St Matthias Group, about 2,500 miles north-west of New Zealand. We were by this time experienced in moving from camp to camp and had acquired all kinds of things to make life as comfortable as possible, all packed into our aircraft for every change of venue. Four aircraft set out every day to patrol a large area of ocean to the north, in case Japanese reinforcements were being sent to New Ireland, New Britain, or Bougainville in the Solomon Islands.

An urgent diversion intruded on these missions on 9 September, when of three of our Venturas tasked to attack one of

Rabaul's protective airfields, two failed to return. A prolonged search was mounted by the Squadron but nothing was ever found of the aircraft piloted by Roye Stevens. On 12 September, however, the Squadron received a message by circuitous means that the crew of the other missing aircraft, piloted by Fred Thomas, had managed to make a dramatic landing on a very short landing strip, the crew surviving in good health. Their aircraft,was never able to take off again, remaining a prisoner of the jungle for ever. Fred Thomas and his crew were flown in a Catalina to Emirau, then by a land aircraft back to Bougainville.

Having been ordered to undertake a special task on detachment from the Squadron, my crew and I flew back to Bougainville on 23 October 1944. When the Squadron had moved to Emirau, some of its aircraft had been left behind for repairs or routine checks. They had to be test flown before being certified as being in order for Squadron use again. This was the task that fell to us. While we were there we also undertook some combat missions, once supporting fifteen United States dive bombers, and joining in a bombing raid near Rabaul. On 11 November we searched the south coast of New Britain but could find no evidence of Japanese activity to attack.

In easy stages between 25 and 28 November I returned to New Zealand to become an instructor on Ventura aircraft and later to pilot Dakota transport aircraft carrying passengers and freight between Auckland and the Pacific Islands. On 3 January 1945 I was promoted to Flight Lieutenant and subsequently had the opportunity to pilot a Lodestar aircraft to various destinations around New Zealand. Notable passengers on these domestic trips at one time were the members of a well-known American dance band which was making a tour of military bases in the country.

This flying work continued through to the end of October 1945. It included the repatriation of New Zealanders who had been prisoners in Japanese hands. This was a particularly satisfying but harrowing job, taking place virtually as my last flight in the service of the Royal New Zealand Air Force.

Hours in the Air 1941-1945 in the Royal New Zealand Air Force

	As 1st pilot, 2nd pilot or instructor	As pupil	As Passenger	Total
Single-engine aircraft	535	53	2	590
Tiger Moth				
Harvard				
Hind				
Vincent				
Twin-engine aircraft	1605	79	169	1853
Oxford				
Hudson				
Ventura				
Anson				
Lodestar				
Dakota				
Overall totals	2140	132	171	2443

When VJ Day – the day of the Japanese surrender - arrived on 14 August 1945, I was in Auckland. I had been flying up and down to the islands bringing people home in Dakota aircraft, a married man of four months. My wife and I went into the city to find that enormous crowds had gathered everywhere. The scene was a spontaneous and understandable reaction to the stresses and strains of six long years of war for New Zealand.

Although I did consider becoming a civil airline pilot, I was happy to give up the Air Force and return to accountancy. After having returned to my old job in the accountancy firm for twelve months, I moved to Wellington as Secretary at the Institute of Chartered Accountants, being responsible inter alia for publishing its monthly journal. Seven years later I came back to the accountancy firm of Nicholls, North and Nicholls, in Christchurch, as a partner. I retired at sixty-two from the firm but took a job at the Canterbury District Law Society, holding it until I was seventy-eight, working on lawyers' Trust Accounts. In having to be in touch with many law firms in that job, I found that none of them properly obeyed the rules.

Well before the war had ended - on 3 April 1945 - Peg and I married in Auckland. Since then we have lived mainly in Christchurch and have four children, eight grandchildren, and a great grandchild. David farms at Rangiora, Denise is a freelance consultant psychologist at Redcliffs, Peter is a builder and photographer at Lyttelton, and Warren works in Wellington in commerce. I continue to enjoy simple activities like walking the dog, going into town, and picking up leaves in the garden. I have been fortunate to have had good health. For many years I enjoyed playing cricket as a batsman and wicket keeper, but I gave it up forty years ago. It has been a long life – but a good one.

~ ~ ~

Jim Tocker flew as pilot in the following aircraft, listed in experiential order.

> Tiger Moth
> Oxford
> Harvard
> Hind
> Vincent
> Anson
> Hudson
> Ventura
> Lodestar
> Dakota

Photographs and the specifications of these aircraft may be found in Part 2, listed in alphabetical order.

Jim Tocker at Harewood as Flying Instructor, March 1942

Hudson in revetment, Whenuapai, New Zealand. Note armed patrol of the site in expectation of possible Japanese invasion, January 1943

This photograph shows the method adopted by the Royal New Zealand Air Force for ferrying fighter aircraft from New Zealand to distant combat stations in the Pacific. Taken in stages, a larger aircraft with a specialist navigator– in this case a Hudson bomber in 1943 – provided the comprehensive navigational capability that the fighters lacked

A completed new airstrip with a second under construction on Ondonga in the Mid-Solomon Islands November 1943. Note the Hudson on the left coming in to land, and two Catalina flying boats at their berths on the water

**A Japanese Zero fighter shot down at Munda in the
Mid-Solomon Islands, December 1943**

**Ventura in 1944. Note the torpedo-shaped extra fuel tank under
each wing and the twin, rear pointing belly guns under the tail**

Venturas in formation, each flying on its port engine only – a photograph believed to have been taken on a publicity flight over Auckland on 21 June 1945 by aircraft from Number 1 Bomber Operational Training Unit

Ventura and crew in April 1944 at Ohakea, New Zealand. L-R: Sergeant Keith Shivas, gunner; Warrant Officer Chum Gardner, navigator/ bomb aimer; Flying Officer Jim Tocker, pilot; Warrant Officer Stuart Cullen, wireless operator/gunner; and Flying Officer Harold Moss, gunner

Morning tea at Bougainville Officers' Camp, September 1944.
L-R: Pat Dignan, Bob Bruce, Fred Thomas, Ted Manthorp
(Adjutant), Hamish Wilson, Rex O'Rourke, Ken Lumsden,
Neville Joynt (Navigator), Ian Rowe (Operations Officer), and
Keith Wilby. The seven men not identified by occupation were
pilots

Ventura over Green Island, an important allied base 130 miles
east of Rabaul, New Britain. The view is looking south-east
over the island to the open sea, with the lagoon below

Part of Green Island atoll showing two landing strips, called Ocean Strip and Lagoon Strip, looking north-west. They were constructed by American Sea Bees (Construction Battalions) within a month of the capture of the atoll by the New Zealand 3ʳᵈ Division on 15 February 1944

Ventura and crew with a passenger at Ohakea, New Zealand, 1944. Jim Tocker is fourth from the left

Wedding Day, 3 April 1945

3 Squadron Reunion, 2 April 1981 at Whenuapai, New Zealand.
Jim Tocker is forth from the right in the back row. In fifth place
is Ian Morrison, a former Head of the Royal New Zealand Air
Force

Chapter 11.

Man of Many Parts

Dave Wilkie

Man of Many Parts

My twin brother Hugh and I were born in Raetihi, in what was called the King Country, on 11 January 1923. Unknown to the family at that time our date of birth was just right to make us eligible – in the event of our survival until that time - for military service at the outset of the Second World War, the war that no one anticipated. We both became aviators but my brother was killed. Having completed a tour of twenty-eight missions, taking 567 hours of operational flying, as pilot on Stirling bombers in 15 Squadron of the Royal Air Force, Hugh was posted as an instructor to Stradishall in Suffolk. The loss rate of Stirlings was high as the aircraft's service ceiling was low relative to that of the Halifax and Lancaster, making them more vulnerable to the enemy defences but also subject to destruction from the bombs falling from friendly aircraft flying at higher altitudes. So the manner of his death was particularly poignant – and, from my point of view, particularly disquieting.

In a Mark 111 Stirling, EJ108, at the Number 1657 Heavy Conversion Unit of the Royal Air Force, Stradishall, Suffolk, in November 1944, Hugh was taking off on an instructional flight at 2235 hours, when he struck and killed three Americans on bicycles as they illegally rode across the runway. No one will ever know if they did this inadvertently or deliberately, perhaps out of bravado, but the point at which they crossed the runway was at a distance from the approaching Stirling that amounted to an act of the utmost folly. Hugh was already committed to the take off. Once in the air, having reported the accident, he was ordered to land at Woodbridge, at a distance of forty-two miles from Stradishall, for a damage assessment. Simultaneously the crew heard a loud noise after which the aircraft immediately began to climb out of control. Hugh ordered the seven trainee bomber crew members to bale out on reaching sufficient height. Six of them successfully completed a landing but their engineer fell out of his improperly adjusted parachute harness and was killed.

Hugh and the flight engineer as their instructors stayed aboard in an attempt to land the aircraft but it crashed out of control at 2330 hours near Little Glenham, seven miles north-east of Woodbridge. At the scene of the collision on the runway at Stradishall, a dinghy cover and a dinghy's emergency rations were discovered, indicating that a wing had been damaged and that the aircraft's dinghy had been released. The dinghy had in fact flown free but remained attached to the aircraft. In wrapping itself around the tail, it had prevented the normal control of the aircraft, leading to ultimately fatal consequences. Both men were killed. Hugh was still only twenty-one and had been awarded the Distinguished Flying Cross on completing his operational tour.

This bizarre accident was certainly rare but not unique, insofar as the destructive effect of a released dinghy in flight was concerned. After the cessation of hostilities in May 1945, a Lancaster bomber was returning to the United Kingdom with repatriated prisoners-of-war when one of them – presumably in a moment of euphoria or inquisitive exploration – apparently pulled the emergency handle located inside the fuselage of the aircraft for releasing the dinghy. The aircraft crashed killing all on board, the dinghy being found wrapped around its tail.

In September 2000, Frank Diamond DFC, AE, Hugh's navigator and friend during his tour on Stirlings, took the trouble to travel all the way from his home in Norfolk, England, to find the family of his lost friend. For me his visit was a poignant experience after so many years without my twin.

My father had a farm of 10,000 acres, at Ore Ore, near Raetihi. It was nearly all bush, but usable for sheep and cattle. Hugh and I were born on the farm. We were a large family in the custom of the times, consisting of three daughters and six sons, Hugh and I being sixth and seventh in seniority. Four of the others are still alive – my eldest sister at a great age in Hastings, an older sister in Wanganui, and two brothers in Tauranga. When I was a year old the family moved to Taranaki, where we had a dairy farm at Okaiawa. Milk was taken in cans by horse drawn wagons to the local dairy factory. In 1928 when I was five years old, the family moved again – this time to a dairy farm at Wangaehu, near

Wanganui. With my twin brother Hugh, and older brothers Ted and Jim, I attended Wangaehu School, during which time the terrible earthquake that destroyed Napier took place. These were years of economic depression, making life for our family very hard.

The farm was owned by my maternal grandmother. When we moved yet again to another dairy farm at Turakina, my oldest brother Donald remained behind to manage it. It is still in family hands today, being managed by my nephew John Wilkie. At Turakina, Hugh and I completed our primary schooling before travelling daily by train to the Martin District High School, my own attendance there lasting only six months.

Father was a beekeeper as well as a dairy farmer. He processed the honey with family help. He used a hot blade to remove the comb, and a centrifuge to extract the honey. We ate our own honey. When my father retired during the later 1930s, he and mother moved to a house in the village near the church. As a teenager I went back to Ore Ore to work on my aunt's farm for several years, staying with her until I enlisted.

One of my earliest recollections of the Second World War was finding out that a cousin had undertaken a correspondence course to qualify for aircrew service in the Royal New Zealand Air Force. He was subsequently offered a fast track training opportunity in the Royal Navy Fleet Air Arm, but on his way to Britain the ship he was sailing in was captured by a German surface raider. Many of the people on it were put ashore on Emirau Island in the north of the Bismarck Archipelago, but most of the military personnel on it, my cousin among them, were taken as prisoners-of-war to Germany. For them it had been a short – if eventful – war. Another cousin went into the Army.

My aunt wanted to keep me back from military service. She applied for my exemption on the grounds that I was in an essential industry. Nevertheless I volunteered in 1941 for the Air Force. I undertook the required correspondence course but found it difficult. I am not sure that I completed it, but I still got in. My twin brother had already preceded me into the Air Force a year earlier.

He trained in New Zealand and was on his final leave – the last time I was destined to see him – just before I reported for service in the Air Force, where I was given the number NZ422955. I spent time at Wigram and also Rotorua for classroom studies. The classes were good for me because I was never good at mathematics in school but it became clear I would be air crew straight away. After completing my induction into the Air Force and the preliminary ground school studies, I had to go overseas for my air training under the Empire Flying Training Scheme, where I flew for the first time. During my training I flew variously in Fort, Anson, and Bolingbroke aircraft.

In January 1943 I went for this training to Canada, arriving at the Number 3 Wireless School at Winnipeg for the first part of it. Our air exercises were carried out at Stevenson Field in basic wireless training and Morse Code, for which we had to achieve so many words a minute. The next stage of training was at the Number 8 Bombing and Gunnery School at Lethbridge, Alberta, in western Canada in July 1943. After that the next posting was to the Number 7 Air Observer School at Portage la Prairie, Manitoba, in August 1943. I finally completed my training at the Number 5 Air Observer School at Winnipeg, Manitoba, between October and December 1943. At this point I was awarded my wing and promoted to Sergeant.

By this time in the Second World War, resources were increasingly needed in the Pacific for the monumental task of winning back the vast conquests of the islands which the Japanese had achieved during 1942. Whereas so many of my fellow New Zealanders who had been through the aircrew training programmes in Canada had been exclusively posted to operational duties in the United Kingdom, for the rest of the war after Japan's entry into it on 7 December 1941, a proportion of newly trained aircrew personnel was allocated to the Pacific. Consequently, I was posted back to New Zealand early in January 1944 with my sights set on serving with the Royal New Zealand Air Force. I actually spent Christmas 1943 on the train travelling westwards across Canada to Vancouver, from where I continued by train down the west coast of the United States via Seattle to San Francisco to embark for my home country.

After some welcome leave in New Zealand, I was posted as a fully trained wireless operator/gunner to the only dive bomber squadron to operate in the Royal New Zealand Air Force. With others, in February 1944, I joined 25 Squadron at the Operational Training Unit at Ardmore, flying Dauntless dive bombers. The Squadron's Commanding Officer was Squadron Leader Theo de Lange. My pilot, Flying Officer Adrian Hayman, and I were assigned to Flight Lieutenant Bob Penniket's Flight of four aircraft. These small aircraft had amassed a good reputation by that time in the Pacific war as a result of their successes when operating from United States aircraft carriers against the Japanese fleets during 1942. They had a crew of two. The pilot released the aircraft's bombs during the dive and had control of the forward firing guns. He also had to undertake most of the navigation but the wireless operator/air gunner also acted as observer and provided the pilot with drift readings and radio bearings, and operated the dorsal guns.

25 Squadron had been formed at Seagrove, near Auckland, on 31 July 1943, initially with only nine aircraft on loan from the United States Marine Corps unit also stationed at Seagrove, the intention being to supply the Squadron with a full complement of eighteen aircraft and their crews at a later date. Building the Squadron and training occupied the second half of 1943, culminating with a celebratory fly past over Auckland City of eighteen Dauntless aircraft on the morning of 6 January 1944, led by Squadron Leader Theo de Lange. At that time it was the largest formation of aircraft that had ever been seen over the city, arousing great interest in the population.

Adrian Hayman and I were assigned to the Reserve Flight for the move to the islands. The main part of the Squadron with forty-one crew members had already left for Bougainville on 29 January 1944. They flew in three Lodestar aircraft and at least one Dakota of 40 Squadron via Norfolk Island to Pallikulo on Espiritu Santo Island. After more extensive training the eighteen aircraft moved on to Henderson Field, Guadalcanal on 22 March, before moving forward to Piva on Bougainville the following day.

The latest arrivals including me were formed into three crews. There was talk of making us the basis for a second Dauntless squadron, Number 26, but on 13 November this idea was shelved. The dive bomber was a diminishing asset at a time when hundreds of fighters were being released from fighter duties as the Allies gained mastery of the air, and large numbers of fighter bombers were available to do the job as effectively. On 21 March 1944 I was sent for training with the American Army Air Force before joining the rest of the Squadron on 14 April 1944 on Bougainville. Two days later I took off on my first operational flight.

I completed one tour in the Dauntless, including eighteen operational missions, before returning on 21 May 1944 to Whenuapai, New Zealand. The Dauntless Number 25 Squadron was then disbanded, all the available crews being assigned to other duties. In August 1944 I was posted to the Number 1 Bomber Operational Training Unit at Ohakea for conversion to the Ventura. In October I was posted to Number 4 Bomber Reconnaissance Ventura medium bomber Squadron in which I completed a second tour, serving first in Fiji until 24 November and then on Emirau Island when the Squadron moved there for combat missions. These lasted until 10 February 1945 when I was posted back to New Zealand.

We frequently flew operationally with the United States Army Air Force for combined attacks. Typically the Dauntless Squadron provided a dozen planes out of a total of about 100 in the air. Maintaining twelve aircraft for service put an enormous strain on ground crews, especially in view of the fact that the total number of aircraft at the Squadron's disposal by that time had dropped to fifteen. Several had been lost in accidents. One was a write off having swerved on landing at Henderson Field on the way to combat stations and hit an oil barrel.

All our operations were against prescribed located land targets, primarily against Rabaul but also some targets on Bougainville itself. The Japanese had a ring of airfields in the

Rabaul area, all well protected by anti-aircraft guns. Our job was to dive bomb the gun emplacements while the accompanying New Zealand Avengers or a wide variety of American medium bombers or fighter bombers attacked the airfields, especially their runways. Gun sites were inevitably as concealed as possible so that it was usually necessary to pinpoint the gun flashes first to identify the target. It was not unheard of for attacking Dauntless aircraft actually to dive down the stream of gunfire from the ground to ensure an accurate bombing strike, although the risk of doing so was tantamount to the foolhardy at times. Fortunately the Japanese gunners were sometimes taken by surprise, but if not, their accuracy could be vitiated by the imminent threat of death and destruction in their being at the end of the dive.

Attacks against Rabaul required up to four hours of flying, usually in the mornings. Area targets such as supply yards and runways - as opposed to specific sites - were usually glide bombed. Without the use of air brakes, aircraft were put into a shallow dive of about 45° at 4,000 feet, the bomb being released at 1,500 feet. The aircraft then pulled out of the glide at 1,000 feet. The bomb load was usually one 1,000 pound bomb but could be one 500 pound and two x 250 pound bombs. In addition we often carried two x 100 pound bombs. On one occasion, 10 April 1944, 100 rounds of defective .303 ammunition were tied around our 100 pound bombs to give greater effect to the shrapnel cover.

On 16 April we took part as one of twelve aircraft from 25 Squadron in an attack on the runways and gun positions at Vunakanau during which ninety-six hits were scored on the runways. The following day we attacked gun positions and runways at Lakunai amid intense anti-aircraft fire which brought down one of our aircraft and damaged another to the point of its being a write off. We were tasked on 19 April against gun positions and supply areas on Matupi Island. The attack was led by 25 Squadron but after a flight of 100 miles into the mission we all had to turn back in the face of bad weather. On 23 April a mission against Rabaul also had to turn back because of bad weather. An attack against gun positions near Lakunai airfield on 25 April was executed but one of our twelve aircraft was damaged by flak. Six aircraft were assigned for an attack against a supply area at Rataval. Despite poor weather conditions the attack was pressed home but with only limited success, which included, however, a direct hit on a petrol dump and a huge explosion. Military installations on Rantan Island, South Bougainville, were attacked on 7 May by six of our aircraft but the dive bombing was hampered by bad weather. Another of our aircraft was lost on 10 May after being hit during an attack on gun positions at Lakunai. It had been hit on pulling out of its dive and crashed into Great Harbour.

The following day the task force sent to attack Vunakanau was compelled by bad weather to seek alternative targets at Tobera and Marawaka, south of Piva. The very next day targets all over the Rabaul region were assigned to us, from Talili Bay to beyond Raluana Point. We provided twelve aircraft, one of which was damaged. Some of the United States aircraft involved were firing rockets against barge traffic. We all landed at Green Island on the way home to re-arm and refuel for an attack on other targets on the coast south of Sorum. 14 May was an unusual day in that, after we had attacked Vunakanau again, Japanese fighter aircraft were seen five miles away doing slow rolls and steep climbing turns. They seemed to be engrossed in their aerobatics. They made no attempt to intercept us. The following day I was in one of the six aircraft sent to bomb a supply area at Chabai in the north of Bougainville but we had to turn for home when engine trouble developed, leaving the other five aircraft to carry out the attack, which they successfully accomplished. On 16 May four aircraft of the Squadron glide bombed the supply area near Tobera. Two of our aircraft had to turn back with engine malfunctions. We all four managed to achieve direct hits on the target.

Four days later on 20 May 1944, all the seventeen remaining aircraft took off from Piva for the last time and landed at Renarde in the Russell Islands, from which the aircrews were flown to Guadalcanal. The following day we all boarded Dakotas for a thirteen hours' flight to New Zealand via Tontouta.

My lasting memories of the eighteen operations in the Dauntless are mostly from the approach to the target. We used to fly to the target area at 14,000 feet but adopted a high speed shallow dive down to 10,000 feet at which point the dive brakes were opened and we plunged at a full dive towards the precise target itself. I could look over the side of the aircraft to see the flashes from enemy guns and then the explosions of the shells. But above all else for me it was an electrifying experience as a wireless operator/ air gunner in a Dauntless during a near vertical dive to the target to be hurtling earthwards backwards, sitting in the rear seat with my back to the pilot. Once the aircraft had been committed to the dive, I was inevitably looking upwards into the sky to witness the explosions and smoke of the ack-ack that had been aimed at us but had passed us by. It was always comforting to see this array, knowing that the shots had all failed to arrive at their intended destination.

Aircraft followed each other down at close intervals and sometimes attacked a target in a V-formation of three. During a dive, the aircraft's longitudinal axis was actually vertical, but owing to lift and wind effects the dive angle was usually 75°. It began by flying slightly to one side of the target at around 10,000 feet and when abreast of it pushing over the vertical and rotating onto the target with the use of the ailerons. By opening the dive brakes the aircraft could dive at a speed of about 300 mph. The pilot released the bomb at 2,500 feet and then pulled out of the dive to level off low on the jungle canopy, at which point I could machine gun anything that looked a likely target. This could be the sources from which tracers were coming, or a hut, or a little boat on the beach. I never saw a Japanese soldier. The Americans had by then gained mastery of the air, offering Hellcats or Corsairs as our escorts. In addition New Zealand fighter pilots were always on the prowl in Kittyhawks and Corsairs, so we were well protected. Although most of my operational missions were against Rabaul and its defences, the targets were not always its anti-aircraft guns. We also used to spray their vegetable gardens with oil to deny them food supplies. As supplies by sea became increasingly difficult for the Japanese garrison in Rabaul, they had to depend on subsistence measures to feed themselves.

For me, in facing skywards in the dive, it was a unique sensation to be plunging backwards, but my seat always gave me a feeling of security and support. Only once were we hit by anti-aircraft fire, which caused a small hole near my cockpit. The twin Browning .303 machine guns jammed quite frequently. This could happen at the most inconvenient times. The precious seconds taken to re-cock the guns usually meant a target forgone or at least a reduction in the number of rounds I was able to fire at it.

Since very few aircrew members other than Americans served in Dauntless dive bombers, I feel a certain amount of satisfaction from having had such an unusual experience. The Dauntless was a successful failure. It made a contribution to the war effort in the air in the Pacific by the Royal New Zealand Air Force by helping to neutralize the important Japanese base at Rabaul. It was a solid aircraft and could take punishment but it was a little slow. Its use was brief but effective.

On my return to New Zealand I had to bid farewell to my pilot, Flying Officer A W B Hayman, who I believe settled in Christchurch after the war and lived until 2001. I underwent the conversion course to Ventura aircraft and was posted to 4 Squadron, which had previously been designated a General Reconnaissance Squadron but had become a Bomber Reconnaissance Squadron. I was first based at Fiji in October 1944 for more training, patrols, and shipping searches. The purpose of shipping searches was the identification of our own ships as well as that of enemy ships, and particularly a search for enemy submarines. We didn't undertake convoy escorting. We moved successively on to Tonga, Tabu, and then to Emirau Island in the Bismarck Archipelago. This last base was the springboard for attacks on New Ireland. New Ireland was divided into three parts for bombing operations – a northern section, a central section, and a southern section. We operated in the middle section for our bombing missions.

We had specific targets, all on land, both coastal and inland. A few houses that we found still standing were blown to bits. We also dropped depth charges on the vegetable gardens and other crops being cultivated by Japanese troops. I completed forty-two operational missions in the Ventura, taking 125 hours, eighteen of the missions being strikes – the same number as I had flown in the Dauntless.

My overall total of operational flying hours was 780 – made up of 676 by day and 104 by night during a total of sixty operational missions – eighteen in the Dauntless dive bomber, eight out of Fiji in the Ventura, and thirty-four from Emirau Island in the Ventura.

I returned finally from 4 Squadron to New Zealand on a C47 Dakota aircraft as a passenger, from Emirau Island via Espiritu Santo to Whenuapai in the North Island of New Zealand. Personnel travelled to and from the Islands of the Pacific by Dakota in this way. Operational aircraft were left at their base while a whole Squadron's aircrews could be rotated for a rest, retraining, a conversion course, or discharge.

I was discharged early in 1945. Having never considered the possibility of staying on in the Air Force, I took the leave due to me and thought about returning to civilian employment. At first I was attracted back to farming, becoming a sharemilker for a farmer in the North Island before working at another farm for an old lady whose husband had died. Her brother later came from Canada to take over the farm, but I stayed with him for a while as his knowledge of farming was limited. I then worked at a butter factory for two or three years, obtaining my cream grading ticket while I was there. My final job in farming followed at a dairy farm before I decided to move to Wellington in 1951 and establish myself in city life.

My wife Keita, whom I married in 1946, was already converted from the country to the town. She had been brought up in the country but loved the town and was particularly attracted to Wellington. When I considered taking a shepherd's job away out in the wild, my wife flatly said, "I'm not going up there." So I had to submit to town life. We had four children – Peter, Charles, Joy, and Debbie, born in that order. The elder son is a photographer in Sydney. The youngest son is in Opotiki, New Zealand, where he and his wife run 'Energy Options', a charity firm, advising on insulating houses and ecologically friendly fires. My two daughters both live in New Zealand, Joy in Otaki, and Debbie in Tauranga.

When we came to Wellington we lived with my wife's family, paying rent for five years. In 1956 the old lady who lived in the house I now live in - where I have lived ever since that year - went to hospital. The house was put up for auction. At the time I had a modest income derived from working at Kilbirnie, rolling a bowling green. I went to the auctioneer to find out how much this house was likely to sell for and came out having bought it. My lawyer arranged a loan of 1,000 pounds sterling to buy the house.

Since then I have had a variety of odd jobs. When I first came to Wellington I worked on the waterfront, then for a car painter, undersealing motor cars for anti-rust and protection to the underbody from flying stones. It was hard work on a bonus basis.

A major move for me came when I went to work at the Miramar Gas Works. It was a filthy job, giving a good income, but after a while I tired of the shift work. I worked at the Watergas Plant to process the coke, producing gas of a low quality but which was injected with oil to improve its quality. I later moved from there into the engine room, where I attained a first class engine driver's qualification whilst working on the job. By then I was in my forties. When natural gas was piped out of New Plymouth the old method of producing it became obsolescent and put us out of work. That's when I first heard the word 'redundancy'. But I obtained government employment, first at Bowen State Building, then at other nearby government buildings, looking after the air conditioning and hot water boilers for the heating. I retired at the obligatory age of sixty.

The twenty-three years since then in retirement have been busy. I started part-time work with a furniture company, making the morning tea for the staff and keeping the tea room clean, but employment seemed to grow on me. Four hours a day became eight and in a few more weeks I was working full time again. I love to read books, the financial papers, and the daily papers, and take a regular interest in international affairs. Since my wife died in 2004 I have maintained my own house, including outside painting, and looking after the garden. I have been fortunate with my health. The prostate cancer that appeared ten years ago I have been able to combat but I recognize that I have been slowing down.

Since 1945, 25 Squadron has held a number of reunions combined with 25 Dive Bomber/Fighter Service Unit. Venues have included Blenheim, Christchurch, and several times in Wellington, the latter being the most central venue for personnel from both the main islands. With the greatly reduced numbers attending and the death of the Commanding Officer, Theo de Lange, they came to an end some years ago. At the last one I attended, Bruce Cullen from Auckland and I were the only former aircrew members present.

The feature of my long life since my wartime service that has given me most satisfaction has been my continued interest in flying. After the war I joined the Territorial Air Force in a radar unit but I had to surrender my wartime rank of Warrant Officer for the junior rank of Leading Aircraftman. I took civilian flying lessons in a wartime Tiger Moth with Wanganui Aero Club, an aircraft that had been sold by the government for civilian use, and went solo on it after four hours and twenty-five minutes with an instructor. That first solo flight on 25 June 1950, in Tiger Moth ZK-AIZ, was memorable for me in more ways than one. I had not flown for eleven months. The Chief Flying Instructor, Ken Fenwick, and I met for the first time that day, yet he sent me into the air. It took three attempts to land. My first approach was too low. The second was too high. The third time I made a greasy landing on the grass.

I finally achieved my pilot's licence on 10 April 1964 in a Piper Cub PA 18 with Wellington Aero Club. Apart from its reminding me of all my wartime flying, I was pleased to achieve this as a tribute to my brother who was denied the chance of a life so unnecessarily.

~~~

Dave Wilkie flew as wireless operator/air gunner in the following aircraft, listed in experiential order.

Fort
Bolingbroke
Anson
Dauntless
Ventura

Photographs and the specifications of these aircraft may be found in Part 2, listed in alphabetical order.

Dave Wilkie at Stevenson Field, Winnipeg, on the Number 39
Course for the training of wireless operators, beside a Canadian
Fleet Fort aircraft used for this purpose

Wireless operator/air gunners of 4 General Reconnaissance Squadron converting to Ventura aircraft at the Bomber Operational Training Unit at Ohakea in August 1944. L-R back row: Pilot Officer Howell; Pilot Officer Leatham; Pilot Officer Shaw; Flight Sergeant White; Sergeant Mitchell; Sergeant Blank; Warrant Officer Connelly; Warrant Officer Brown. L-R front row: Pilot Officer Shanahan; Sergeant Anderton; Warrant Officer Silver; Sergeant Hinty; Sergeant Northmore; Sergeant Burgess; Flight Sergeant Wilkie

Number 4 Bomber Reconnaissance Squadron at Emirau Island late in 1944. Flight Sergeant Dave Wilkie is fourth, and his pilot, Sergeant Trevor Adams, is third, from the right hand end of the back row. Their navigator, Sergeant Hugh Kelleher, is at the extreme left hand end of the third row from the front

Wartime Tiger Moth in civilian ownership and freshly painted
as used for post-war private pilot training

Officers of Number 4 BR Squadron at Emirau, November 1944

Dave Wilkie in 1964 with the Piper Cub PA18 BTV aircraft he
flew in training for his private pilot's licence, which he
achieved in a similar aircraft BQN

Chapter 12

Navigating Different Fields

Jack Wright

Navigating Different Fields

Being a fourth generation New Zealander is a matter of some pride for me. My great grandparents on my father's side of the family, in coming to New Zealand from Cornwall, were true pioneers among those who laid the foundations of what New Zealand has become. On my mother's side, my great grandparents hailed from Scotland and Ireland.

I was born on 16 April 1923 in Hamilton. I grew up there with my younger brother and sister, completing my schooling at the local Primary School and then at Hamilton High School. On leaving high school I took a job in the Department of Justice in Hamilton as a Cadet, employed from 8 April 1940 on elementary clerical work in the Courts. Even before I had started work, New Zealand found itself at war after 3 September 1939, so the expectation for me as for every other young man in his upper teens was to be called up for military service sooner or later. I became eligible on reaching my eighteenth birthday and was eventually ordered to report to the Army for initial training in September 1941, but as I was transferred in my civil service job to Tauranga, my military service was postponed until January 1942.

Before enlistment, I found that I was allocated to a medical unit but this was not to my liking. I applied for a transfer, but the Colonel in command - who had the job of building a new unit - was naturally unwilling to permit comings and goings. On discussing the matter with my father, I discovered that he knew that the Army needed clerks. Consequently, on the first day of my arrival at Kensington Camp, Whangarei, when the range of duties was explained, I held my hand up for the Orderly Room – a job which clearly did not appeal to the majority. I was duly assigned to the job and within a few months I was promoted to the rank of Sergeant. The Orderly Room was the name given to the office for the administration of the whole unit. The term had its origins in the British Army in the old colonial days. The title was misleading in nature but was continued in use as the title for the administrative centre and hub of any Army unit. It was the place where personnel reported on arriving at the unit, where records were kept, and where overall control of ongoing events was exercised.

Although the job content in itself was not irksome to me, as I had already committed myself to clerical work when I joined the staff of the Department of Justice in Hamilton as a junior, and although as a Sergeant my pay was very attractive, being in excess of my wages in the Courts, I fundamentally felt ill at ease in the Army. I had originally wanted to join the Air Force but my father withheld the parental consent that was needed for applicants under the age of twenty-one. My father had been in the First World War, spending his twentieth birthday on the ocean bound for the war in Egypt. I wanted to do the same. Under pressure from my earnest pleas, he eventually signed my papers. Evidently, the demand for aircrew members took precedence over other commitments to the extent that I transferred out of the Army into the Air Force in September 1942. I had to report to the Aerodrome Defence Unit at Milsom, near Palmerston North, where, after induction procedures had been completed, I settled down to a routine of two days of classroom studies, one day of fatigues, and one day on guard duty.

At the end of the year I was sent home on leave from which I went to the Initial Training Wing at Rotorua from 1 January 1943 until the beginning of March. The work there was confined to elementary aeronautical studies in the classroom. After more leave I was ordered to report to Wellington at the end of March. A few days later I boarded the USS *Monticello,* which crossed the Pacific Ocean war zone safely to arrive at the Panama Canal. I had my twentieth birthday in Panama City. The ship then passed through the Canal and commenced its long voyage northwards across the Caribbean Sea to the western Atlantic Ocean en route for New York. The ship ahead of us through the Panama Canal from Curacao had been torpedoed, so we were on high alert. We reached New York just before Easter, docking at Staten Island, where we were met by Royal Canadian Air Force Officers. Our number included 250 New Zealanders and 100 Australians.

When we disembarked into the dockside sheds, the mood of everyone was expectant and excited in anticipation of leave in New York after the Easter Parades. Contrary to all our hopes, however, the windows and doors of the train were locked. We were railroad prisoners being firmly transported away from the fleshpots of New York to our serious preparations to be airmen in Canada, travelling overnight by train in sleepers across Canada, through Winnipeg to Brandon, Manitoba, fifty of us staying at Brandon. We wanted leave to go into Winnipeg, where former Royal Flying Corps members who had flown in the First World War had set up an organization with their daughters and friends to meet every aircrew trainee to ensure him of a welcome and offer generous hospitality.

I was posted to Number 5 Air Observers' School, Winnipeg, where at long last I actually came into contact with a real aircraft, and the chance of taking to the air - which had been the mainspring of my determination to enlist in the Air Force. The day's work consisted pretty regularly of ground school for half a day and flying for half a day. The classroom studies introduced more advanced subjects in the field of navigation. The flying consisted of exercises to implement and apply the knowledge gained in the classroom. The aircraft in use was the Avro Anson, famed for its stability and benign characteristics as a flying machine. Two erstwhile navigators usually accompanied the pilot. It fell to the task of one of the trainees to cope with the one famous disability of the Anson. The Mark 1 of this aircraft was bereft of a mechanical means to raise the undercarriage. It had to be laboriously wound up by hand, requiring over 300 turns of a winch. The best that can be said for this mighty chore was that it enabled a trainee to get some physical exercise and keep fit.

All the pilots were Canadians, mostly known as 'bush pilots', reflecting their pre-war occupation in the back blocks engaged in agricultural work of one kind and another. The people on the station were Canadian Pacific Railways personnel drafted into war work for the purpose. After spending a while in hospital, I was granted leave to spend time with a family I had met, which lived in St Paul, Minnesota. When I returned to Winnipeg, I finally graduated on 31 October 1943, but later than my friends, as I had lost time through hospitalization and mid-course leave. For my end of course leave, I travelled to Duluth, Minnesota, the port city at the extreme western end of Lake Superior, to see the family of a boy with whom I had exchanged stamps during my growing up years in New Zealand. I returned for a second visit to the family in St Paul before taking the train to New York to sample the sights, sounds, smells, and excitement of the city which had been denied me on arriving there by ship. After a few days, I caught a bus to Montreal, and then took a train to Nova Scotia, where large numbers of newly qualified navigators and other aircrew members were assembled while waiting for onward transport by sea either to the European or Pacific theatres of war. So many of them were destined never to retrace their steps to their homelands.

After a few days twenty of us were sent back to New Zealand, mostly from the Number 7 Air Observers' School. One other man and I argued that being from Number 5 Air Observers' School, we should not be included in the group. We were given the chance to change but we accepted orders. In retrospect our decision to do so probably increased our percentage chances of survival as our alternative destination would have been Europe, where the loss rate in Bomber Command became horrendous during 1943. The members of my course - other than the two of us who went to the Pacific - were posted to Europe.

It was nothing if not an interesting but circuitous train journey by which I was dispatched from Halifax, Nova Scotia, on the Atlantic seaboard in the far east of Canada, to San Francisco on the Pacific Coast of California. We were put in a railway carriage which was attached to a variety of trains, taking a week to progress via Montreal, Quebec, Chicago, Kansas City, Albuquerque, and finally to San Francisco. I actually spent a whole month in that famous latter city, based at Fort McDowell on Angel Island, before embarking on the USS *General John Pope* for a voyage of two weeks to Noumea in New Caledonia. The ship was used for troop carrying United States forces engaged in the war against the Japanese, which I too was on my way to join. I spent Christmas of

1943 in Noumea before being transported by air in a United States Army Air Force Dakota to Auckland.

After some leave I was posted to Ohakea, where the Operations Officer wanted to see my log book and astro-navigation records. Apparently I was wanted as a replacement for a New Zealand trained navigator who had been stood down. On completing a conversion training course there, I was posted to Number 3 Squadron, flying PV1 Venturas and Hudsons. We took our own aircraft to the war zone. At the last moment during a flight over Wanganui I asked the pilot to dip the aircraft as a signal to my girl friend Connie to tell her I was on my way.

Our route was via Whenuapai in New Zealand, then Norfolk Island, and Espiritu Santo, a major American base, where we stayed a while for training flights. Our combat posting took the Squadron first to Guadalcanal where we undertook acclimatization measures, flying training in tropical conditions, and patrols in earnest. On the whole, living conditions were difficult in the islands. Guadalcanal in particular was a depressingly primitive place. With tropical rain storms there could be mud everywhere, accompanied by a formidable heat. Diseases and dangerous insects constantly threatened all of us as temporary residents. We took our own aircraft to the airstrips at Piva on the west side of Bougainville. I was subsequently put on detachment at Green Island, before finishing off the tour based on Emirau Island in the north of the Bismarck Archipelago.

On returning to New Zealand at the end of my first tour, I completed a general reconnaissance course at New Plymouth. Two of us on the course were Canadian trained, all the other members being ex-pilot instructors. After the course I was posted in April 1945 to Hobsonville to join Number 4 Squadron at Whenuapai, leaving New Zealand a month later for a return visit to Emirau Island, before moving on to Mokerang on Los Negros in the Admiralty Group.

During August, we were on patrol one day when we heard that the war was over. The pilot immediately said he wanted a course for base as the war was over and we were going home. We actually didn't leave the war zone until September, when two PV1 Venturas, including my crew, acted as navigation aircraft for twelve Corsair fighters that were returning to New Zealand. They flew in formation with us, sometimes finding it hard to maintain station, and sometimes peeling away to break the boredom but keeping well in sight of us. Hovever, we got them all home, in easy stages.

I completed 127 hours and 40 minutes of operational flying, and 69 hours and 10 minutes of non-operational flying for my first tour. The second tour consisted of 49 hours and 10 minutes of operational flying, and 41 hours and 45 minutes of non-operational flying. I flew a total of fifty missions for the two tours combined.

Apart from a malfunctioning engine occasionally, the aircrew of which I was the navigator was fortunate enough to survive without serious mishap. The PV1 Ventura, however, had a few bad habits. Its fuel system could cause trouble. When we were at Emirau Island, one crew faced a serious problem soon after take off. The pilot notified base that he had to return. The aircraft was seen to be rising and falling as it came towards the airstrip. The pilot was given permission to jettison fuel from the tanks which were full. On landing it was found that one member of the crew had died from asphyxiation. Fuel had to be dumped through a vent at the back of the aircraft but a rubber connection had perished in the tropical climate, causing a life-threatening condition in the aircraft.

During my own second tour, we were once scheduled for a dawn patrol. The Operations Officer for the day was new to the Squadron. We had to be called at 0200 hours to prepare in time for daybreak. It was pouring with rain as it can only rain in the tropics, but he insisted that we became airborne. We waited until day broke to see ourselves safely off the strip. Although the rain by then had eased, we were still reluctant to take off, but eventually did so. We were but only a few minutes in the air when we were told to dump some petrol and come back. I protested about dumping the petrol in view of the danger, but we found a reef which seemed to be a good place to jettison our load of depth charges. About two hours after returning from our aborted flight, a jeep came looking for the skipper and me. Staff members had wrongly determined that we had dropped the depth charges in a shipping lane, so we had to reassure them that that wasn't the case. Depth charges were timed to explode at a given depth in the sea, being a weapon primary designed for attacking submerging enemy submarines. But if we fixed a tent peg in the nose of the depth charge it could be used as a blast bomb on land. Its explosion could spread 360°on the surface. In particular, this proved a handy weapon with which to destroy the Japanese Army's crops in the plantations on Bougainville.

Apart from our regular convoy escort work, we made many raids on many areas throughout Bougainville - and specifically on Rabaul in New Britain, and targets on New Ireland, The American Army had pursued a policy of by-passing substantial enemy forces which then had to be kept quiescent by constant air attacks. We were shot at on nearly every attack, but particularly over Rabaul. It was good practice to go low into the attack so that enemy gunners had little time to go into action. In addition the low elevation required of their guns exacerbated their problem. Since the missions against these land targets were always carried out in daylight, I invariably felt vulnerable to enemy guns, despite the best we could do to neutralize their effectiveness.

On one occasion we were tasked from Piva to drop leaflets at Numa Numa and then Kieta, with an American Major as a passenger. Our first run over the target area at Numa Numa was uneventful, but when we were over the dropping zone at Kieta, the port engine suddenly cut out. As we were flying at only 400 feet, the resultant drop in speed from 190 to 100 knots instantly alarmed us, as the stalling speed of the PV1 Ventura was 90 knots. We quickly jettisoned the rest of the leaflets advising Japanese soldiers to surrender. Then we went systematically through the aircraft to throw every movable object out to lighten the aircraft as we made for areas under cumulus cloud to take advantage of prevailing up-draughts to gain some height on our one engine. At the same time the Captain ordered everyone to prepare for ditching in the sea, and broke radio silence to inform base of our predicament, in the hope that a Catalina flying boat could be sent to shadow us and rescue us from the sea if necessary.

We headed for the Buka Passage at the north end of Bougainville Island, which separated Buka Island from the main Island. It ran in an east-west direction, heavily protected by two enemy airstrips. Another Ventura joined us at this point, but both of us passed through the Passage without seeing the enemy. We decided to make for Torokina on the west side of Bougainville rather than attempt to fly over the jungle to our base at Piva. After making a safe landing, the American Major congratulated the pilot on his flying. When he asked the upper gunner how he would have reacted if he, the Major, had panicked, he received the assurance that if he had made one foolish move he would have been hit so hard he would have had no further interest in the proceedings.

In contrast, shipping patrols were usually benign in nature but could be quite exciting on occasion. Every ship leaving port - mainly from the western seaboard of the United States – sailed to arrive at a prescribed time at its destination port. A ship was not expected to undertake any interim reporting in the interests of its own safety, potentially vulnerable as it was to enemy aircraft or submarines. As a consequence, ships could be in an unexpected location or in an expected location at the wrong time. The Squadron had the job of plotting the whereabouts of ships so that their movements could be compared with what was expected of them, and of finding lost ships. On one occasion we were looking for a ship that we never found, but instead found another ship that wasn't expected. On another we were looking for a given ship but found the *Mariposa* troopship. All ships had a four letter code which we were appraised of, and which we used to extract an identification signal from them. This they often were reluctant to do. When we asked them who they were, they usually replied but sometimes failed to reply out of caution, indifference, or incompetence. The cure for any recalcitrance was to fly around the ship at a threatening height while opening the bomb doors. This gesture was unfailingly sufficient for the ship's crew to produce the flags and lamps to clarify their identity.

With the cessation of hostilities, and having completed our escort of the Corsair fighters back to New Zealand in September 1945, I was granted leave before returning to civilian employment in the Department of Justice in December 1945, where I stayed for forty years, destined to be a civil servant for life. My wife Connie was a homemaker and relished the idea of a permanent base, her own background giving rise to her attitude. During our engagement, when I suggested that I could opt to stay in the Air Force, she was less than enthusiastic. We married on 30 November 1946.

Consequently, as my pre-war employment was available for me - in line with the general policy that employers were required to offer their former jobs to returning servicemen - I applied to the Department of Justice and was posted to Rotorua at the beginning of 1946. I stayed there until 1950 when I was transferred to the Magistrate's Court, Wellington. This was the first of a series of promotions which took me to a position working in the Head Office. The job involved work for all the diverse divisions which formed the Department of Justice - the Courts, Prisons, Land and Deed, Patents, and Probation. In the postwar period in fact, quite a lot of rationalization of the organization was required. I was not keen to take up the appointment but after discussion, agreed to a review at the end of the year. I didn't change my mind, but as it happened a fortuitous event intervened to avoid an impasse. The Minister of Justice, the Right Honourable (later Sir John) J R Marshall, wanted a new senior private secretary. I was appointed to the post with immediate effect, and worked with him for eighteen months.

Then Mr S T Barnett, the permanent Head of the Department of Justice asked me to see him. He as much as told me that I was wasting my career time working at Parliament, as there had been a change of Government, that I was only on secondment and that he wanted me back. My transfer was made the very next day to work in the Prisons Division. I was secretary of the Parole Board, before being appointed to the inspectorate, covering all disciplines in the Department, and travelling all over the country for five years. Then I applied for a vacancy in the Courts division as Deputy Registrar, Wellington. My final office was that of Registrar General of Births, Deaths and Marriages, and Chief Electoral Officer for New Zealand. In my capacity as Chief Electoral Officer,

311

I was responsible for the organisation of five national elections. After retiring, my wife and I undertook some of the travelling that Connie had originally been reluctant to do, and which the nature of my employment had not required. This included trips to Australia to see Connie's family.

In a quantum leap of contrasting occupation I was invited to a conference of Pacific Countries on Vital Statistics Practices in Asia in Manilla in 1977, to present a paper and run a seminar. Both large and small countries attended, including China, Indonesia, Philippines, and the United States. While I was there, one of the Americans approached me to ask if I would be willing to be on the United Nations list of consultants. I assented, but a year later, when I was asked to go to Nepal, as a registration officer, I was not permitted to go, as a national election was pending in New Zealand.

With Connie, after retiring in 1980, I attended an aircrew reunion in September in Winnipeg, where I had trained. On our return I received a letter offering me a one year appointment to work for the United Nations Commission for Africa (UNECA) as Regional Adviser in Civil Registration and Statistics. Connie was able to accompany me to the countries that had been British Colonies to meet the national adviser who had been appointed in each country to administer registrations. Each of them was an experienced officer drawn from other countries. My task was to give them encouragement and any assistance they needed. We went first to headquarters in Addis Ababa, Ethiopia, for three weeks for orientation and briefing purposes, before travelling via Nairobi in Kenya, to Zambia, from where we visited Somalia, Tanzania, Zimbabwe, Swaziland, Botswana, and Ghana. It was a busy and hardworking assignment but of course an unparalleled opportunity to become acquainted with the enormous African Continent, its social, economic, and cultural conditions, and problems. It was personally satisfying to be able to make use of my knowledge and experience of the sophisticated mechanisms for population statistics - that had taken several centuries to develop elsewhere - available in those parts of Africa where they were absent but needed.

312

I have been a licensed lay preacher of the Presbyterian Church for over fifty years and have remained active in the Church to the present day. Other activities that I have been able to sustain over the years included serving as an Officer at battalion and national levels of The Boys' Brigade, and the editor of its national magazine for nearly thirty years. I have also been secretary of the Wellington Branch of the Brevet Club for veteran airmen, a life member of it, and a member of the Hutt Valley Philatelic Society, the Masonic Order, and the Presbytery. Until 1962 I was a member of the Air Force Active Reserve, flying as second navigator in Dakota, Bristol Freighter, and Hastings aircraft in Number 40 Squadron. My long life has been full of contrasts around the complete and stable career that I was able to pursue in the Civil Service, with a family of four sons and a daughter, seven grandchildren and two great-grandchildren.

~ ~ ~

Jack Wright flew as navigator in the following aircraft, listed in experiential order.

> Anson
> Hudson
> Ventura
> Dakota
> Bristol Freighter
> Hastings

Photographs and the specifications of these aircraft may be found in Part 2, listed in alphabetical order.

Jack Wright at the Initial
Training Wing for aircrew,
Rotorua, 10 January 1943

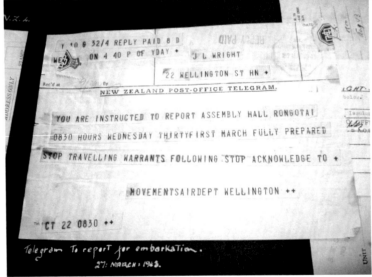

Telegram ordering Jack Wright to report in Wellington at 0830
hours on 27 March 1943 for embarkation to Canada

Jack Wright on the right with Andries Vermeulen during their navigator training, Winnipeg, June 1943

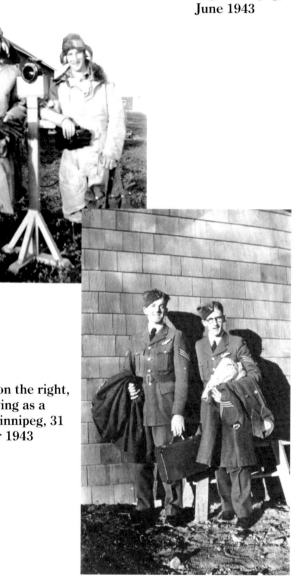

Jack Wright, on the right, on qualifying as a navigator, Winnipeg, 31 October 1943

Wrecked Japanese transport and barge (on the beach) on
Guadalcanal from 1942.

Wrecked Japanese submarine on Guadalcanal in the Solomon
Islands from 1942.

Living quarters for one Ventura air crew on Los Negros Island in the Admiralty Islands in 1944. This tented accommodation was manufactured in the United States and was widely used in the Pacific among allied units

Warrant Officer Jack Wright in February 1945

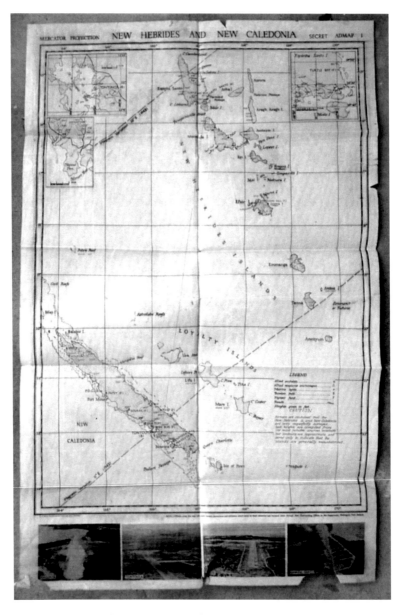

Wartime map of the New Hebrides and New Caledonia used by
aircrew, marked Secret

318

Momote Chapel on Los Negros Island in 1945. The notice board indicates Sunday Service times for Catholics at 0630 hours, for Protestants at 1230 hours, and Mormons at 1330 hours

Number 4 Squadron PV1 Ventura aircrew outside their living quarters on Los Negros in 1945.

L-R: Flight Sergeant F W Chisholm, air gunner; Warrant Officer A D Robertson, pilot; Flight Sergeant M B Macpherson, air gunner; Warrant Officer J L Wright, navigator; and Warrant Officer A Blank, wireless operator/air gunner

Jack Wright's crew in front of their PV1 Ventura of Number 4
Squadron at its jungle parking bay at Los Negros in 1945. L-R:
Flight Sergeant M B Macpherson, air gunner; Warrant Officer
J L Wright, navigator; Warrant Officer A Robertson, pilot;
Warrant Officer A Blank, wireless operator/air gunner; and
Flight Sergeant F W Chisholm, air gunner

References

Primary sources

Churchill, Winston S. (1951) *The Second World War*, Volume 4. Cassell, London

Cochrane, Wing Commander, The Honourable R. A., RAF (1936) *Air Aspect of the Defence Problems of New Zealand*. Report, December, National Archives, Wellington.

Cochrane, Group Captain, The Honourable R. A., RAF (1938) *Report on RNZAF*. Letter to his successor, 20 December, National Archives, Wellington.

Craven, W. F., and J. L. Cate (1948-58) *The Army Air Forces in World War II*.

7 Volumes. University of Chicago Press, Chicago

Encyclopaedia Britannica

Encyclopaedia of New Zealand (1966). A. H. McLintock, Government Printer, Wellington

Encyclopaedia of World War II (1978). Simon and Schuster, New York

Gillison, D., and G. Odgers (1957) Royal Australian Air Force 1939-45, Volume I. Australian War Memorial, Canberra

Gillison, D., and G. Odgers (1962) Royal Australian Air Force 1939-45, Volume II. Australian War Memorial, Canberra

McGibbon, I. C. (1981) Blue Water Rationale. Historic Publications Branch, Wellington

Official History of New Zealand in the Second World War 1939-1945. War History Branch, Department of Internal Affairs, Wellington, New Zealand.

Baker, J. V. T. (1965) *War Economy Documents* (1949) (3 Volumes)

Gillespie, O. A. (1952) *The Pacific*

Ross, J. M. (1955) *Royal New Zealand Air Force*

Stevens, W. G. (1958) *Problems of 2 NZEF*

Thompson, H. L. (1959) *New Zealanders with the Royal Air Force*, Volume III

Waters, S. D. (1956) *Royal New Zealand Navy*

Wood, F. L.W. (1958) *Political and External Affairs*

Richards, D., and H. Saunders *(1953) The Royal Air Force 1939-1945*, Volume II: *The Fight at Odds*. HMSO, London

Supplementary sources

Adlam, Lance (1991) *The Quest for Wings*. Dunmore Press, Palmerston North

Bentley, G. (1969) *RNZAF, A Short History*. A.H. and A.W. Reed, Wellington

Collier, Basil (1969) *The War in the Far East*. Heinemann, London

Driscoll, Ian (1972) *Flight Path South Pacific*. Whitcombe and Tombs, Christchurch

Driscoll, Ian (1979) *Airline*. Shortland Publications, Auckland

Ewing, R., and R. Macpherson *(1986) The History of NZ Aviation*. Heinemann, Auckland

Green, William and Gordon Swansborough (1976 and 1977) *Japanese Army Fighters in WW2* (2 volumes). Macdonald and Janes, London

Harrison, P. (1997) *The Golden Age of NZ Flying Boats*. Random House, Auckland,

Holmes, Frank (2004) *Jungle Bomber*. Frank Holmes, Wellington

Horn, Alex (1992) *Wings Over the Pacific*. Random Century, Auckland

Ingham, Wally (1990) *The Avengers*. Aviation Historical Society of New Zealand, Wellington

Ingham, Wally (1991) *We Also Served*. Aviation Historical Society NZ, Wellington

Liddell Hart, B. H. (1970) *History of the Second World War*. Cassell, London

McIntyre, Donald (1972) *Sea Power in the Pacific*. Arthur Barker, London

Rusbridger, James and Eric Nave (1991) *Betrayal at Pearl Harbour*. Simon and Schuster, New York

Sekigawa, Eiichiro (1974) *Japanese Military Aviation*. Ian Allen, London

Thomas, D. A. (1978) *Japan's War at Sea*. Andre Deutsch, London

Vader, John (1970) *Pacific Hawk*. McDonald, London

PART TWO

Aircraft used by the veterans either for training,
conversion or combat

The photographs are representative of the type of aircraft in question, irrespective of the variations in name, specification and uses it may have had as a result of being manufactured in different countries or employed by different Air Forces. The same aircraft type could be subject to many changes to its construction, equipment, armament, and purpose, usually signified as different *Marks* of the aircraft. The veterans in this book in some cases flew in more than one *Mark* of the same aircraft. With few exceptions, the general data only for each aircraft type are presented.

Measurements are given to the nearest inch.

Photographs by Permission of the Air Force Museum, Christchurch, New Zealand.

Anson

1. Purpose

  Mark 1: General reconnaissance with a crew of 3 – pilot, navigator, gunner

  Mark T.21: Navigation trainer with a crew of up to 6 – regular crew plus trainees

2. Description

  Low wing monoplane, fabric covered metal fuselage, wooden wings and wooden tail

  Mark 1: Hand operated, *Mark T.21* power operated, retractable undercarriage

3. Manufacturer

  A V Roe & Company Limited at Newton Heath (Manchester), Chadderton (Manchester) and Yeadon (West Yorkshire)

4. Engines

  Mark 1: Two 350 hp Armstrong Siddeley Cheetah 1X

  Mark T.21: Two 420 hp Armstrong Siddeley Cheetah 15 or 17

5. Dimensions

  Mark 1: Wingspan 56 feet 6 inches. Length 42 feet 3 inches. Height 13 feet 1 inch. Wing Area 410 square feet

  Mark T.21: Wingspan 57 feet 6 inches. Length 42 feet 3 inches. Height 13 feet 10 inches. Wing Area 440 square feet

6. Weights

  Mark 1: Empty 5, 375 pounds. Loaded 8,000 pounds

  Mark T.21: Empty 7,766 pounds. Loaded 10, 306 pounds

7. Performance

  Mark 1: Maximum speed 188 mph at 7,000 feet. Cruising Speed 158 mph. Initial climb rate 720 feet per minute. Range 790 miles. Service ceiling 19,000 feet

Mark T.21:   Maximum speed 171 mph at 5,000 feet. Cruising speed 149 mph. Initial climb rate 700 feet per minute. Service ceiling 16,000 feet. Range 660 miles

8. Armaments

Mark 1:   Two .303 guns, one fixed forward, one in the turret. Bomb load 360 pounds

9. Actual Uses and Users

The Anson, introduced in 1936, and famed for its easy handling, was used for pilot and navigator training in numerous squadrons in the United Kingdom, Canada, and elsewhere throughout the Second World War. 11,022 were delivered.

Its use as a combat aircraft was confined to work in many squadrons of Coastal Command for convoy escort work in the early years of the Second World War. An Anson, on 6 September 1939, made the first attack by an RAF aircraft on a U-Boat. 148 Squadron in Malta was also equipped with the Anson. It was used for training purposes by Bomber Command in Numbers 7, 44, 51, 58, 61, 76, and 144 Squadrons. Transport Command used it in Numbers 24, 48, 233, 437, 512, and 575 Squadrons of 46 Group, and in 147, 167, and 187 Squadrons of 110 Wing. 510, 516 and 544 Squadrons used it for transport duties, and 116 and 527 Squadrons for Radar Calibration. Post-war, the Anson was used for Communications purposes by all Commands.

Avenger

1. Purpose

Torpedo bomber with a crew of three – pilot, gunner, and radio operator

2. Description

A mid wing all metal monoplane, with retractable undercarriage and vertically folding wings for storage on aircraft carriers. Manufacturer's designations XTBF-1, TBF-1, TBF-1C, XTBF-2, and XTBF-3. The aircraft supplied to the Royal New Zealand Air Force were the TBF-1 variant

3. Manufacturer

Grumman Aircraft Engineering Corporation, Bethpage, New York

4. Engines

One 1,700 hp Wright R-2600-8, with three-bladed propeller

5. Dimensions

Wingspan 54 feet 2 inches. Length 40 feet. Height 16 feet 5 inches.

Wing area 490 square feet

6. Weights

Empty 10,080 pounds. Loaded 15,905 pounds

7. Performance

Maximum speed 271 mph at 12,000 feet. Cruising speed 145 mph. Initial climb rate 1,430 feet per minute. Service ceiling 22,400 feet. Range 1,215 miles

8. Armaments

One fixed forward firing .3 inch gun. One dorsal .5 inch gun. One ventral .3 inch gun. One 1,600 pounds torpedo or equivalent load in bombs. All three members of the crew could operate guns from their respective stations. Avengers operated by the Royal New Zealand Air Force in the Pacific were used to carry a usual load of 4 x 500 pound bombs or the equivalent in smaller or larger bombs or other munitions, but not torpedoes.

9. Actual Uses and Users

9,836 Avenger aircraft of several variants in total were built during the Second World War. Avengers of the later variants, developed for a range of different tasks, served in a number of Air Forces and Navies until 1954. A total of 958 went to the British Fleet Air Arm.

The Avenger was designed to replace the ill-fated Devastator which suffered annihilation at the Battle of Midway, 4 -7 June 1942, when thirty-six out of forty-one carried by the United States aircraft carriers Hornet and Enterprise were destroyed in desperate but futile attacks against the Japanese fleet. The prototype first flew on 1 August 1941 and first saw action in the same battle, on 4 June 1942, albeit inauspiciously, since five of the six aircraft dispatched from United States fleet carriers were shot down without hitting their targets. The Royal New Zealand Air Force operated 48 aircraft between 1943 and 1959. They served as dive bombers operated by Numbers 30 and 31 Squadrons in the Pacific Islands. Thereafter they were used for crew training and target towing.

Battle

1. Purpose
Light bomber with a crew of three – pilot, navigator, gunner.

2. Description
Low wing monoplane of all metal, stressed skin construction and retractable undercarriage.

3. Manufacturer
Fairey Aviation Company Limited, Stockport, Cheshire. Sub-contracted by Austin Motor Company Limited, Longbridge, Birmingham.

4. Engines
One 1,030 hp Rolls-Royce Merlin I, II, III, or V.

5. Dimensions
Wingspan 54 feet. Length 52 feet 2 inches. Height 15 feet 6 inches.

Wing area 422 square feet.

6. Weights
Empty 6,647 pounds. Loaded 10,792 pounds.

7. Performance
Maximum speed 241 mph at 13,000 feet. Cruising speed 210 mph.

Climbing rate 4.1 minutes to 5.000 feet. 21.4 minutes to 20,000 feet.

Service ceiling 23,500 feet. Range 1,050 miles.

8. Armaments
One fixed .303 Browning gun forward, one Vickers K gun aft.

Bomb load 1,000 pounds.

9. Actual Uses and Users

In the belief that the Battle, introduced in 1937, represented a developmental leap over the obsolescent biplanes of the 1930s, the Royal Air Force equipped twenty-two home bomber squadrons with it, including four Polish Squadrons. Of these, Numbers 12, 15, 40, 88, 103, 105, 142, 150, 218, and 226 Squadrons were sent to France after the commencement of hostilities and served there during the early months of the Second World War. Until April and May 1940, there was little activity. Then Germany systematically attacked and overran all the countries from Denmark westwards to France - the German ground forces operating in irresistible conjunction with the Luftwaffe. The Battles fell an easy prey to single-seat fighters and ground fire, proving obsolescent in every performance department, and were virtually wiped out. Number 98 Squadron served in Iceland equipped with Battles.

Some Battles were used by 611 and 616 Auxiliary Squadrons. A few Battles were converted for pilot training. 624 were delivered. The last Battle to be produced left the works on 2 September 1940. Outstanding orders totaling 235 aircraft were cancelled. After the Battle's demise as a combat aircraft, large numbers of them were shipped to Canada for use in air gunnery training and as target tugs.

Beaufort

1. Purpose

Torpedo bomber with a crew of four – pilot, navigator, bomb aimer, wireless operator/air gunner.

2. Description

Mid wing monoplane with retractable undercarriage of all metal, stressed skin construction. Manufacturer's designation Type 152.

3. Manufacturer

Bristol Aeroplane Company Limited, Filton, Bristol.

4. Engines

Two 1,130 hp Bristol Taurus VI.

5. Dimensions

Wingspan 57 feet 10 inches. Length 44 feet 7 inches.

Height 12 feet 5 inches. Wing area 503 square feet.

6. Weights

Empty 13,107 pounds. Loaded 21,228 pounds

7. Performance

Maximum speed 265 mph at 6,000 feet. Cruising speed 200 mph. Normal range 1,035 miles. Maximum range 1,600 miles. Endurance 6 hours.

8. Armaments

Varied between *Mark I* and *Mark II:* Two .303 guns in the nose and the dorsal turret. Some aircraft were also equipped with a .303 gun in a blister under the nose and two beam guns. Bomb load 1,500 pounds or 2,000 pounds, or one 18 inch torpedo of 1,605 pounds or mines.

9. Actual Uses and Users

The Beaufort was the mainstay torpedo bomber of Coastal Command of The Royal Air Force from 1940 to 1943, replacing the obsolescent Vickers Vildebeest biplane. The prototype first flew on 15 October 1938, the first aircraft being delivered to 22 Squadron at Thorney Island in October 1939, which used them for the first mine laying operation of the war on the night of 15 April 1940 and also to drop the first 2,000 bomb of the war. A total of 955 of the *Mark I*, and 166 of the *Mark II* were built to equip 22, 42, 86, 217, 415, and 489 Squadrons in home waters and 39, 47, 203, and 217 Squadrons in the Middle East. They saw service in the North Sea, the English Channel – notably against the three German capital ships which escaped from Brest via the Channel, the Atlantic Ocean, and the Mediterranean Sea.   217 Squadron operated from Malta and 39 Squadron from the Western Desert. They were also operated by the Royal Australian Air Force in the Pacific.

Bolingbroke

1. Purpose

Light bomber or reconnaissance aircraft with a crew of three –
pilot, and two further aircrew members to handle the navigation, wireless and gunnery.

2. Description

A midwing monoplane of all metal, stressed skin construction
with retractable undercarriage. The manufacturer's designation
Types 149 and 160.

3. Manufacturer

Fairchild Aircraft Limited, Longueuil, Province of Quebec, Canada

4. Engines

Marks I and *III:* Two 840 hp Bristol Mercury VIII.

Mark IV: Two 920 hp Bristol Mercury XV.

Marks IV and *IV-T:* Two 920 hp Bristol Mercury XX.

Mark IV-C: Two 850 hp Wright Cyclone G3B .

Mark IV-W Two 750 hp Pratt and Whitney Twin Wasp Junior
SB4G.

5. Dimensions

Marks I, II, and *IV:* Wingspan 56 feet 4 inches. Length 42 feet 9
inches.

Height 9 feet 10 inches. Wing area 469 square feet.

6. Weights

Marks I, II, and *IV*: Empty 9,800 pounds. All-up weight
12,500-14,400 pounds.

7. Performance

Maximum speed 295 mph. Service ceiling 31,500 feet. Range
1,950 miles

8. Armaments

One fixed Browning .303 gun firing forward and twin .303 guns in the dorsal turret.

Bomb load 1,000 pounds internally and 320 pounds externally.

9. Actual Uses and Users

The Bolingbroke, like the Bisley and Beaufort, was derived from the original Blenheim *Mark I* which first flew on 25 June 1936 and was seen as an innovative aircraft, designed to replace the obsolescent Hawker Hind biplane, as part of an urgent development programme to modernise the Royal Air Force in the face of possible hostilities in Europe. Many *Marks* of the Blenheim and Bolingbroke were introduced over the following years. Blenheims were withdrawn from service in Bomber Command on 18 August 1942 but continued in other forms and for different tasks elsewhere. The Bolingbroke, introduced in 1939 in Canada, was used for advanced training purposes but Bolingbrokes were also formed there into a reconnaissance squadron for use against the threatened expansion of Japanese forces from their initial tenuous hold in the Aleutian Islands. A total of 626 were delivered.

Bristol Freighter

1. Purpose
Bulk freight carrier but convertible for short haul passenger transport with a crew of two to four, depending on cargo/passenger and civilian/air force usage

2. Description
High wing all metal monoplane with fixed undercarriage. Central locking for the two nose doors which opened outwards and sideways for vehicle loading. Wing racks and bomb release mechanism fitted for aerial re-supply operations and air-sea rescue equipment dropping. Manufacturer's designation Type B170. The standard version known as *Mark 31*

3. Manufacturer
Bristol Aeroplane Company Limited, Filton, Bristol

4. Engines
Two 1,980 hp Bristol Hercules 735, fourteen cylinders, with four-bladed propellers

5. Dimensions
Wingspan 108 feet. Length 68 feet 4 inches. Height 26 feet 3 inches

6. Weights
Empty 27,229 pounds. Freight 10,000 pounds or 35 passengers.

Maximum at take-off 44,000 pounds

7. Performance
Maximum speed 225 mph at 3,000 feet. Climb rate 10 minutes to 10,000 feet. Service ceiling 23,000 feet. Range with 12,000 pound payload 820 miles

8. Armaments
Nil

9. Actual Uses and Users

Designed to carry a large payload over short distances, this aircraft was produced in three main versions, *Mark 31, Mark 31E,* and *Mark 32*. It was supplied for civilian uses all over the world. The 200th aircraft was delivered on 16 January 1953 to Air Charter Limited in Britain, a company using it for the transport of tourists and their cars across the English Channel.

Its military version was used by the Air Forces of Australia, Burma, Canada, Iraq, New Zealand, and Pakistan, being used to transport field guns, Jeeps, and military stores. Twelve aircraft were supplied to the Royal New Zealand Air Force, serving from 1951 to 1977 in Numbers 1, 3, and 41 Squadrons. They became a familiar sight when used later as a means of transport between the main islands for civilian traffic.

Catalina

1. *Purpose*
Ocean reconnaissance with a crew of eight or nine

2. *Description*
High wing monoplane flying boat of all metal, stressed skin construction, the wing being mounted above the fuselage on a central pillar supported by double struts to the fuselage. Manufacturer's designation Model 28

3. *Manufacturer*
Consolidated Aircraft Corporation, San Diego, California

4. *Engines*
Two 1,200 hp Pratt and Whitney Twin Wasp R-1830, S1C3-G

5. *Dimensions*
Wingspan 104 feet. Length 65 feet 2 inches. Height 17 feet 11 inches. Wing area 1,400 square feet

6. *Weights*
Empty 14,240 pounds. Loaded 27,080 pounds

7. *Performance*
Maximum speed 190 mph at 10,500 feet. Cruising speed 179 mph. Initial climb rate 900 feet per minute. Service ceiling 24,000 feet. Range 4,000 miles. Normal maximum flight time 17.6 hours, but this was often exceeded

8. *Armaments*
One .303 gun in the bows, two in each side blister amidships, and one in a ventral position aft of the step. Bomb load up to 4,000 pounds

9. *Actual Uses and Users*
Famed for its exceptional endurance time in the air, the Catalina first entered service with the United States Navy in 1936 but attracted the interest of the Royal Air Force which ordered fifty

late in 1939. On 26 May 1941 a Catalina found the *Bismarck* again after it had slipped through British naval forces, another shadowing the ship until it could be brought to action. The Victoria Cross was awarded to two Catalina pilots for attacks on U-boats. The 196th and last U-boat to be sunk by Coastal Command was destroyed by a Catalina on 7 May 1945. Over 650 were built for the Royal Air Force covering seven *Marks* altogether, serving in the Indian Ocean at Madagascar and Ceylon, and in West Africa, as well as Britain for service in the Atlantic. Squadron Numbers 119, 190, 202, 209, 210, 240, 330, 333, and 422 of Coastal Command, and 162 of the Royal Canadian Air Force were equipped with the Catalina in Europe. Overseas Squadrons included Numbers 191, 205, 209, 210, 212, 240, 244, 259, 262, 265, 270, 321, 413, 490, and 628. In the Pacific Islands, Numbers 5 and 6 Squadrons of the Royal New Zealand Air Force were equipped with Catalinas.

Corsair

1. *Purpose*
Single seat fighter aircraft primarily intended for use on aircraft carriers

2. *Description*
Gull-shaped, low wing monoplane, of all metal construction with retractable undercarriage, and foldable wings. Data given for the variant with the manufacturer's designation F4U-1

3. *Manufacturer*
United Aircraft Corporation's Vought-Sikorsky Division at Stratford, Connecticut, and its Chance Vought Division at Dallas, Texas;

Brewster Aeronautical Corporation, Long Island City, New York; and the Goodyear Aircraft Corporation, Akron, Ohio

4. *Engines*
One Pratt and Whitney 2,000 hp R-2800-8 with three-bladed propeller. Later variants were fitted with engines of 2,450 hp

5. *Dimensions*
Wingspan 41 feet. Length 33 feet 4 inches. Height 16 feet 1 inch.

Wing area 314 square feet

6. *Weights*
Empty 8,982 pounds. Loaded 14,000 pounds.

7. *Performance*
Maximum speed 417 mph at 19,900 feet. Cruising speed 182 mph. Climb rate 2,890 feet per minute. Service ceiling 36,900 feet. Range 1,015 miles

8. *Armaments*
Six .5 inch guns in the wings. Later variants carried up to 4,000 pounds of bombs

9. Actual Uses and Users

The Corsair was widely regarded by the United States as one of the two best carrier based fighters of the Second World War, and in some ways superior even to the Mustang. It combined the smallest possible airframe with the largest possible engine, coming into front line war service in 1943, remaining in production for over ten years and in service until 1965. 12,681 of its many variants were produced. It was credited with the destruction of 2,140 enemy aircraft in the Pacific theatre of war for only 189 losses at enemy hands during a total of 64,051 missions by United States forces. The Royal Air Force received 2,012 Corsairs and the Royal New Zealand Air Force 370, the latter for combat in the islands as a replacement for the Kittyhawk.

Dakota

1. Purpose

Military transport with a crew of three – pilot, navigator and wireless operator - and twenty-eight troops or alternative equivalent freight.

2. Description

A twin engined low wing monoplane with retractable undercarriage of all metal, stressed skin construction.

3. Manufacturer

Douglas Aircraft Company Incorporated, Santa Monica, California.

4. Engines

Two 1,200 hp Pratt and Whitney Twin Wasp R-1830-92

5. Dimensions

Wingspan 95 feet. Length 64 feet 6 inches. Height 16 feet 11 inches.

Wing area 987 square feet.

6. Weights

Empty 16,865 pounds. Loaded 25,200 pounds and a maximum of 31,000 pounds.

7. Performance

Maximum speed 230 mph at 8,500 feet.

Cruising speed 185 mph.

Initial climb rate 1,130 feet per minute.

Service ceiling 23,200 feet.

Range 1,500 miles but 2,125 maximum.

8. Armaments

Nil

9. Actual Uses and Users

The Dakota became the most famous military transport aircraft of all time, a total of 13,300 being produced. It first flew on 18 December 1935 and became the mainstay transport for both the United States Army Air Force and later the Royal Air Force from 1941, over 1,200 of them serving the latter in all theatres of war and for diverse purposes until they were withdrawn in 1950. They were used as ambulances, freighters and personnel carriers. They towed gliders, carried paratroops, engaged in re-supply missions for paratroop assaults in Europe and the Chindits in the Burma jungle, and in the post-war period were used for communication purposes and dropping leaflets to Malayan rebels. In many parts of the world this aircraft is still used for local tourist purposes and short flights for the public at air displays.

Dauntless

1. Purpose

Dive bomber, primarily to operate from aircraft carriers, with a crew of two – pilot and wireless operator/ air gunner. The latter also had some navigation and observation duties, and could fly the aircraft from the rear cockpit

2. Description

Low wing, all metal monoplane with retractable undercarriage and arrester hook. It could operate from a carrier without a catapult

3. Manufacturer

Douglas Aircraft Company, El Segundo, California, and Tulsa, Oklahoma.

Manufacturer's designations SBD 1-5, 5A, XSBD-6, and SBD-6

4. Engines

One 1,200 hp Wright R-1820-60 with three-bladed propeller

5. Dimensions

Wingspan 41 feet 6 inches. Length 33 feet. Height 12 feet 11 inches.

Wing area 325 square feet

6. Weights

Empty 6,675 pounds. Loaded 10,855 pounds

7. Performance

Maximum speed 245 mph at 15,800 feet. Cruising speed 144 mph.

Initial climb rate 1,190 feet per minute. Service ceiling 24,300 feet.

Range 1,100 miles

8. Armaments

Two fixed forward firing .5 inch guns. Two flexible .3 inch dorsal guns. Up to 1,600 pounds of bombs externally mounted under the fuselage and one 325 pound bomb under each wing

9. *Actual Uses and Users*

The earliest variants of the Dauntless went into service with the United States Navy at the end of 1940. The later SBD-3 variant was widely used to equip its aircraft carriers at the time of the entry of the United States into the Second World War, distinguishing itself in the Battle of Midway by sinking the Japanese aircraft carriers *Akagi, Kaga, and Hiryu* on 4 June 1942. A total of 5,936 Dauntless aircraft were built, 68 being operated between 1943 and 1945 by the Royal New Zealand Air Force, which formed 25 Squadron with them for dive bombing in the Pacific Islands in 1944.

Fort

1. Purpose
Aircrew training for instructor and trainee, with dual controls

2. Description
Low wing semi-cantilever monoplane. The wings are separate with no centre section. Metal skin fuselage, fin, and tail plane, all fabric covered. A fixed undercarriage enclosed with distinctive streamlined fairings.

Enclosed, independent cockpits in tandem fitted with emergency release devices. Manufacturer's designation Model 60.

3. Manufacturer
Fleet Aircraft Company, Canada

4. Engines
One 250 hp or 350 hp Jacobs radial air-cooled

5. Dimensions
Wingspan 36 feet. Length 26 feet 2 inches. Height 11 feet 2 inches.

Wing area 200 square feet

6. Weights
Empty 1,850 pounds. Loaded 2,900 pounds

7. Performance
Model-L with the 250 hp engine: Maximum speed 164 mph. Cruising speed 150 mph. Landing speed 58 mph. Initial climb rate 1,000 feet per minute. Service ceiling 15,000 feet. Cruising range 690 miles

8. Armaments
Nil

9. Actual Uses and Users
Compared with other Second World War training aircraft, such as the Tiger Moth and the Harvard, the Fleet Fort was produced

in modest numbers and confined to uses for training purposes in Canada. Although primarily intended for use for the advanced initial training of pilots to fly fighter and other single-engine aircraft, it could be used for the training of other members of aircrew, such as navigators and wireless operators.

Gordon

1. *Purpose*
Daylight bomber and general purpose aircraft with a crew of two
– pilot and gunner.

2. *Description*
Biplane of metal structure, fabric covered.

3. *Manufacturer*
Fairey Aviation Company Limited, Hayes, Middlesex, England.

4. *Engines*
One 525 hp Armstrong Siddeley Panther 11A.

5. *Dimensions*
Wingspan 45 feet 9 inches. Length 36 feet 9 inches. Height 14
feet 2 inches.

Wing area 438½ square feet.

6. *Performance*
Maximum speed 145 mph at 3,000 feet. Cruising speed 110
mph. Initial climb rate 1,000 feet per minute. Service ceiling
22,000 feet. Range 600 miles.

7. *Armaments*
One Vickers gun forward, one Lewis gun aft. Bomb load 460
pounds.

8. *Actual Uses and Users*
The Gordon was first flown in 1930 and remained with a few
first-line squadrons in the United Kingdom and the Middle East
until as late as 1938, after which they were used for several years
as target tugs in gunnery schools in the United Kingdom, and in
New Zealand for pilot training. The first Gordons were fitted
with Napier Lion engines, which were replaced in the second
type by Panther radial engines, requiring changes to the oil, fuel,
and electrical systems, together with some structural modifica-

tions to the forward fuselage, permitting the forward gun to be outside the fuselage. The second type had an improved performance, including a better take-off when fully loaded. It remained in production until 1934, a total of 160 being produced for the Royal Air Force, as well as a version for the Fleet Air Arm known as the Seal.

In 1931, Number 40 Squadron in the United Kingdom was the first to receive it. Gordons were then sent to Number 6 Squadron to replace its obsolescent Bristol Fighters in Egypt and Palestine. Numbers 35 and 207 Squadrons with Gordons were sent to the Middle East to reinforce the Royal Air Force there when Italy attacked Abyssinia in 1935. Number 14 Squadron served in Transjordon with them, as did 45 Squadron in Egypt, and 47 Squadron at Khartoum.

Harvard

1. Purpose

The advanced training of pilots, primarily for those intended to fly single-engined fighter aircraft.

2. Description

Low wing monoplane of all metal and stressed skin construction, with a retractable undercarriage and two seats for the instructor and trainee with dual controls.

3. Manufacturer

North American Aviation Incorporated, Inglewood, California.

This company also manufactured an aircraft known as the BT-14 in the United States but as the Yale in the Royal Air Force as used in Canada. The Yale resembled the Harvard in appearance, having a similar purpose and construction.

4. Engines

One 550 hp Pratt and Whitney Wasp R-1340-49.

5. Dimensions

Wingspan 42 feet. Length 29 feet. Height 11 feet 8 inches.

Wing area 253 square feet.

6. Weights

Empty 4,158 pounds. Loaded 5,250 pounds.

7. Performance

Maximum speed 205 mph at 5,000 feet. Cruising speed 170 mph. Initial climb rate 1,350 feet per minute. Service ceiling 21,500 feet.

Range 750 miles. Maximum flight time 3.9 hours.

8. Armaments

Although generally used as an unarmed trainer, the Harvard could be fitted with 2 x .303 Browning guns for gunnery training. Small bombs could also be carried when the aircraft was used for operations as it was on rare occasions in unusual places and circumstances, notably against the Mau Mau in Kenya and Malaysian terrorists in the post-war period.

9. Actual Uses and Users

A total of over 5,000 Harvards of various *Marks* were delivered from December 1938 onwards. The last pilots to qualify in England on them did so at Number 3 Flying Training School, Feltwell, England on 23 March 1955, but Harvards continued to be used after that date by University Air Squadrons in the United Kingdom. It was prominently used for pilot training in Britain, Canada, Southern Rhodesia (now Zimbabwe), Australia, and New Zealand throughout most of the Second World War.

Hastings

1. Purpose
Civil airliner with military derivatives C1 and C2 as strategic transports for fifty passengers and/or freight with a crew of five

2. Description
Low wing monoplane with retractable undercarriage of all metal construction

3. Manufacturer
Handley Page Limited, Cricklewood, London NW2

4. Engines
Four Bristol Hercules 106 14 cylinder air-cooled radials of 1,675 hp each

5. Dimensions
Wingspan 113 feet. Length 82 feet 8 inches. Height 22 feet 6 inches.

6. Weights
Loaded 82,000 pounds

7. Performance
Maximum speed 348 mph at 22,200 feet. Ceiling 26,500 feet.

Range 4,250 miles

8. Armaments
Nil

9. Actual Uses and Users
The Hastings was conceived as a post-war transport aircraft for the Royal Air Force to replace the Avro York which had become dated. It was designed in 1945, the prototype first flying on 7 May 1946. Subsequently, twenty-five aircraft were delivered to the British Overseas Airways Corporation for use on the many European international routes that were being opened up. The first of the two military versions of the aircraft first flew on 25 April 1947. Fifty of the C1 version and 100 of the C2 were then

delivered to the Royal Air Force. Those that were manufactured in time took part in the Berlin airlift. A minor variant was produced for meteorological reconnaissance. Four aircraft as a C3 variant were built for New Zealand, and four as a C4 variant to carry important political and military passengers.

Heyford

1. Purpose
   Daylight heavy bomber with a crew of four

2. Description
   Biplane with fixed undercarriage, the fuselage being flush with
   the upper wings, in unusual contrast to the practice in biplanes
   of placing it flush with the lower wings

3. Manufacturer
   Handley Page Limited, Cricklewood, London NW2

4. Engines
   Two 575 hp Rolls-Royce Kestrel III, 12 cylinder V, liquid cooled

5. Dimensions
   Wingspan 75 feet. Length 58 feet. Height 17 feet 6 inches.

6. Weights
   Empty 16, 900 pounds

7. Performance
   Maximum speed 142 mph at 13,000 feet. Ceiling 21,000 feet.

   Range 900 miles

8. Armaments
   Three machine guns. 2,800 pounds of bombs

9. Actual Uses and Users
   The Heyford, as successor to the Handley Page Hinaidi, was the
   last biplane heavy bomber to serve with the Royal Air Force. It
   was designed in 1927, the prototype taking to the air in June
   1930. It went into production two years later and entered service
   with 99 Squadron in July 1933. The production of variants,
   Marks I, IA, II, and *III* successively continued until September
   1936, a total of 122 being built, including 70 of the *Mark III.*
   Heyfords remained in front line service until 1937, when they
   were relegated to aircrew training duties

Hind

1. Purpose

Light day-bomber and general purpose aircraft with a crew of two – pilot and gunner

2. Description

Biplane of fabric covered, all metal construction, with a cut-away gunner's cockpit, a fixed undercarriage, and a tail wheel instead of the customary skid

3. Manufacturer

Hawker Aircraft Limited, Kingston, Surrey, England. The General Aircraft Company undertook the conversion of 124 Hinds to be training aircraft

4. Engines

One 12 cylinder, fully supercharged, liquid cooled 640 hp Rolls-Royce Kestral V

5. Dimensions

Wingspan 37 feet 3 inches. Length 29 feet 7 inches. Height 10 feet 7 inches

6. Weights

Empty 3,251 pounds. Loaded 5,298 pounds

7. Performance

Maximum speed 186 mph at 16,400 feet. Climb rate 6,560 feet in 4 minutes. Service ceiling 26,400 feet. Range 430 miles

8. Armaments

One Vickers gun firing forward and one rear firing Lewis gun.

Bomb load of 500 pounds carried externally under the wings

9. Actual Uses and Users

The Hind was intended as an interim replacement for the Hart, pending the arrival of the new generation of monoplane light bombers in the form of the Blenheim and Battle. The prototype made its first flight on 12 September 1934. Hinds remained operational until 1938, a total of 528 having been built. It was variously used by some twenty-five regular squadrons of the Royal Air Force until then, being the last of the biplane light bombers to have first line service, but continued in use in eleven Auxiliary Air Force squadrons until just before war began in September 1939. A number of Hinds were supplied to the Royal New Zealand Air Force and used for training purposes in the early part of the Second World War.

Hudson

1. Purpose

General reconnaissance with a crew of five - pilot, navigator, wireless operator, and two gunners

2. Description

Mid wing cantilever monoplane of all metal, stressed skin construction, with retractable undercarriage

3. Manufacturer

Lockheed Aircraft Corporation, Burbank, California

4. Engines

Two Wright R-1820-G 102A, 1,100 hp nine cylinder radial air cooled Cyclone for *Marks I, II,* and *III.* Two Pratt and Whitney Twin Wasp for *Marks IV* and *V*

5. Dimensions

Wingspan 65 feet 6 inches. Length 44 feet 4 inches. Height 11 feet 10 inches.

Wing area 551 square feet

6. Weights

Empty 12,536 pounds. Loaded 18,500 pounds

7. Performance

Maximum speed 275 mph. Cruising speed 223 mph. Landing speed 72 mph.

Service ceiling 24,500 feet

8. Armaments

Two fixed .303 Browning guns in top of fuselage in front of the pilot. Turret with .303 Browning guns located just short of the tailplane. One .303 gun in the beam position on each side of the fuselage. One .303 Browning gun in a retractable tunnel under the fuselage towards the tail. Bomb or depth charge load of

1,400 pounds internally stowed. Anti-submarine rockets were fitted to later *Marks*

9. *Actual Uses and Users*

The Hudson was a military development of the Electra and found favour with the Royal Air Force for maritime reconnaissance in Coastal Command. Hudsons themselves destroyed or shared in the destruction of twenty-five U-boats. A total of 2,934 was delivered for use mainly from United Kingdom bases but also by a number of squadrons in the Mediterranean. They saw front line service from 1939 to 1943 when surviving aircraft were relegated to liaison, transport, and training duties. The Hudson was supplied to the Royal New Zealand Air Force for maritime reconnaissance and strike operations in the Pacific Islands from 1942.

Kittyhawk

1. Purpose

Single seat fighter bomber.

2. Description

Low wing monoplane of all metal stressed skin construction, with retractable undercarriage.

3. Manufacturer

Curtiss Airplane Division of the Curtiss-Wright Corporation, Buffalo,New York.

4. Engines

Mark III: One 1,600 hp Allison V-1710-73 or 81.

A Rolls-Royce Merlin was fitted to the *Mark II*.

5. Dimensions

Wingspan 37 feet 3 inches. Length 33 feet 4 inches. Height 10 feet 7 inches.

Wing area 236 square feet.

6. Weights

Empty 6,350 pounds. Loaded 8,500 pounds.

7. Performance

Maximum speed 346 mph at 5,000 feet. Climb rate 15,000 feet in 9 minutes.

Service ceiling 29,000 feet. Normal range 810 miles.

Maximum range 1,190 miles.

8. Armaments

Six .50 calibre guns, three in each wing and fittings for a total of 1,000 pounds of bombs, usually consisting of one 500 pound bomb under the fuselage and 2 x 250 pound bombs, one under each wing.

9. Actual Uses and Users

Developed from the Tomahawk, the Kittyhawk first entered service with the United States Army Air Force in May 1941. Over 3,000 Kittyhawks were delivered to the Royal Air Force and the Air Forces of Canada, South Africa, Australia, and New Zealand, including 560 of the *Mark I*, 1,500 of the *Mark IA*, 616 of the *Mark III*, and 586 of the *Mark IV*. Those delivered to the Royal Air Force were used exclusively in the Western Desert, Sicily and Italy, in close support of the Army and as escorts for medium bombers.

In Canada they were used for fighter affiliation and other advanced training purposes. In the Pacific it was widely used on operations by the Australian and New Zealand Air Forces.

Lodestar

1. Purpose
   Commercial transport and air liner with flight deck for two seats
   (*Model 14*) or three seats (*Model 18*)

2. Description
   Mid wing cantilever monoplane of all metal construction and retractable undercarriage, with cabin seating for fourteen passengers (*Model 14*) or twenty passengers (*Model 18*) and a steward-
   ess

3. Manufacturer
   Lockheed Aircraft Corporation, Burbank, California

4. Engines
   Two 750 hp Pratt and Whitney Hornet, or 900 or 1,050 hp Twin
   Wasp, or 900 or 1,000 hp Wright Cyclone, radial air cooled, ac-
   cording to the variant.

   Model 18: Two 1,100 hp Wright Cyclone or two 1,200 hp Pratt
   and Whitney Twin Wasp

5. Dimensions
   Model 14: Wingspan 65 feet 6 inches. Length 49 feet 10 inches.
   Height 11 feet 10 inches. Wing area 551 square feet. *Model 18A*:
   Length 55 feet 10 inches

6. Weights
   According to version: Empty 11,290 to 12,195, loaded 17,500 to
   18,500 pounds

7. Performance
   With the Pratt and Whitney Hornet Model 18-07 750hp SIE3G
   engines:

   Maximum speed 236 mph at 7,000 feet. Cruising speed at 70%
   power 214 mph.

Initial climb rate 1,275 feet per minute. Service ceiling 20,400 feet. Cruising range at 50% power 2,030 miles

8. Armaments

Nil

9. Actual Uses and Users

This aircraft was the progenitor of the Hudson and the Ventura to both of which it gave its characteristic general shape. Designed as a commercial carrier, many versions were produced and some were adapted to be military passenger and transport aircraft by the United States Army and Navy. It was adopted in 1941 by the Royal Air Force primarily as a service passenger aircraft, notably in the Mediterranean and African theatres of war, where it was also used as an air ambulance and transport for war materials. The later *Model 18* was an easier aircraft to handle than the *Model 14* and proved to be a useful aircraft for wartime purposes. A small number of Lodestars were used for passengers and freight purposes between New Zealand and the Pacific Islands by the Royal New Zealand Air Force.

Moth Minor

1. Purpose
Single seat aircraft for private ownership and club use

2. Description
Low wing light monoplane, with either an open cockpit or coupé top of French design, and fixed undercarriage

3. Manufacturer
The de Havilland Aircraft Company Limited, Hatfield, England, and Bankstown Aerodrome, Sydney

4. Engines
One 80 hp de Havilland Gipsy Minor

5. Dimensions
Wingspan 36 feet 7 inches. Length 24 feet 5 inches.

Height 6 feet 4 inches. Wing area 162 square feet

6. Weights
Empty 960 pounds. Loaded 1,550 pounds

7. Performance
Maximum speed 118 mph. Cruising speed 100 mph. Initial climb rate 590 feet per minute. Ceiling 18,400 feet. Range 300 miles

8. Armaments
Nil

9. Actual Uses and Users
Introduced in 1937, a total of 73 was delivered. Australian built aircraft were used by the Royal Australian Air Force, a number of them surviving in private hands after the Second World War. A few were in use by the Royal New Zealand Air Force, a small number being sold to private buyers after 1945. Its Air Force use seems to have been confined to runabout purposes.

386

Norseman

1. Purpose

Transport for passengers or freight and a variety of other uses.

2. Description

High wing monoplane, with steel tube structure, fabric covered.

3. Manufacturer

Noorduyn Aviation Limited at St Laurent and Montreal, Quebec, Canada.

4. Engines

One Pratt & Whitney Wasp rated as 550 hp at 5,000 feet.

5. Dimensions

Wingspan 51 feet 8 inches. Length 32 feet. Height 10 feet 1 inch.

Wing area 325 square feet.

6. Weights

As passenger aircraft: Empty 3,816 pounds. Loaded 5,447 pounds.

7. Performance

Maximum speed 170 mph at 5,000 feet. Cruising speed 150 mph at 5,000 feet.

Climb rate 16 minutes 15 seconds to 5,000 feet. Service ceiling 17,000 feet.

Range 600 miles. Range with maximum tankage 1,150 miles.

8. Armaments

Nil

9. Actual Uses and Users

The Norseman was designed to be a versatile aircraft for a variety of uses and users in diverse climatic conditions throughout Canada. A large number were ordered by the Royal Canadian Air Force for the training of wireless operators and navigators under the Empire Air Training Scheme. In 1942 the United States Army Air Force placed a large contract for the aircraft.

Many trainee aircrew members from Australia and New Zealand joined those from Canada in using this aircraft in the training schools across Canada before being posted to the United Kingdom.

Oxford

1. Purpose

An advanced training aircraft for aircrew members routed to fly multi engined aircraft with a crew of three – pilot, navigator and wireless operator/gunner

2. Description

Low wing monoplane of wooden structure, with plywood skin.

Manufacturer's designation AS 10 for *Marks I* and *II,* AS 46 for *Mark V.*

3. Manufacturer

Airspeed (1934) Limited at Portsmouth and Christchurch, Hampshire, England.

Subcontracted by de Havilland, Standard Motors, and Percival Aircraft.

4. Engines

Two 370 hp Armstrong Siddeley Cheetah X.

Two 450 hp Pratt and Whitney Wasp Junior in the *Mark V.*

5. Dimensions

Wingspan 53 feet 4 inches. Length 34 feet 6 inches. Height 11 feet 1 inch.

Wing area 348 square feet.

6. Weights

Mark II: Empty 5,380 pounds. Loaded 7,600 pounds.

Mark V: Empty 5,670 pounds. Loaded 8,000 pounds.

7. Performance

Mark II: Maximum speed 188 mph. Climb rate 960 feet per minute.

Service ceiling 19,500 feet.

Mark V: Maximum speed 202 mph. Climb rate 2,000 feet per minute.

Service ceiling 21,000 feet

8. *Armaments*

Normally nil but sometimes with a dorsal rear gun turret

9. *Actual Uses and Users*

The Oxford entered service in 1937 as the first twin-engined advanced trainer. Nearly 400 were in use by the outbreak of war in September 1939. By July 1945 a total of 8,751 had been built. They were used in the Middle East, Australia, Canada, New Zealand, Southern Rhodesia (now Zimbabwe), and universally in the United Kingdom. Having been intended for training all members of aircrew, the *Mark I* had a dorsal turret for gunnery training. The *Mark II* was mainly used for pilot training. They served in ten squadrons for anti-aircraft co-operation duty, and were used also for air ambulance, radar calibration and communications duties. They were finally withdrawn in 1954.

Tiger Moth

1. Purpose
Initial pilot training with two seats — instructor and trainee pilot.

2. Description
Biplane of mixed wood and metal construction, fabric covered.

Manufacturer's designation DH 82.

3. Manufacturer
de Havilland Aircraft Co Limited, Hatfield, Hertfordshire.

Subcontracted by Morris Motors.

4. Engines
One 130 hp de Havilland Gipsy Major.

5. Dimensions
Wingspan 29 feet 4 inches. Length 23 feet 11 inches. Height 8 feet 9 inches.

Wing area 239 square feet.

6. Weights
Empty 1,115 pounds. Loaded 1,770 pounds. Maximum at take-off 1,825 pounds

7. Performance
Maximum speed 109 mph at 1,000 feet. Cruising speed 93 mph.

Rate of climb 673 feet per minute, 23.5 minutes to 10,000 feet.

Service ceiling 13,600 feet. Range 302 miles. Endurance 3 hours.

8. Armaments
Nil

9. Actual Uses and Users

One of the most famous military pilot training aircraft of all time, the Tiger Moth was widely used in many countries around the world. It entered service with the Royal Air Force in February 1932 and was still in use in 1951 with the Volunteer Reserve. By September 1939 over 1,000 had been delivered to the Royal Air Force. Wartime production in Britain totalled 4,005. A further 2,949 were built in Australia, Canada and New Zealand. They were used by all the Elementary and Reserve Flying Training Schools in the United Kingdom and the Commonwealth Countries. Most wartime pilots received their initial training in the Tiger Moth.

Valetta

1. Purpose

Medium range military passenger and freight transport with a crew of four, 34 troops, or 20 fully equipped paratroops, or the equivalent freight

2. Description

Mid wing, all metal, stressed skin construction, with retractable undercarriage. Manufacturer's designation Type 607

3. Manufacturer

Vickers-Armstrong Limited, Weybridge, Surrey, England

4. Engines

Two 1,975 hp Bristol Hercules 230

5. Dimensions

Wingspan 89 feet 3 inches. Length 62 feet 11 inches. Height 19 feet 6 inches.

Wing area 882 square feet

6. Weights

Empty 24,854 pounds. Loaded 36,500 pounds

7. Performance

Maximum speed 294 mph at 5,500 feet. Cruising speed 172 mph.

Climb rate 8 minutes to 1,000 feet. Maximum range 1,410 miles or 360 miles with 34 troops, or 530 miles with 20 paratroops. Service ceiling 22,200 feet

8. Armaments

Nil

9. Actual Uses and Users

The prototype made its maiden flight on 30 June 1947. It was a military variant of the Viking civil airliner, first entering service with Number 240 Operational Conversion Unit of the Royal Air

Force in 1948, and was intended to replace the Dakota in Transport Command and in the transport squadrons of the Middle East and Far East Air Forces. It was used for a variety of purposes, including troop-carrying, freight, glider-towing, ambulance duties, and supply dropping. They assisted Hastings aircraft during the Suez Crisis late in 1951 to carry 17,000 troops and airmen into the zone and flew 2,700 members of Service families back to England. Valettas of the Far East Transport Wing dropped over 2,000 tons of supplies to troops in the jungle during the operations in Malaya against communist guerillas, and millions of leaflets urging them to surrender. A later version of the aircraft served to train navigators at the Numbers 1 and 2 Air Navigation Schools and the Royal Air Force College at Cranwell. In July 1961, Valettas of 233 Squadron took part in the Kuwait operations from their base at Aden. The last Valetta produced for the Royal Air Force was completed on 29 September 1952.

Ventura

1. Purpose

Medium bomber with a crew of four in the United Kingdom – pilot, navigator/bomb aimer, wireless operator/gunner for the rear firing gun in the retractable tunnel, and gunner for the upper turret. In the Pacific a fifth crew member was carried to operate the tunnel gun.

2. Description

Mid wing monoplane with retractable undercarriage, of all metal, stressed skin construction. Manufacturer's designation V-146.

3. Manufacturer

Vega Aircraft Corporation, an affiliate of Lockheed Aircraft Corporation, Burbank, California.

4. Engines

Two 2,000 hp Pratt and Whitney Double Wasp GR 2,800 S1A4-G.

5. Dimensions

Wingspan 65 feet 6 inches. Length 51 feet 2 inches. Height 11 feet 10 inches.

Wing area 551 square feet.

6. Weights

Maximum Loaded 31,077 pounds.

7. Performance

Maximum speed 300 mph. Cruising speed 260 mph. Service ceiling 25,000 feet. Range 1,000 miles.

8. Armaments

Two fixed .50 inch calibre guns operated by the pilot. Two depressable .303 inch calibre guns in the nose. Two or four .303 inch calibre guns in the dorsal turret and two .303 inch calibre guns in a rear firing ventral position from a retractable tunnel. Bomb load 4,000 pounds.

9. Actual Uses and Users

Developed from the Lodestar transport to replace the company's Hudson in the Royal Air Force which had been in service with Coastal Command, the Ventura embodied features in design which reflected the operational experience gained with the Hudson. It first flew on 31 July 1941 but the actual 394 deliveries began only in the summer of 1942 and fell far short of the original contract of 675. It made its first operational flight on 3 November 1942 and served in Numbers 21, 464, and 487 Squadrons of Bomber Command. It was withdrawn in 1943 but continued in 519 and 521 Squadrons of Coastal Command, and 299 Squadron of Transport Command, serving also in 13, 500, and 624 Squadrons in the Middle East. Over 390 were widely used in Canada, South Africa, Australia, and New Zealand.

Vildebeest

1. *Purpose*
Land based torpedo bomber with a crew of three – pilot, ob-server/gunner, and bomb aimer

2. *Description*
Biplane with fixed undercarriage, half covered with streamlined fairings. An all-metal tubular structure and metal skin. Data for *Mark IV* are featured herewith

3. *Manufacturer*
Vickers Armstrong Limited, Weybridge, Surrey, England

4. *Engines*
One Bristol Perseus VIII, 9 cylinder radial air-cooled

5. *Dimensions*
Wingspan 49 feet. Length 37 feet 8 inches. Height 14 feet 8 inches

6. *Weights*
Loaded 8,500 pounds

7. *Performance*
Maximum speed 156 mph. Ceiling 17,000 feet. Range 630 miles

8. *Armaments*
Two machine guns: one Vickers firing forwards, one Lewis gun firing backwards. One torpedo or 2,200 pounds of bombs

9. *Actual Uses and Users*
The Vildebeest was ordered in 1932 as a replacement for the Hawker Horsley. Production started in 1933, a total of 152 air-craft as *Marks I, II*, and *III* being completed by 1936. A further contract for a final variant with a more powerful engine, the *Mark IV*, was placed in December 1936, production ending in 1937 with an overall total of 209. These aircraft were the only bomber aircraft of their generation to see service in the Second World War, being on station in Singapore at the time of the Jap-

anese entry into the war at the end of 1941 and during their attack on Singapore early in 1942. Those remaining in existence were evacuated and destroyed in Sumatra in March 1942. In New Zealand, Number 3 Squadron was still equipped with the Vildebeest until the arrival of Hudson aircraft in 1942. Obsolescent by the start of the Second World War, the remaining aircraft were relegated to training duties there and elsewhere.

The only known Vildebeest in the entire world is currently being reconstructed at the Air Force Museum, Wigram, Christchurch, New Zealand, from scrapped remains recently discovered and identified.

Vincent

1. Purpose

A general purpose aircraft with three seats – pilot, observer/bomb aimer, and gunner.

2. Description

Biplane with fixed undercarriage of all metal, tubular construction, fabric covered.

3. Manufacturer

Vickers (Aviation) Limited, Weybridge, Surrey, England.

4. Engines

One 660 hp Bristol Pegasus IIM3.

5. Dimensions

Wingspan 49 feet. Length 36 feet 8 inches. Height 17 feet 9 inches.

Wing area 728 square feet.

6. Weights

Empty 4,229 pounds. Loaded 8,100 pounds.

7. Performance

Maximum speed 142 mph at 4,920 feet. Initial climb rate 765 feet per minute.

Service ceiling 17,000 feet. Normal range 625 miles. Maximum range 1,250 miles.

8. Armaments

One Vickers gun firing forward and one Lewis gun in the rear cockpit firing backwards.

9. Actual Uses and Users

The Vincent, as a modified version of the Vildebeest, entered service in the Royal Air Force late in 1934 for general duties with squadrons in a variety of overseas stations. Although it was fated to become obsolescent with the appearance of monoplane aircraft of far superior performance characteristics at the advent of the Second World war, some of the 197 aircraft delivered remained in service throughout the period, seeing action as late as 1941 in Iraq. Some of these aircraft were made available to other users for training purposes and reconnaissance duties, notably with the Royal New Zealand Air Force in the early 1940s. Its main service days were spent with Numbers 5, 27, 28, and 31 Squadrons in India, with 8 in Aden, with 45 and 47 in Egypt, with 55, 84 and 244 in Iraq, with 207 and Number 1430 Flight in Sudan, and with 223 Squadron in Nairobi.

Walrus

1. *Purpose*

   Air/Sea Rescue with a crew of four – pilot, navigator, wireless operator/gunner, and gunner.

2. *Description*

   Biplane amphibian with pusher engine, fitted for catapulting from naval ships, with wooden hull and fabric covered, metal wings.

3. *Manufacturer*

   Saunders-Roe Limited, East Cowes, Isle of Wight, England.

4. *Engines*

   One 775 hp Bristol Pegasus VI.

5. *Dimensions*

   Wingspan 45 feet 10 inches. Length 37 feet 7 inches. Height 15 feet 3 inches.

   Wing area 610 square feet.

6. *Weights*

   Empty 4,900 pounds. Loaded 7,200 pounds.

7. *Performance*

   Maximum speed 135 mph at 4,750 feet. Cruising speed 95 mph. Initial climb rate 1,050 feet per minute. Service ceiling 18,500 feet. Range 600 miles.

8. *Armaments*

   Two Vickers K guns in the bows and amidships.

9. *Actual Uses and Users*

   Under another name the prototype of this aircraft first flew on 21 June 1933. It was adopted by the Royal Air Force as the Walrus in 1935. A total of 741 of two types were built, including some for the Fleet Air Arm and some for the Australian government.

The output of Type I went mostly to the Fleet Air Arm but 216 were ordered early by the Royal Air Force which then supplemented them with the Walrus II, the type mostly used for Air/Sea Rescue by Numbers 269, 275, 276, 277, 278, 281, and 282 Squadrons in the United Kingdom, and by 283, 284, 293, and 294 Squadrons in the Middle East. 624 Squadron used it on mine-locating duties. A small number of this aircraft were in use by the Royal New Zealand Air Force during the Second World War, mainly for training purposes.

410

Wellington

1. *Purpose*

    Long range night bomber with a crew of six – pilot, navigator, wireless operator, bomb aimer, and two gunners.

2. *Description*

    Mid wing monoplane. Wellington *Marks I C* and *III*: Metal geodetic structure, fabric covered. Manufacturer's designations Type 415 (*I C*), Type 417 (*III*).

3. *Manufacturer*

    Vickers-Armstrongs Limited, at Weybridge, Surrey; Chester; and Blackpool, England.

4. *Engines*

    Mark I C: Two 1,000 hp Bristol Pegasus XVIII

    Mark III: Two 1,500 hp Bristol Hercules XI

5. *Dimensions*

    Wingspan 86 feet 2 inches. Length 64 feet 7 inches (60 feet 10 inches for the *Mark III*). Height 17 feet 5 inches. Wing area 840 square feet.

6. *Weights*

    Empty 18,556 pounds. Loaded 28,500 pounds (29,500 for the *Mark III*).

7. *Performance*

    Mark I C: Maximum speed 235 mph at 15,500 feet. Initial climb rate 1,120 feet per minute. Service ceiling 18,000 feet. Range 1,200 miles with bomb load of 4.500 pounds or 2,550 miles with 1,000 pounds.

    Mark III: Maximum speed 255 mph at 12,500 feet. Initial climb rate 930 feet per minute. Service ceiling 19,000 feet. Range 2,200 miles with bomb load of 1,500 pounds or 1,540 miles with 4,500 pounds.

8. Armaments

Two .303 guns in each of the nose and tail turrets (four in the tail turret for the *Mark III*), plus two manually operated .303 guns in beam positions. Maximum bomb load 4,500 pounds.

9. Actual Uses and Users

Introduced in 1937, Wellingtons served as mainstay bombers during the early years of the Second World War, their last bombing operation for Bomber Command taking place on the night of 8 October 1943. They served in fifty-two Bomber Command squadrons, dropping a total of 42,440 tons of bombs from British bases. They served in fourteen Coastal Command squadrons and were widely used for many purposes in the Mediterranean, including bombing operations into 1945. A total of 11,461 was produced.

Many *Marks* were manufactured for the wide variety of uses found for this versatile aircraft, particularly after its useful life as a bomber came to an end with the advent of its four-engined successors. These included continued extensive work in Flying Training Command.

413

Alan Paisey was born in 1928 in Swindon, Wiltshire. After military service and other employment, he settled for a career in the education system. Following teaching appointments in London Secondary Schools, he worked in teacher education and retired as head of the Administrative Studies Division, Bulmershe College, University of Reading. He gained BA, BSc(Econ), and MPhil degrees from the University of London, and a PhD degree from Brunel University at the Henley Administrative Staff College.

His previous publications include eight books and sixty articles in Britain, the United States, Australia, and New Zealand on educational management. Now living in retirement in New Zealand, he has recently worked on a range of publications on veterans of the Second World War. These include three volumes on surviving veteran aircrew - Volume1: The United Kingdom; Volume 2: The Mediterranean, Africa and India; Volume 3: The Pacific Islands, all published by Compaid Graphics.

In his professionally related field, with Jian Li, recent publications include *International Transfer Pricing in Asia Pacific* (2005), and *Transfer Pricing Audits in China* (2007), both published by Palgrave Macmillan.

Other Books Available

With Luck To Spare

By

Douglas Hawker D.F.C

ISBN 190060415-9
A5, 270 pages.

This book tells the story of the voluntary military service of one of New Zealand's longest-living Lancaster pilots. He survived a full tour of operational flying from Britain with Bomber Command, achieving the position of Flight Commander of B Flight with 630 Squadron at East Kirkby, Lincolnshire.

His story is based upon his meticulous personal diary records, as well as his official professional flying records. The text, both in respect of his early life and Air Force experience throughout, is full of uniquely observed incidents and written with a sense of humour, substantiated by logical analysis.

Distinctively for a text of war time bombing combat missions, the narrative is enriched with technical and operational data, in which the author took an interest beyond the necessities of his pilot duties, together with research data on contingent losses and events from national archives that have only become accessible in recent years. It includes the record of a negative mission involving a celebrated Wing Commander which other accounts have concealed.

Included is a previously unpublished personal account of the experiences of Allied bombing from aircrew members who were delivering them and Germans and Japanese who were suffering them.

It was published to mark the 60th anniversary of the period of greatest effort by Bomber Command during the Second World War

Fate From The Sky

By

Karel Adriaens

ISBN 190060420-5
A5, 224 pages

An unexpected and sometimes unwelcome event can so often change the direction of our lives. The story told in this book turns on the part played in the life of a young Dutchman during the Second World War by the discovery of an injured aircrew from a stricken Lancaster bomber. Karel Adriaens after this event became an active member of the resistance operating aganinst German forces who had occupied his country after the blitzkrieg in 1940.

The book relates in detail the strange happenings of his life and the extraordinary assignments he undertook as a young man working with the Resistance, his escapes from death and captivity, amid the crumbling but vengeful German regime towards the end of the Second World War. It is based on the author's diaries kept secretly but in coded form and his private papers and other records. The narrative recalls the many close bonds between Britain and Holland that were forged in 1940 in the aftermath of the German invasion of the Netherlands.

In particular, it highlights the contribution made by the many members of Royal Air Force aircrews who came from other countries and became involved with Dutch people. The text includes a previously unpublished, remarkable cameo about a New Zealand airman who fought and died in the author's area but whose identity became clarified many years after the war had ended. An extraordinary chance discovery of a personal possession at a crash site led to a heart-warming act of friendship between Dutch and New Zealand families.

Let Nought Deter

A Perspective on Hospital Services in War and Peace

Gil Laurenson

Let Nought Deter

By

Gil Laurenson

ISBN 190060422-1
A5, 274 pages

The author of this book returned from the Second World War after four years with the first general hospital created for the support of New Zealand military forces. It was successively established in Britain, Egypt, Greece, Egypt again, and finally in Italy.

His experiences - involving three extensive voyages by sea across the world in wartime conditions, working in Britain for casualties from German bombing, travelling around Britain at war, the Herculean management efforts repeatedly needed, being overrun by the enemy in Greece, and travelling around the war-torn Mediterranean - are set in their respective general and local, prevailing military contexts. The account provides an insight into the internal structure of a large military hospital, its flow of patients, notably from the Battle of Alamein, and war zone epidemics such as jaundice and venereal disease, punctuated by many surprising and sometimes dramatic events.

The book covers the author's subsequent career as Chief Executive Officer to the North Canterbury Hospital Board for twenty-two years, during which he undertook a world study of hospital services under World Health Authority auspices on behalf of the New Zealand government.

The text is based on meticulous official records salvaged by the author, his personal diaries, and a range of other documentary sources, supplemented by his own vivid recollections, and is enriched by over 100 photographs and documents, many of unique status, drawn from his extensive collection.